Master Your

THE ART OF MARTIAL MIND POW

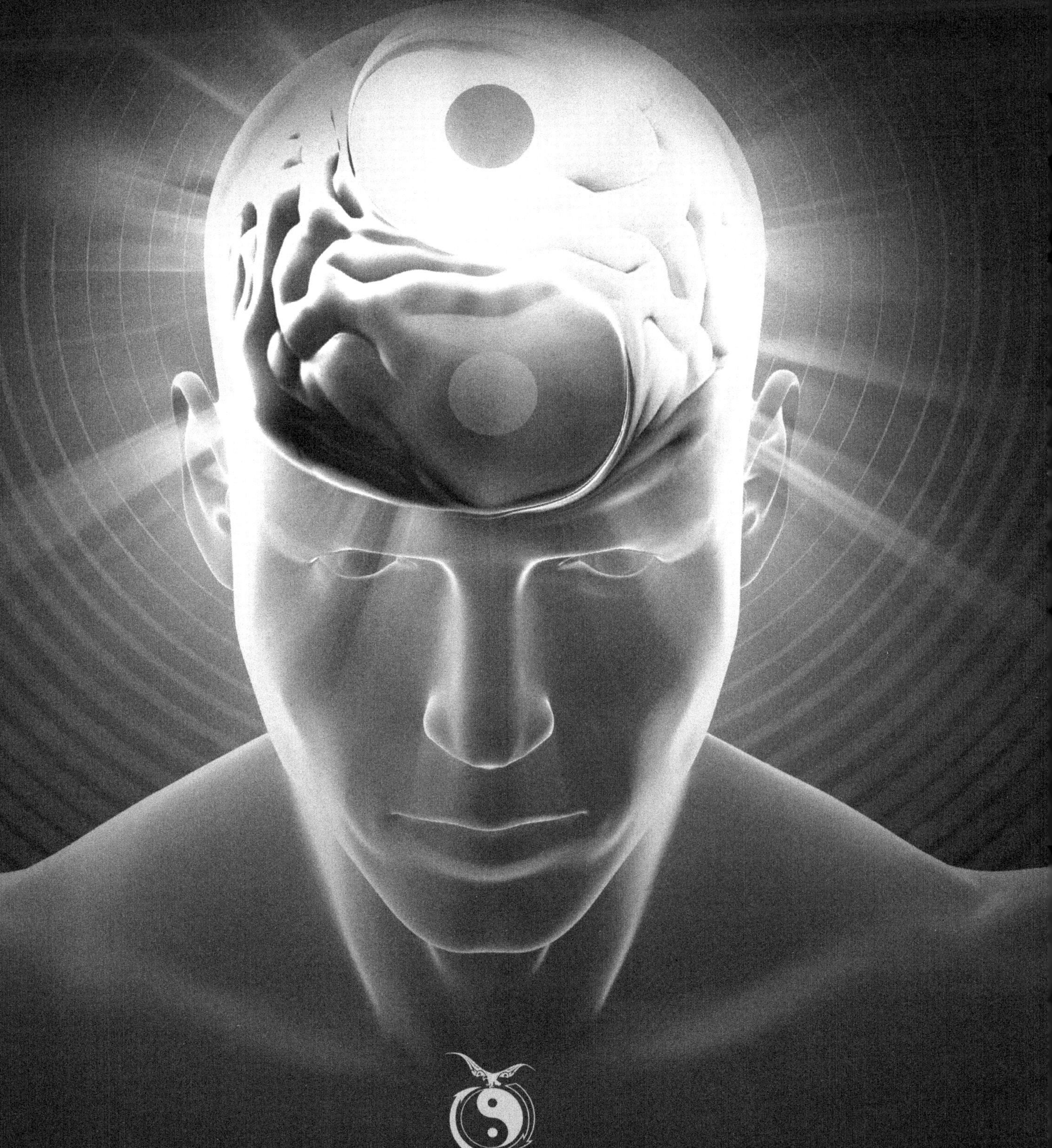

9 STEPS TO SELF-MASTERY INSPIRED BY BRUCE LEE

LAK LOI

Master Your Life

The Art of Martial Mind Power

Lak Loi

A Book Inspired by Bruce Lee

Dedication

I am truly grateful to the universe and the masters who have educated, inspired and empowered me on my journey to write this book. I would like to sincerely thank you — you know who you are.

I dedicate this book to my mum and dad for giving me this wonderful life; my family and friends for giving me the experiences that lent lessons towards this book; my wife, Nina, for being my rock and pointer to the truth; my children, Kieren and Sacha, for keeping my inner child and light alive and shining bright; and the main man who has given me a purpose and true way of life, Bruce Lee.

Peace, respect and love,

Lak Loi

Foreword

By Tim Tackett, *First Generation Instructor in Bruce Lee's Kung Fu, Jeet Kune Do*

I have known Lak since 2007, and he is my flagship London representative.

Lak is a fun, friendly, loyal and respectful friend, who is always willing to serve selflessly, in a true professional manner. He is not only a highly trained martial artist physically under my tutelage, but a highly insightful and philosophical teacher mentally too. He is a great example of a true teacher, a pointer towards finding your own truth.

Lak has a direct lineage to Bruce Lee himself, and is a third generation instructor in Bruce Lee's martial art and philosophy of Jeet Kune Do.

Bruce Lee taught Dan Inosanto.

Who in turn taught myself, Bob Bremer & Jim Sewell (first generation).

I then taught Kwoklyn Wan (second generation).

Both Kwoklyn and I taught Lak (third generation).

Lak is a knowledgeable and expert teacher in the martial art and philosophy of Bruce Lee's Kung Fu, called Jeet Kune Do or JKD for short, and brings to the table a professional background in investment banking, business development, personal development and elite fitness coaching.

Lak is the Leading Authority on the application of Bruce Lee's teachings for personal development, and has truly transcended Kung Fu in his unique way. He has pioneered the use of Bruce Lee's Kung Fu to **Use Martial Movement** to help **Move the Mind** to **Move You Towards Your Own Abundance**. His mission has always been to preserve and promote Bruce Lee's martial art and philosophy of JKD to keep Bruce's spirit alive, so we can discover our personal expression of Bruce's art towards our personal liberation, self-actualisation and achieve our goals.

Lak also made it his personal mission to create awareness in the world that Bruce Lee was not only the most prolific martial artist physically, but also mentally; he used this philosophy to help enrich people's lives, making Kung Fu a way of life. Few know that Bruce Lee majored in philosophy at the University of Washington in the USA. Lee wanted to be known as an 'Artist of Life' before he was known as a 'Martial Artist'. His realisation of artistry of life was born through understanding the martial arts.

Lak has coined the term 'Physical and Mental Cultivation', which is the essence and ultimate expression of martial artistry at its highest form, encompassing both sides of this coin. It is this martial mindset that Lak has beautifully engineered into this book, into an easy-to-follow process of self-mastery, so you can **Get the Life You Want.**

Lak fittingly calls this mindset '**Martial Mind Power**', and the process... '**Master Your Life**'.

Enjoy the journey!

Tim Tackett.

By Don Green, *Executive Director, The Napoleon Hill Foundation, America's Largest Personal Development Organisation, Founded by Dr Napoleon Hill, Bestselling Author of Think and Grow Rich*

Lak Loi has been deeply inspired by Bruce Lee, and discovered how Lee was inspired by Dr. Napoleon Hill's famous book, Think and Grow Rich when Mr Loi made the connection that Bruce had set himself a 'Definite Chief Aim' based on Dr Hill's philosophical works.

Mr Loi realised that the premise of Lee's success was built on a mindset instilled by Dr. Hill's famous philosophy, 'what the mind can conceive and believe, it can achieve'. This gave birth to Mr Loi's concept of using the Martial Mindset inspired by Lee combined with Mind Power inspired by Dr Hill, which led him to coin the term Martial Mind Power. Mr Loi takes the reader through nine steps to self-mastery, to allow you to determine your success in life.

Each one of you has Martial Mind Power to discipline your mind and body to cultivate your self-mastery. If you do not learn to take this power back, your life will be controlled by external forces leading to your misguided misery. I urge you to read this book and then apply Mr Loi's Martial Mind Power teachings in order to cultivate your self-mastery, to live the life you dream of.

Don Green

By Andrew J. Staton, *Jun Fan Journal Columnist for Martial Arts Illustrated Magazine and Authority in Bruce Lee's Legacy*

Jeet Kune Do was the name Bruce Lee gave to his way of martial arts training whilst in Los Angeles, before this he had taught a style called Jun Fan Gung Fu (literally Bruce Lee's Gung Fu which was adapted from the Wing Chun Style of Kung Fu). But in the late 1960's he wanted to free his students of style, system and method and never meant Jeet Kune Do to be a Martial Art, but more the process by which the student could liberate themselves from the limitations which traditional Martial Arts had.

To this aim Bruce taught his students to be mentally & physically strong. These days the physical element is still the easiest to be taught, but the development of Mind Power using the Martial Mindset is still weak in some areas where ever Bruce Lee's combat philosophy is being developed.

Like all JKD instructors they must develop their own teaching skills, to let their students grow in such a way that they can accept knowledge, without limiting themselves on growth or being bound by technique or style.

Lak has seen the freedom in releasing the mind from day to day restraints and passing on his passion by inspiring, educating and empowering his students, so that they can live their lives to their truest potential and align themselves towards their personal liberation, self-actualization and achieve their personal success goals... which was Bruce Lee's main aim. Lak calls this... Martial Mind Power.

This book goes beyond its initial target and sets out a self-discipline guide for ALL who become dedicated to cultivating their own Self-Mastery.

Andrew J. Staton

By Chris Kent, *First Generation Instructor in Bruce Lee's Jeet Kune Do and Author of Liberate Yourself - A Guide to Personal Freedom*

If you are sincerely interested in discovering (or perhaps re-discovering) your real self, actualizing your true potential, and living life to the fullest, then Master Your Life is a must-read.

Combining many of the philosophical principles and concepts utilized by the legendary martial artist, Bruce Lee in his own process of personal liberation with up-to-date research concerning knowledge and learning as well as modern training principles and processes, Lak Loi has masterfully distilled an encyclopedic wealth of knowledge and information about personal growth and development into a single, action equals results-oriented book.

Master Your Life is a powerful call to action for anyone who wishes to empower themselves, take control of their own destiny, and be the architect of their own dreams. Read it today.

Chris Kent

Disclaimer

The author and publisher have made every effort to ensure that the information and advice in this book help to serve the reader to create positive life changes.

The author and publisher do not assume and hereby disclaim any liability to any party for any loss, damage, disruption or death caused by the information, advice, errors or omissions, whether they exist from negligence, accident or any other cause.

The author and publisher advise the reader to take full responsibility and control for their actions, health and safety, and to know their limits when undertaking any of the advice and engaging in any of the exercises, drills and activities described in this book. If the reader has any medical conditions, then they should seek consent from their physician before engaging in any physical activity, and ensure that any equipment is safe and well maintained. They should avoid taking any risks beyond their level of experience, ability, aptitude, training and comfort.

Copyright

Illustrations by Nathan Cole
www.NathanCole.me

First published 2016
by Rowanvale Books Ltd
Imperial House
Trade Street Lane
Cardiff
CF10 5DT
www.rowanvalebooks.com

A CIP catalogue record for this book is available from the British Library.
ISBN: 978-1-910832-56-1

Contents

'Life itself is your teacher,
And you're in a constant state of learning...'

Bruce Lee

0
Get ready to kick ass

Introduction

About Lak Loi

I, Sifu Lak Loi, am a true White Collar Warrior. I have been a City and Wall Street consultant since 1997, and currently work in London as a senior consultant. I spend my evenings practicing and teaching Bruce Lee's martial art and philosophy of Jeet Kune Do ('The Way of the Intercepting Fist') — check out www.LakLoi.com

I have a direct lineage to Bruce Lee himself, being a third generation instructor in Jeet Kune Do, certified under the famous Wednesday Night Group under the living legend, Sifu Tim Tackett, and his European director, Kwoklyn Wan.

The purpose of my martial arts school is to:

> *'Preserve and promote Bruce Lee's martial art and philosophy of Jeet Kune Do, to help define and teach the core curriculum, not to confine us but to liberate us, and to discover our personal expression of Bruce's martial art and philosophy.'*

My personal mission statement is:

> *'My chief definite purpose is to educate, inspire and empower people, so that they can live life to its truest potential... so they can align themselves towards their personal liberation, self-actualisation and achieve their personal success goals.'*

I use Bruce Lee's teachings, fused with personal development and elite fitness coaching, to cultivate people's lives both mentally and physically through a series of exciting physical and philosophical classes, experiences, workshops and online courses.

I call it... Martial Mind Power.

The premise of Martial Mind Power is developed on Dr Napoleon Hill's philosophy:

> *'What the mind can conceive and believe, it can achieve.'*

Similarly, Bruce Lee also quoted:

'As you think, so shall you become.'

In addition to my martial artistry and instructorship in Jeet Kune Do, I hold a Bachelor of Science (Honours) degree in Computer Science/Software Engineering from the University of Birmingham. I am also a fully qualified personal trainer and certified CrossFit elite fitness coach, specialising in training specific population groups including: chair-based elderly; chronically ill and diseased persons; ante-post natal women; children; and elite athletes. Furthermore, I am an NLP practitioner and instructor in hypnotherapy.

The Littlest God (Part I)

Let's start with a little story.

It wasn't long after the gods had created humankind that they began to realise their mistake. The creatures they had created were so adept, so skilful, so full of curiosity and the spirit of inquiry that it was only a matter of time before they would start to challenge the gods themselves for supremacy.

To ensure their pre-eminence the gods held a large conference to discuss the issue. Gods were summoned from all over the known and unknown worlds. The debates were long, detailed and soul-searching.

All the gods were very clear about one thing. The difference between them and mortals was the difference between the quality of the resources they had. While humans had their egos and were concerned with the external, material aspects of the world, the gods had spirit, soul and an understanding of the workings of the inner self.

The danger was that sooner or later the humans would want some of that too.

The gods decided to hide their precious resources. The question was, where? This was the reason for the length and passion of the debates at the Great Conference of the Gods.

Meaning of Chinese Characters

To understand the meaning of Martial Mind Power, I would like to go back to the ancient art of Chinese writing.

Chinese characters do not spell a word, but rather communicate an idea, concept or philosophy, if you may.

It is these very ideas, concepts and philosophies that have kept the Chinese community intact over the past four thousand years.

Dialects, on the other hand, are simply a means to how the ideas are pronounced. The language of ideas, concepts and philosophies remains constant.

The Meaning of Shi or Si

Mandarin and Cantonese are the two most popular dialects of Chinese, with Mandarin being the official language of China.

Figure 2: Chinese character for 'Shi' or 'Si'.

This Chinese character is pronounced 'Shi' in Mandarin, or 'Si' in Cantonese.

Since Chinese characters depict ideas, concepts and philosophies, 'Si' has multiple meanings, such as:

- A master.
- A teacher.
- A tutor.
- A mentor.
- A coach.
- When you model someone of excellence, such as a martial artist, musician, actor, doctor, lawyer — or any specialist for that matter.

Here are some examples of some 'Si' names used commonly in Kung Fu:

師父	Sifu	That's your martial arts father
師母	Simo	That's his wife, your kung fu mother
師姐	Sijei	That's an older kung fu sister
師兄	Sihing	That's an older kung fu brother
師妹	Simui	That's a younger kung fu sister
師弟	Sidaai	That's a younger kung fu brother
師公	Sigung	That's Sifu's teacher, my kung fu grandfather
師祖	Sijou	That's a kung fu ancestor

Figure 3: Different Chinese words beginning with 'Si' and their meanings.

Therefore, 'Si' means:

- Someone who looks out for you.
- Someone who cares for you.
- Someone who is helping you to grow and prosper.
- In the martial arts, it means someone who would give up his or her life for you in your defence.

What Does Fu Mean?

Figure 4: Two different representations of the Chinese word 'Fu'.

The two new characters next to the 'Si' are both pronounced as 'Fu'.

The first 'Fu' character means father or elder male (left-hand side), whereas the second 'Fu' character means teacher or to teach (right-hand side).

What Does Sifu Mean?

Now you understand what 'Si' and 'Fu' mean, you can put them together to mean your teacher and Kung Fu father.

Sifu signifies a really special relationship between a teacher and his students, to whom he gives special skills and teachings, dedicating his time, effort, energy and resources to develop his students' Kung Fu. This saves the student time, and accelerates them to becoming an expert, not just in martial arts, but in life. For example, in China the head chef of a restaurant is called 'Sifu'.

They have a special skill which has taken years to develop, hone and perfect, which they can pass onto you so that you too can become an expert in that skill and take it further. These individuals are known as 'Sifus'.

What Does Kung Fu Mean?

Many believe that 'Kung Fu' just refers to Chinese martial arts and combative styles, systems, methods and so on. This is INCORRECT!

The meaning of 'Kung Fu' or 'Gung Fu' is

'To develop expertise or **excellence** *in skills and abilities,*
through **hard work** *and* **practice** *over time.'*

That means you can have Kung Fu in anything, so long as you are excellent at it.

For example:

- Bruce Lee had the Kung Fu of martial artistry and gave the most exciting performances on the big screen, introducing martial arts to the western world with his blockbuster movie 'Enter The Dragon' in 1973, earning over $25 million dollars in the US, and estimated at over $200 million dollars worldwide.
- Albert Einstein had the Kung Fu of physics, having discovered the theory of relativity amongst a plethora of other profound scientific discoveries, having won the Nobel Prize in 1921 for the Photoelectric Effect and his research in Theoretic Physics.
- Usain Bolt has the Kung Fu of 100 metre sprinting, having won Gold in the 2012 Olympics.

You get the idea, THAT'S RIGHT!

What Is the Idea of Kung Fu?

Kung Fu, then, is a prolific ideology for life and not just for martial arts, which means:

- To **model excellence** in your life.
- To **self-actualise**, so you can be the best you can be.
- To help **develop others** Kung Fu.
- To **live a Kung Fu life** of excellence.

How Do You Develop Kung Fu?

To live a life of excellence, a life of Kung Fu, you must always work on developing and maintaining your:

- Self-harmony.
- Self-humility.
- Self-patience.
- Self-mind.
- Self-discipline.
- Self-openness.
- Self-alertness.
- Self-awareness.
- Self-focus.
- Self-presence.
- Self-thoughts.
- Self-belief.
- Self-attitude.
- Self-certainty.
- Self-motivation.
- Self-courage.
- Self-esteem.
- Self-confidence.
- Self-expression.
- Self-integrity.
- Self-emotion.
- Self-respect.
- Self-truth.
- Self-flow.
- Self-happiness.
- Self-power.
- Self-efficiency.
- Self-action.
- Self-passion
- Self-purpose.
- Self-rhythm.
- Self-fitness.
- Self-control.
- Self-excellence.
- Self-love.
- Self-spirit.
- Self-actualisation, and
- SELF-MASTERY.

As they say, there is a time and place for everything. The moment YOU DECIDE to adopt the right attitude and mindset is the moment you take the first step on the path TO LEADing A KUNG FU LIFE. Excellence cannot be achieved without deciding this. Any Tom, Dick or Harry can learn a skill or ability, and become technically good at it. That is not excellence — that is just becoming a Technician. Someone who can emanate the essence of that skill or ability into other areas of life with purpose is known as a Practitioner.

That my friend, is excellence. *That* is KUNG FU!

How Can You Start Cultivating Your Kung Fu?

As Bruce Lee once said:

'Knowing is not enough,

one must apply.

Willing is not enough,

one must do.'

To be excellent, to develop your Kung Fu, you must live and experience excellence by practising until you get perfect, whatever it is you choose to develop your Kung Fu in.

In Kung Fu, we have a '1,000:10,000' rule. This rule states that it takes 1,000 repetitions of DOING something with good form and function to be able to proficiently execute the technique. It takes another 10,000 repetitions to truly understand that technique so that you can perform it subconsciously and BECOME the technique (not just do the technique). That would be considered to be a Black Belt level, or 'Technician' level.

To transcend the understanding of that technique into every corner of your life takes application above and beyond technical performance, that is when you simply BE. That would be 10th Degree level or 'Practitioner' level.

I am a Practitioner of the Kung Fu way of life, and this book is simply me just BEing me, and helping you to FIND YOUR TRUE WAY.

What Made Me Decide?

I am a true white collar warrior. In the daytime I work for investment banks in both the City and on Wall Street, and have been a senior consultant since 1997. By night I practice and teach Bruce Lee's martial art and philosophy of Jeet Kune Do (JKD or 'The Way of the Intercepting Fist'). I am a third generation instructor or Sifu in JKD. I found the corporate world and the 'rat race' to be egotistical, dehumanising, apathetic, spiritually dead, unfulfilling and meaningless. I had a realisation that in the City and on Wall Street, I made a living, but I did NOT make a life.

I am a firm believer that:

'People are more important than the system.'

That's when I DECIDED to take my power back and improve my life. Once I Mastered My Life, I wanted to give something back to the community and environment by spreading love, light and laughter through my martial teachings; to help people like you take control and responsibility for your life and master it, so that you too can discover your Definite Major Purpose in life.

Ultimately, I want to enable you to LIVE A KUNG FU LIFE — a life OF EXCELLENCE.

What Is My Motive?

Inspired by Bruce Lee and the Kung Fu Way, I decided to **Master My Life** and give something back to the world by helping to educate, inspire and empower people. You can **MASTER YOUR LIFE** and live it to its **truest potential** and achieve **excellence** by cultivating the **Thirteen Pillars of Luck** which are:

Number	Pillars of Luck
1	Peace
2	Possibility
3	Perception
4	Positivity
5	Pluckiness
6	Poise
7	Projection
8	Pleasure
9	Prosperity
10	Purpose
11	Passion
12	Planning
13	Practice

Table 1: The thirteen Pillars of Luck for living life to its truest potential

In doing so you will align yourself to and push yourself towards your **personal liberation** and **self-actualisation**, and will **achieve your success goals** in life, so you can:

'Do what you love, and love what you do.'

Bruce Lee is still regarded as the best martial artist of all time. However, Bruce wanted to be known as an 'Artist of Life' first and foremost; someone who is in the pursuit of **BEing EXCELLENT** and **LIVE A KUNG FU LIFE** in order to **SELF-ACTUALISE** to **BE THE BEST YOU CAN BE**. However, the mental side of his brilliance was overshadowed by his physical side, as he wowed millions across the globe on the big screen with his fighting prowess and amazing physique. One of my personal missions is also to create an awareness that Bruce Lee was also an 'Artist of Life', and these insights will be shared through this gift, this book called **Master Your Life**, inspired by Bruce Lee himself.

Ever since I decided to give something back, my life and the lives of many others have completely changed for the better. Seeing people achieve their success goals and fulfil their Definite Major Purpose in life is the biggest compliment of my work.

This book will help you to create and **LIVE A KUNG FU LIFE** by helping you to **DEVELOP YOUR MARTIAL MIND POWER.**

What Are the Nine Stages of Self-Mastery?

The Martial Mind Power matrix below describes how the thirteen Pillars of Luck have been arranged into nine stages of how to **Master Your Life**. This is a 'black belt' programme which will help you to progress through the self-mastery process in an easy-to-manage way.

All teachings use martial art and philosophy (i.e. Kung Fu), personal and business development and success coaching skills and expertise to help you to:

'Move your body, move your mind, move to success.'

Belt	Pillars of Luck	Chapter	Success Goals
1. Red	Peace	**'Stillness'** Master your peace	• Empty your mind • Switch the noise off in your head • Stop being 'busy being busy' • Take a step back to see the big picture • Attain a state of clarity • Connect to Mother Nature, yourself and humanity • Create a state of peace and harmony for emotional management • Enjoy the present and live in the now • Achieve inner harmony and happiness • Prime yourself for success • Switch OFF to Switch ON!
2. Yellow	Possibility	**'Empty your teacup'** Master your mind	• Open your mind. • Remove obstacles that prevent you from achieving success • Enjoy new experiences, learn and grow • Open the door to success!
3. Orange	Perception	**'Possess an eagle eye'** Master your alertness and awareness	• Open your eyes and switch yourself ON • Start to see new opportunities and ways • Create a state of alertness and awareness • Get on top of your game • Stay ahead of the curve • Control and direct your own life • Swoop in and take the new opportunities • Soar to success!

Belt	Pillars of Luck	Chapter	Success Goals
4. Green	Positivity	**'Think & become'** Master your confidence & self-belief	• Create a sense of calmness • Get clarity so you can see clearly • Have absolute certainty • Tap into your unlimited potential • Take massive action • Get massive results • Get massive belief and confidence • Think success, be success!
5. Blue 1	Pluckiness	**'Waatah!!!'** Master your fears	• Learn and understand what fear is • Develop a healthy respect for fear • Accept and recognise your own fears • Understand how to control fear • Conquer your fears • Scream to success!
6. Blue 2	Poise Projection	**'Honestly express yourself'** Master your communi-cation and influencing skills	• Learn the art of how to express yourself with honesty and integrity • Know yourself • Develop tools and skills to communicate effectively with poise, confidence, and act 'as-if' • Learn how to invest in emotional content • Make it your own • So you can win friends, influence people and enrich relationships with your family, friends, loved ones and colleagues • Express your way to success!
7. Purple	Pleasure	**'Be like water'** Master your flow	• Be adaptable and flexible to cope with any situation • Overcome obstacles that stand in your way • Create calm and clarity • Create a sense of vision and happiness • Achieve whatever ends you desire • Find your flow • Flow to success!

Belt	Pillars of Luck	Chapter	Success Goals
8. Brown	Prosperity purpose passion	**'Power side forwards'** Master your visions	• Understand what power side forwards means • Accept and recognise areas of your life that need improvement to create harmony and balance in all areas of your life • Find your passion so you can love what you do, do what you love • Create a burning desire • Understand and calibrate your strengths and weaknesses • Identify how to use what you got to your maximum advantage by putting your strengths forward • Discover your definite major purpose in life • Create a vision • Identify creative opportunities • Power forwards to success!
9. Black	Planning Practice	**'Stay ahead'** Master your success	• Develop an understanding of rhythm and broken rhythm • Develop an understanding of The Rhythm Of Life • Find your own rhythm • Orchestrate your success strategy to overcome obstacles and challenges • Dance to your own rhythm • Stay ahead of your success!

Table 2: The nine stages of self-mastery… Master Your Life Black Belt Programme

In traditional Kung Fu fashion, it's time to DECIDE TO BECOME EXCELLENT. It's time to read and start to TAKE ACTION NOW…

How This Book Works

This book is split into nine key chapters, each relating to a definitive step of the self-mastery process. Each stage has a belt colour associated with it, making it easier for you to track your progression to Master Your Life and Become a Black Belt in Self-Mastery.

In each chapter, I pose a number of Do-It-Yourself Interactive Challenges so you get a first-hand experience of the teachings by means of questions, exercises and drills — both mental and physical. These interactive challenges are scattered throughout the book, and are to be carried out in one of three ways, explained within the 'activity boxes' and they are either:

Think — to be completed on your own.

Pair — to be completed with a partner.

Share — to be completed in small groups with family, friends or colleagues.

In some of the group interactive challenges, there is an appointed Leader that directs the rest of the group through the exercise to get the best results, and often the person who is at the centre of the exercise is nominated as 'it', being the key person going through the learning experience like in a children's game of 'tag'.

Demonstrations of the *Do-It-Yourself Interactive Challenges* can be found on our website on www.MartialMindPower.com/Resources

Anyone can take part in these challenges, even without any prior martial arts experience. All that I ask is for you to Keep an Open Mind for the possibility to Tap into Your Infinite Potential, and Give 100% of Yourself for the best results. As I like to say:

'The more you put in, the more you will get out!'

Are you ready to Become a Master Now ?

The Littlest God (Part 2)

The gods debated where to hide their precious resources.

Some suggested hiding these resources at the top of the highest mountain. But it was realised that sooner or later the humans would scale such a mountain.

And the deepest crater in the deepest ocean would be discovered.

And mines would be sunk into the earth.

And the most impenetrable jungles would give up their secrets.

And mechanical birds would explore the sky and space.

And the moon and the planets would become tourist destinations.

Even the wisest and most creative of the gods fell silent, as if every avenue had been explored and found wanting.

Until the littlest god, who had been silent until now, spoke up.

'Why don't we hide the resources inside each human? They'll never think to look for them there.'

1 Stillness

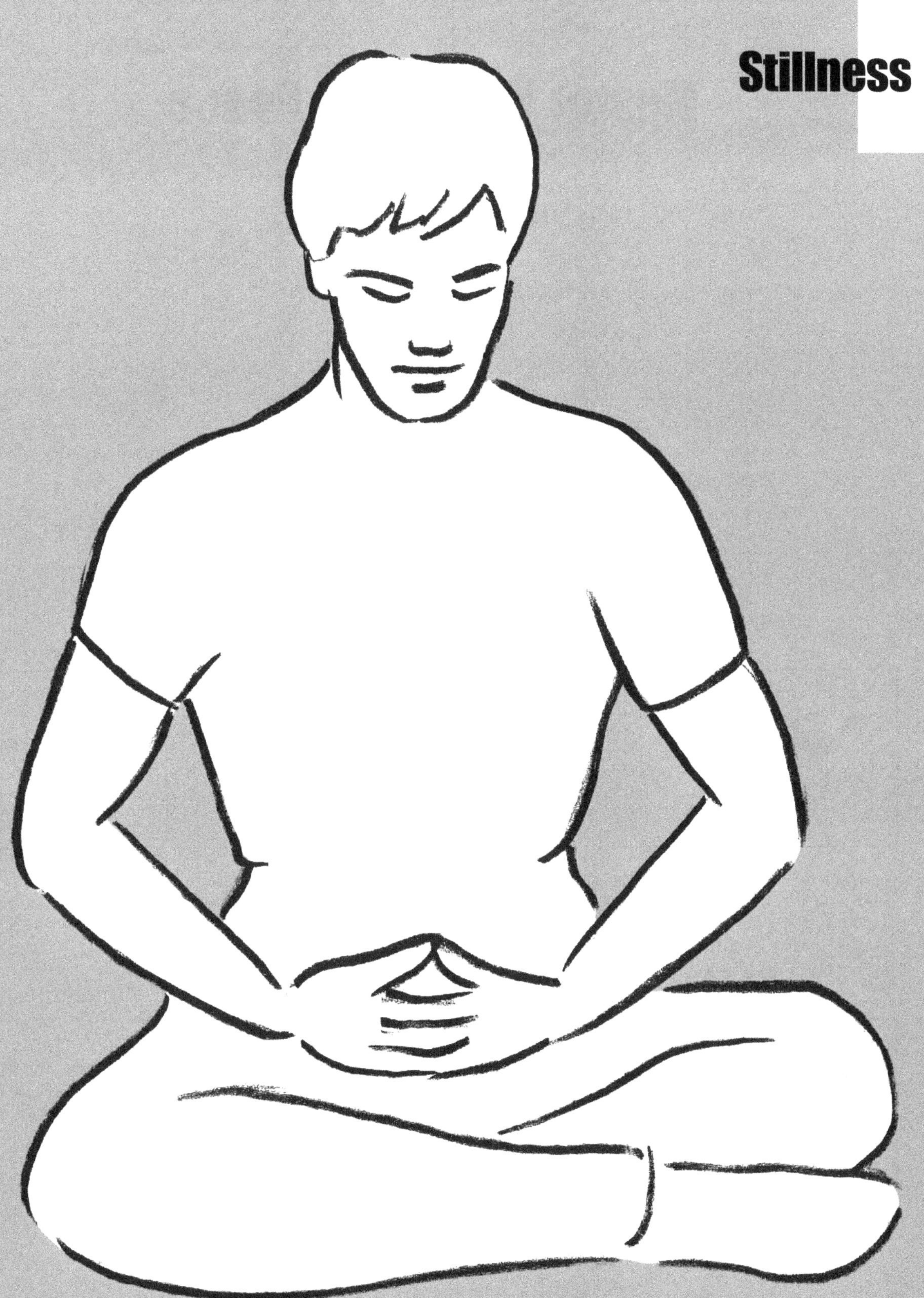

Stillness

STAGE 1 — RED BELT

Master Your Inner Peace

What's the Problem?

So, who is this **Stillness** stage of your self-mastery journey aimed at?

- People who are too 'busy being busy' and caught up in a rut, a routine, or the rat race.
- People who are walking around with blinkers on, and they have lost sight of the bigger picture.
- People who are not present anymore, and are walking around in a zombified and disassociated state.
- People who are disconnected from Mother Nature, themselves and humanity.

Objective

Outcomes and Results Question
What outcome(s) and result(s) do you expect to get when you start to **Practice the Art of Stillness**? Take ten minutes to list down all the positive changes you would like to see, hear and feel.

Being still is not about being static or silent in one place. Stillness is a different matter entirely. Stillness demands that we **look inside** of us **whilst everything is going on outside** of us. Without trying to control what's occurring on the inside or the outside. **Without judgement**. In the presence of **motion** and **chaos**, yet **finding tranquillity** in its **BE**ing.

Examples Question
Can you think of any examples when you **Need to Be Still**, but you are not? Take ten minutes to make a list of the times and scenarios you fail at being still. What was the outcome of the situation, and how did you feel afterwards?

Do you sometimes find yourself:

- Too busy to think, let alone eat and exercise?
- Unable to think straight?

- Unsure whether you're coming or going?
- Having too much on your plate and feeling overwhelmed?
- Making mistakes because you cannot keep juggling all the balls in the air?
- Feeling like the quality of your work is suffering because you have a high quantity of work to deal with?
- Feeling like you're out of your depth, and cannot see the wood for the trees?
- Feeling trapped in the rat race?
- Feeling like you're stuck in a rut?
- Walking around like you've got blinkers on?
- Feeling like you're at a loss?
- Feeling like your life is out of control, and you cannot keep up with everything?
- Feeling like a zombie in a movie?
- Feeling disconnected from yourself and other people?
- Not spending any time in nature, and unable to remember the last time you did?

If you have answered 'yes' to any of the above, then you're in for an AMAZING TRIP.

Stillness is based on Bruce Lee's martial philosophy:

'The stillness in stillness is not the real stillness;
Only when there is stillness in movement does the universal rhythm manifest.'

This stage of your self-mastery journey will help you to:

Belt	Pillars of Luck	Chapter	Success Goals
1. Red	Peace	**'Stillness'** Master your peace	• Empty your mind • Switch the noise off in your head • Stop being 'busy being busy' • Take a step back to see the big picture • Attain a state of clarity • Connect to Mother Nature, yourself and humanity • Create a state of peace and harmony for emotional management • Enjoy the present and live in the now • Achieve inner harmony and happiness • Prime yourself for success • Switch OFF to Switch ON!

This stage is broken down into five key substages as follows:

1. Switch off the Noise in Your Mind.
2. Stop Being Busy Being Busy.
3. Stillness.
4. Stillness Exercises.
5. Take a Step Back to See the Big Picture.

Are you ready to **Switch OFF to Switch ON?**

Warm Up

Let's jump right in and start warming up by answering the following questions:

Question
What do you think '**Stillness**' means? Take five minutes to define.

Question
What do you think '**Switching Off the Noise in Your Mind**' means? Take five minutes to define.

Question
What do you think '**Stop Being Busy Being Busy**' means? Take five minutes to define.

Question
What do you think '**Take A Step Back to See The Big Picture**' means? Take five minutes to define.

Question
Would you like to learn how to **Be Still So You Can Move to Success?** (Yes or No)

If you answered 'yes' to the last question, then you're in the right place. So, let's BE STILL AND MOVE TO SUCCESS!

Storm Before the Calm

The storm brewed over the lake.

The clouds began to collate over the lake, creating a gloomy and dark atmosphere.

I could taste the electricity in the air, indicating that it was about to rain.

And then suddenly, a strike of lightning opened up the heavens.

The rain began to pour fiercely, as the water droplets bounced off the lake's surface creating a layer of mist.

And then — BA-BOOM! A bolt of lightning came crashing down on a tree in the far distance. The tree was Still standing.

The wind blew intermittently, causing me to close my eyes when the water hit me in the face with a cold shock.

The rain ran down my face, and I could taste the crisp rainwater as my clothes got dripping wet.

I started to feel colder and colder.

The lake now looked like one big mud pool.

Switch Off the Noise in Your Mind

How Meditation Changes Your Brain

Dr Sarah McKay, a neuroscientist, wrote the following article, titled 'A Neuroscientist Explains How Meditation Changes Your Brain'. The article reads as follows:

> *'Do you struggle, like me, with monkey-mind? Is your brain also a little unsettled, restless, capricious, whimsical, fanciful, inconstant, confused, indecisive, or uncontrollable? That's the definition of 'monkey mind' I've been given!*
>
> *If you need more motivation to take up this transformative practice, neuroscience research has shown that meditation and mindfulness training can cause neuro-plastic changes to the grey matter of your brain.'*

A group of Harvard neuroscientists interested in mindfulness meditation have reported that brain structures change after only eight weeks of meditation practice.

Sara Lazar, PhD, the study's senior author, said in a press release:

> *'Although the practice of meditation is associated with a sense of peacefulness and physical relaxation, practitioners have long claimed that meditation also provides cognitive and psychological benefits that persist throughout the day.'*

To test their idea, the neuroscientists enrolled sixteen people in an eight-week mindfulness-based stress reduction course. The course promised to improve participants' mindfulness and well-being, and reduce their levels of stress.

Everyone received audio recordings containing forty-five-minute guided mindfulness exercises (body scan, yoga, and sitting meditation) that they were instructed to practice daily at home. To facilitate the integration of mindfulness into daily life, they were also taught to practice mindfulness informally in everyday activities such as eating, walking, washing the dishes, taking a shower and so on. On average, the meditation group participants spent an average of twenty-seven minutes a day practicing some form of mindfulness.

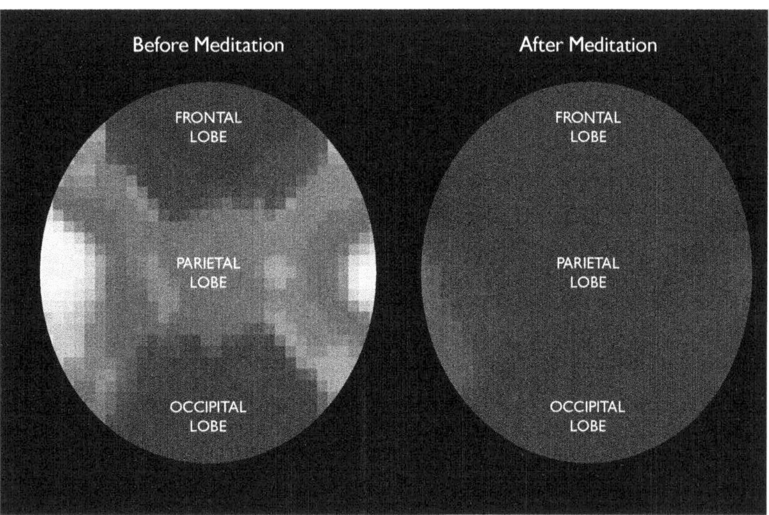

Figure 5: Magnetic Resonance Images (MRI scans) of a participant's brain activity before and after mindfulness exercises.

Magnetic resonance images (MRI scans) of everyone's brains were taken before and after they completed the meditation training, and a control group of people who didn't do any mindfulness training also had their brains scanned.

After completing the mindfulness course, all participants reported significant improvement in measures of mindfulness, such as 'Acting with Awareness' and 'Non-Judging'.

What was startling was that the MRI scans showed that mindfulness groups increased grey matter concentration within the left hippocampus, the posterior cingulate cortex, the temporal-parietal junction and the cerebellum; brain regions which are involved in learning, memory, emotion regulation, sense of self and perspective taking!

Britta Hölzel, the lead author on the paper says:

> *'It is fascinating to see the brain's plasticity and that, by practicing meditation, we can play an active role in changing the brain and can increase our well-being and quality of life.'*

Sarah Lazar also noted:

> *'This study demonstrates that changes in brain structure may underlie some of these reported improvements and that people are not just feeling better because they are spending time relaxing.'*

To learn more about how meditation changes the brain, please watch Sarah Lazar's TEDx Cambridge talk on our website, amongst many more resources on this topic, at www.MartialMindPower.com/Resources

Meditation Exercise

The following is a wonderful meditation script titled 'Abundance', which was written by **David Key**, my Sifu in NLP and hypnotherapy. You can purchase a copy of this meditation on DVD from David's website on **www.Auspicium.co.uk**

Abundance Meditation
Now sit safely and comfortably in a chair, sofa or simply lay down, whilst a friend, family member or loved one reads the **Abundance Meditation Script** below to you in a soothing and calming voice. You can put on some tranquil background meditation music or binaural beats, to help you go into a deeper state of relaxation for maximum benefit. Enjoy the trip.

Abundance Meditation Script

Now is the time when your mind and body are preparing to go into a different way of being for a while.

I'll be speaking quietly with you.

(And there'll be some relaxing music in the background.)

As you take time out.

And perhaps listen to me for a while.

Before **drifting off** into a refreshing, **deep sleep.**

And this is something your body knows how to do naturally.

And follow my instructions to get the results **effortlessly.**

And you may prefer to allow my voice to wash over you, as you allow any tension to just **melt away.**

Allowing the sounds to carry you and **fade into the background.**

And you may just want to find a spot above eye level, and notice what you're noticing.

Just allow your eyes to blink easily and effortlessly.

And, if you prefer, allow your eyelids to blink together, or even flutter, before you **close your eyelids now.**

And just be aware that you are in a safe place, a peaceful place, and you know that you are in control as you **fall asleep naturally** with your sounds, thoughts and feelings that are all natural.

As a **deeper** part of you knows how easy it is to **drift off to sleep.**

As your **conscious mind floats away** successfully.

Your conscious mind can **relax,** and your unconscious can just allow you to take a deep breath in through your mouth and hold it, for a second, 3, 2, 1 as you go into a beautifully peaceful quiet place.

And **deeper still.**

As you're lying where you're lying or sitting, I want you to know that you can really **start to relax now.**

Because it is **easy to relax.**

You just have to decide to **close your eyes.**

And allow yourself to dream by imagining you're lying on a beautiful beach.

And as you're lying there looking up at the beautiful sky, I want you to see a cloud, and just notice it.

Notice the colour, of one fluffy white cloud.

Just **drifting and drifting**, peacefully slowly, as you lay there still.

And imagine that cloud starting to evaporate, just like any tension that you may have had in your body up until right now.

Just imagine that the tension **floating** out just right there, and dissolving with the warmth of the sun, stroking your skin comfortably, that's right.

And now as you just peacefully sleep, while feeling any tension **float away**, you can listen to the sounds and notice what you're noticing.

Start to notice your toes starting to relax, and notice the feeling of comfort washing over you.

As your muscles around your ankles **soften**, that's right.

And moving those feelings gently over your calf muscles now, moving that feeling of **relaxation** around your knees.

And now moving that **relaxation** to your thighs, and gently to the back of your legs and around your waist.

And the more you notice the feelings of relaxation soothing your muscles and body and your mind, the more you're starting to **notice that physical relaxation** and **being still** is all part of the process of going **deeper and deeper** into beautiful **deep sleep.**

And now listen.

Move that **relaxation** up through your spine, back and stomach.

And move it gradually up to your shoulders.

And perhaps, if you had any tension in your teeth, **relax** your jaw.

And move that **relaxation** sensation around your neck and cheek muscles.

And gently around your eyelids. Are getting **heavier and heavier.**

Because you know you can open your eyes at any time.

But perhaps that's not what you want to do.

Because as you drift off into a **deeper state of relaxation** you can just feel any desire to open them up disappear into that cloud as it **floats away easily** into the air now.

Now as you listen to the sound of my voice will go with you, I just want you to imagine the number 100 in your mind's eye.

And I want you to start counting backwards all the way down, **doubling your relaxation** with each count.

That's right.

Ninety-nine, going even **deeper.**

Ninety-eight, feeling even sleepier now.

Ninety-seven, allowing the numbers to just disappear, as you go **deeper still.**

Ninety-six.

By the time you get down to ninety, you'll find that the numbers just fade away, as you **drift** and **drift** into a **deep sleep.**

Ninety-five, **double your relaxation,** as you **relax,** continuing to count down.

As you go even **deeper** still... that's right.

Ninety-four, noticing the numbers just disappearing into the background.

Ninety-three, make them disappear.

Ninety-two, continue to count back in your mind as you go even **deeper still.**

Ninety-one, with each number as you count down, all the way down.

And now, as your unconscious mind listens carefully,

As you become even more **relaxed,** I want you to think about

Your financial goals you want to achieve.

The material goals you desire.

And the **richness** you want in your life.

It can be anything.

Imagine the perfect scenario for accomplishing these goals.

You wake up everyday, ready to create and **move forward** towards your objectives.

It's easy to get out of bed to start your day, because you know you will **feel good.**

You will **feel great** all day, knowing that at the end of the day, you will be another step closer to **achieve your abundance.**

And you know everything will fall into place perfectly.

You are consistently moving forward.

You are able to overcome any financial challenge.

Everything seems possible, everything is within your grasp. Everything is within reach for you.

You extend your arm and hold on and you constantly **reach higher and higher.**

You have **resolved all past obstacles.**

You have overcome all past issues in your life.

That's right.

Feel confident and strong, you know you are putting all your skills and talents to good use to **earn abundantly.**

You can overcome one challenge after another easily, which only gives you **more energy,** which only gives you **more abundance, more fulfilment.**

A life of richness.

It doesn't just have to be wealth.

You can replace all the old habits with new ones, positive ones; you are able to achieve your financial goals.

You are at the top now, and the view is magnificent.

Every obstacle you overcame, you look upon as a triumph.

And you would do it all over again in a blink of an eye, **confidently knowing.**

You **feel accomplishment.**

Goals and dreams that have been there for many years whilst you have been focussing your energies are finally being realised.

You are **successful and proud.**

Family, friends and people see yourself as successful, and **have respect for yourself.**

Notice how **happy you are.**

See yourself as intelligent, caring, strong, tenacious and successful.

You deserve to **feel confident and respected.**

You are of **worldly abundance.**

Now bring that feeling from the future and realise that you can accomplish anything.

You are **confident and strong.**

You fill your life with positive choices, you **fill your life with positive people and thoughts** unconsciously — you don't have to think about it.

Now imagine your life six months from now, and go into the future now.

Notice what you have become, and how successfully you have worked on your financial goals.

You have had many successes and overcome many obstacles.

You feel more **fulfilled** than you ever have.

You have realised that once you accomplish one financial goal, it's easy to accomplish any goal.

Say in your mind, **'It was easy.'**

Say it to yourself, **'This is easy.'** That's right.

It was so easy, that it makes you **smile**.

So you can accomplish many more.

Financial goals to create that life of richness.

Feel fulfilled and satisfied by your successes.

Everyone around you wishes they were as **motivated** as you.

People aspire to be you and be as motivated as you.

Look at yourself two years from now.

Imagine walking in front of the mirror. What does your skin look like? What do your eyes look like? What are they saying to you?

How are you standing?

What are you saying to yourself?

What are other people saying to you?

That's right. You are still motivated and succeeding in everything that you put your mind to.

You're tenacious and you have resolve to keep going, and keep going.

Every goal now is coming more easily.

Because you feel so satisfied with every step, you **feel the energy** coming as you accomplish one goal after another.

Your life now is **filled with better habits, positive habits, and feel fulfilled**.

Others envy you, and want to succeed just as you have done.

That's right.

You now look forward to all the challenges that come your way, because you know you will face them head on and accomplish them.

Life looks promising.

You're now excited about your future, and you know now that you are the reason for the success in your life.

You did it, and you feel very proud of yourself.

I want you to imagine now that you are standing on the top of a flight of stairs.

Twenty steps that take you all the way down to a beautiful place.

This place has some rich treasure stored away in a gold treasure chest, and you have the key to **unlock your true abundance and your true potential**.

That's right.

Now, you are going to slowly start walking down the steps, going **even deeper** with each step that you go down, while you **double your relaxation** and **triple your confidence**.

You will feel totally rich and confident by the time you reach this place.

Now take the first step **down**, twenty.

Nineteen, eighteen, seventeen, sixteen, fifteen, fourteen, thirteen, twelve, eleven, ten, nine, eight, seven, six, four, five, seven, three, two, one.

That's right.

And in this beautiful place I want you to just **relax** as you see that golden treasure chest.

I want you to walk over to it.

And take a key and unlock it.

And now, you will, **find inside the answer**, how you can **create a life of abundance** on the **inside**, the **answers on the inside**.

See the answer now… **inside**.

That's it, good.

The answer can remain in your unconscious mind.

Your unconscious mind can remember what to do in order to **create a life of abundance effortlessly and quickly** — good.

Now, your unconscious mind is listening carefully.

Perhaps when you wake up, or within a few hours of waking up, or even less than that.

You will have a different feeling inside; it's called **confidence**.

That's right.

That's it.

You are now **confident**.

Appropriately.

And the more that you think about achieving your goals, the more confident you will become.

Now imagine yourself in the future, seeing yourself standing confidently, hear yourself speaking confidently.

What are you saying to yourself?

What are other people saying to you?

See other people in admiration of your confidence and your positive manner.

Take those feelings now, and move forward one year from now.

And see yourself in the mirror, standing confidently.

Communicating confidently with other people.

And notice how good that feels.

Now take that feeling ten years into the future, see what you're seeing, notice what you look like, and how good that feels.

Now, bring those feelings back to now.

Now in the past, you've lost your phone or your keys and you couldn't remember where you put them.

Because you **forgot**. Forgetting is so easy.

You **forget**, you forgot.

You've been to a party, and introduced to someone new, and you **forget** their name in a matter of moments. It's OK.

Because forgetting is so easy.

You **forgot**, you forget.

There's been a time when you've walked into a room, and you didn't even know why you were there.

Because you forgot, because **forgetting is so easy**.

You **forget**, you forgot.

So now, as your unconscious mind listens carefully, I want you to find those stairs and look up.

And I want you to find that beautiful white light which is healing energy shining down on you.

This is a sign for you to come out of this relaxing sleep.

And in a moment, I am going to count from ten all the way up to one.

And you will wake up one-tenth of the way coming up. Feeling more **awake**, more **alive** than ever before.

And when I get to one, you can open your eyes, stand up, and stretch out.

Feel good because you can **feel great** confidently.

Ten, nine, eight, seven, six, five, four, three, two —

And get ready now, here we go, stretch out — one.

Stop Being Busy Being Busy

In this section we are going to explore how you can **Stop Being 'Busy Being Busy'**. So here goes…

Question
When you ask someone *'How's it going?'* what kind of responses do you typically get? Take five minutes to list as many responses as you can think of.

In my experience, I have noticed some of the most common responses are usually along the lines of:

- Really busy.
- Busy running around.
- Crazy busy.

Question
When people respond with *'crazy busy'*, do you think this is a *boast* or a *complaint*? (Boast or Complaint)

This type of typical response is usually a boast disguised as a complaint.

Question
What *kind of response* do you give back when someone states they are *'crazy busy'*? Take five minutes to list as many responses as you can think of.

In my experience, the typical response to that is usually something like:

- That's a good problem to have.
- Better than the opposite.
- It's better to be busy than twiddling your thumbs.

Question
What *kind of person* gives the 'crazy busy' response? Take five minutes to list as many types of people who would respond in this way.

It is *not* people who are working more than one minimum wage job back-to-back. Those people are simply tired, exhausted, knackered and dead on their feet. It is almost always people who:

- Are ambitious.
- Have a self-imposed business.
- Have taken on work and obligations voluntarily.

Question
Can you give some examples of things you are *'crazy busy'* doing? Take five minutes to list as many things you can think other people are busy doing as well.

In my experience, people tend to be busy doing…

- Classes and activities they've encouraged themselves or their kids to take on.
- Developing new business ideas to take over the world.

The Busy Paradox

People are busy because of their own ambition or drive or anxiety, because they're addicted to the business of 'Busyness' and dread what they might have to face in its absence.

Almost everyone I know is busy. They feel anxious and guilty when they aren't either working or doing something to promote their work.

The Diary

Question
Do you keep a diary? (Yes or No) This includes diaries on smart phones such as calendars, schedules, reminders, timetables and alarms.

People seem to be so busy these days that they have to diarise time with family and friends.

Question
Put your hands up if you diarise time with your family and friends? (Yes or No)

Does that feel right when you say it back to yourself? (Yes or No)

Recently, I wrote to a friend to ask if he wanted to do something this week. He answered back that he didn't have a lot of time, but if something was going on then I should let him know so he could rearrange his diary to squeeze in a meeting. I went on to clarify that my question was not a heads-up on a future invitation, but rather, it *was* the invitation! His busyness was like a vast, churning noise through which he was shouting at me. I gave up trying to shout back over the noise.

Clear When it is Calm

Question
What are the disadvantages of living in a state of busyness and noise? Take five minutes to list as many disadvantages as you can of being busy or living with a churning noise in your mind.

Typically, busyness creates negative emotions such as:

- Stress.
- Confusion.
- Feelings of being overwhelmed.
- Feelings of being worthless and insignificant.

Bruce Lee quoted:

'A tranquil lake when disturbed becomes muddied
and clear when it's calm.'

Therefore, the big idea is to calm your thoughts and emotions like water — *then* you will have clarity. If our thoughts and emotions are stirred, they become like muddied water, and we can end up making mistakes or missing opportunities because we cannot see them.

Chinese philosopher Chuang Tzu wrote:

'If water derives lucidity from stillness,
how much more the faculties of the mind.'

Busy Children

Question
Have you got any children? (Yes or No)

Even children are busy now. They have their own timetables. If it's not school from 8:45 a.m. to 3:15 p.m. then it's extracurricular activities after school or even on the weekend.

Parents are trying their best to ensure their children stand-out in their academic careers, due to the ever increasing KPI (Key Performance Indicator) world that we live in.

Children come home at the end of the day as tired as grown-ups who have been slogging it out in a 'factory' all day long.

Question
Do your children do any extracurricular activities? (Yes or No) What is their typical weekly timetable? Take ten minutes to consider your children's timetables.

How do your children look and feel at the end of a typical school day? Take five minutes to describe in detail the state of your children after a day at school, how they look, feel and sound.

Remember when you were at junior and secondary school. How did your school day look back then? Take five minutes to list your typical school day and after school activities.

I remember when I was at junior and secondary school. Every day after school I'd have two to three hours of free play.

I'd go and:

- Knock for all my pals and arrange a game of football on the street (when there were less cars on the road) or a local park.
- Watch *Take Hart*, an arts and crafts TV program. I'd then scour the house for empty boxes, empty tissue rolls and whatever else I could find to make anything from cardboard robots to pencil drawings (we couldn't afford expensive oil paints back then).
- Watch a movie on VHS tape recorders which I'd rent from the local video store with money I'd earn by doing errands around the house for my mum and dad.
- Listen to music and record new songs directly from the radio onto cassette, because we could not afford to buy music.
- Play computer games when they eventually loaded from cassette.
- Play fight with my brother, which often ended up in a real fight.

All these activities provided me with valuable skills and insights that remain valuable to me today — particularly the fighting skills.

Those free hours became the model for how I wanted to live the rest of my life... with a flair for arranging events and activities, self-expression through motion using martial arts and sports and, most of all, have a FREE, CREATIVE MINDSET & PLAYFUL HEART

Question
What is your Childhood Blueprint? Take fifteen minutes to think about the things you did as a child, and how they have trickled their way into the way you live your life now.

Think about all the fun playful childhood things that you used to do which you have supressed or even deleted from your life. Would you like to bring them back now?

Busy Hysteria

Question
Where do you think this **Busy Hysteria** comes from? Take five minutes to think about the sources of *'busy hysteria'.*

The present hysteria is not a necessary or inevitable condition of life; it's something we've chosen, if only by our submission to it.

Tim Kreider is the author of *We Learn Nothing*, a collection of essays and cartoons. He quotes:

> *'Not long ago I Skyped with a friend who was driven out of the city by high rent and now has an artist's residency in a small town in the south of France. She described herself as happy and relaxed for the first time in years.*
>
> *She still gets her work done, but it doesn't consume her entire day and brain. She says it feels like college — she has a big circle of friends who all go out to the cafe together every night. She has a boyfriend again. (She once ruefully summarised dating in New York: 'Everyone's too busy and everyone thinks they can do better.')*
>
> *What she had mistakenly assumed was her personality — driven, cranky, anxious and sad — turned out to be a* DEFORMATIVE EFFECT OF HER ENVIRONMENT. *It's not as if any of us wants to live like this, any more than any one person wants to be part of a traffic jam or stadium trampling or the hierarchy of cruelty in high school — it's something we collectively force one another to do.'*

Roots of the Busy Hysteria

The busy hysteria comes from:

- Existential reassurance.
- Hedge against emptiness.
- Give your life some significance.

It is obvious that your life cannot possibly be silly, trivial or meaningless if you are so busy, completely booked, in demand every hour of the day. Right? WRONG!

In one of my roles in the City with one of the UK's largest investment banks, I was told that I could not take my lunch hour to go to the gym or take lunch for that matter, in case they needed me for something urgent. I was told that I was paid to work, not have lunch — and definitely not go to the gym! I remember specifically being told that I didn't get paid to go to the gym… even if it was in my lunch hour.

So, it's hard to see this pretence of indispensability as anything other than a form of 'INSTITUTIONAL SELF-DELUSION'.

How Busyness Creeps into Our Lives

Tim Kreider wrote:

> *'More and more people in this country no longer make or do anything tangible. I can't help but wonder whether all this* HISTRIONIC EXHAUSTION *isn't a way of covering up the fact that* MOST OF WHAT WE DO DOESN'T MATTER.
>
> I AM NOT BUSY. I AM THE LAZIEST AMBITIOUS PERSON I KNOW. *Like most writers, I feel like a reprobate who does not deserve to live on any day that I do not write, but I also feel that four or five hours is enough to earn my stay on the planet for one more day. On the best ordinary days of my life, I write in the morning, go for a long bike ride and run errands in the afternoon, and in the evening I see friends, read or watch a movie. This, it seems to me, is a sane and pleasant pace for a day. And if you call me up and ask whether I won't maybe blow off work and check out the new American Wing at the Met or ogle girls in Central Park or just drink chilled pink minty cocktails all day long, I will say, what time?*
>
> *But just in the last few months, I've insidiously started, because of professional obligations, to become busy. For the first time I was able to tell people, with a straight face, that I was 'too busy' to do this or that thing they wanted me to do. I could see why people enjoy this complaint; it makes you feel important, sought-after and put-upon. Except that I hate actually being busy. Every morning my inbox was full of e-mails asking me to do things I did not want to do or presenting me with problems that I now had to solve. It got more and more intolerable until finally I fled town.'*

Question

Do you feel like you are busy? (Yes or No)

What kinds of things are you typically busy doing other than your daily work? Please take five minutes to list all the things that are keeping you busy and taking up your time.

In my experience, real-life examples typically include:

- Reading and replying to emails.
- Reading and replying to text messages.
- Taking and making voice calls.
- Surfing the net.
- Watching TV.
- Playing computer or video games.
- Checking Facebook and other social media sites.

Question

How can you **Escape from the 'Busy Trap'**? Take five minutes to think about how you can avoid the *'busy trap'.*

Escaping the Busy Trap

Some of the simpler choices include:

- Switch OFF your TV/radio — no news, no shows, no movies.

- Switch OFF your computer — no emails, no social media, no internet.
- Switch OFF your mobile — no texts, no voice calls, no internet.

Simply put, you should Disconnect from Being Busy by PRESSing THE OFF SWITCH and Immerse Yourself in the World!

Immerse Yourself in the World

Question
How can you Immerse Yourself in the World? Take five minutes to think about what 'immerse yourself in the world' means, and how you could do that.

It is a simple formula, which spells ON, and it stands for:

- O is for Own — Spend time on your Own
- N is for Nature — Spend time in Nature

That is to learn the art of BEing STILL.

This 'Stillness' stage is the art of learning and practising stillness the aim of which is to 'Switch OFF to Switch ON!'

Jar in Your Mind

Picture you have a jar filled with the purest, clearest water ever, from your mind.

Notice how clear, crisp and sharp the water is.

Notice how you can see clearly through the water.

Now picture you also have several jars containing samples of coloured sand.

Each colour of sand reflects your negative thoughts and emotions of anger, confusion, frustration, worry, sadness, anxiety and ego.

See the coloured sand jars in front of you.

Now, pick a jar of sand containing the colour that reflects how you feel and what you're thinking right now, and pour it into the clear jar of water.

Notice how the sand gently falls to the bottom of the jar of water.

Now you start to stir your water, and notice how it creates a vortex spinning inside the jar like a tornado.

Notice how the coloured sand of your negative thoughts and emotions start to muddy your water.

Notice how your vision is blocked through the jar of your water.

Notice how you cannot see through.

Stillness

<u>Question</u>
What Does **Stillness** mean to you? Take five minutes to define.

In my experience, people typically think stillness means:

- Idleness.
- Stopping.
- Silence.

Bruce Lee famously quoted:

'The stillness in stillness is not the real stillness;
only when there is stillness in movement does the universal rhythm manifest.'

Stillness is not just a vacation, an indulgence or a vice; it is as indispensable to the brain as vitamin D is to the body, and if deprived of it we suffer a mental affliction as disfiguring as rickets.

The space and quiet that stillness provides is a necessary condition for standing back from life and seeing it whole, for making unexpected connections and waiting for the wild summer lightning strikes of inspiration — it is, paradoxically, necessary to getting any work done.

Thomas Pynchon wrote:

'Idle dreaming is often of the essence of what we do.'

<u>Question</u>
Can you think of any examples of **Stillness Dreaming** that led to some **Profound Inspiration** with prolific results? Take five minutes to think about some examples.

Here are some profound ideas born in stillness:

- Archimedes discovered the principle of displacement during his famous *'Eureka'* (meaning *'I found it'*) moment whilst bathing.
- Newton discovered gravity whilst chilling under a tree watching apples falling.
- Physicist Neils Bohr was led by images in his dreams to discover the structure of the atom.
- Chemist Friedrich Kekule fell asleep and dreamt how the benzene ring was formed.
- Robert Louis Stevenson, author of *Strange Case of Dr Jekyll and Mr Hyde*, claimed that he got many of his best stories from his dreams.

His story is full of stories of inspirations that come in idle moments and dreams. It almost makes you wonder whether loafers, goldbricks and no-accounts aren't responsible for more of the world's great ideas, inventions and masterpieces than the so-called 'hardworking'.

Stillness Exercises

Indirect Relaxation

The first stage of Stillness is 'Indirect Relaxation'. This includes creating a state of relaxation using fun games and activities.

<u>Zen Counting</u>

<u>Pair</u>
Another person reads this script to you in a calm and soothing voice.

<u>Objective</u>
To mentally relax and still the mind; to create a sense of self-control and of being present in the now.

<u>Requirements</u>
None.

<u>Time</u>
Ten minutes.

<u>Set up</u>
Sit up tall, comfortably and securely in your chair or on the floor with your eyes closed.

<u>Tasks</u>

1. Breathe in **gently**.
2. Start mentally counting from fifty to twenty, counting even numbers on each out-breath, and odd numbers on each in-breath.
3. When you get to twenty, count on the out-breath only, and breathe in normally on the in-breath.
4. When you reach zero, stop counting and **just be** aware of your natural breathing as you **sit still and relaxed**.
5. Be aware of how **happy and harmonious you feel now**, whilst sitting **relaxed still**.
6. Be aware of how **brave and courageous you feel now**, whilst sitting **relaxed still**.
7. This is the feeling of **being centred**.
8. Get used to being still, as you **relax** here **still** for another two or **'free'** minutes.
9. As you **absorb the stillness**, prepare to open your eyes over the next six or **'heaven'** minutes.
10. Breathing normally... **relaxed and easy**, learning to **be in control of yourself**

11. Let the breath flow free as your body controls your relaxation and stillness.
12. As the numbers start to disappear the closer you get to zero, which shows you are becoming more aware.
13. Just be aware of your sensations and thoughts, with a comfortable feeling of contentment and ease.
14. (Let the person relax in stillness for six to seven minutes).
15. In a moment, I am going to count back from ten to one. You will come back to full awareness, feeling energetic and switched on one tenth on each count. Ten, nine, eight, feeling more aware, seven, six, five, feeling energy flowing through every cell of your body, four, three, two, fully switched on, aware and energetic, and one, back in the room. Open your eyes.

Alphabet Ball Pass

Share
Three or more people, where one person is the nominated leader.

Objective
To allow you to switch off your critical faculty with a fun game and establish team building by working in a group and creating communication. The movement activates your body to improve motor skills such as coordination, balance and core strength.

Requirements
One or more different sized and textured balls (e.g. tennis ball, football, etc.) and a music player.

Time
Ten minutes.

Set up
Group forms a large circle.

Tasks
1. One person starts with one ball.
2. The person with the ball calls out 'A' and then passes the ball to another person in the circle.
3. The person now in possession of the ball calls out the next letter of the alphabet and passes the ball to another person.
4. Repeat step three until you reach 'Z'.

Progressions
1. To make things interesting, the leader can throw more balls into the circle, and you continue calling out the next letter of the alphabet.
2. Sit on floor, and pass and catch the ball with your feet whilst calling out the next letter of the alphabet.

3. Play music, and the ball is passed around. When the music stops, the person in possession of the ball calls out the next letter of the alphabet.
4. Play music, and the ball is passed around. When the music stops, everyone just freezes and becomes still.

Kung Fu Statues

Share
Three or more people, where one person is the nominated leader.

Objective
To let inhibitions go and break through your limitations, and to increase positive energy in the room.

Requirements
Music. It is recommended to use some upbeat martial arts themed music. Alternatively, choose a happy and upbeat song that the participants will recognise.

Time
Ten minutes.

Set up
Group forms a large circle.

Tasks
1. The leader demonstrates some martial arts poses that the participants must do when the music stops, for example: Horse Stance; Bow Stance; Cross Stance; Drop Stance; Cat Stance. Check out some poses on our website at www.MartialMindPower.com/Resources
2. The leader demonstrates the stances to all the participants, so they can practice them first.
3. The leader starts to play the music.
4. When the music stops, the participants must freeze whilst displaying one of the martial arts poses. The participants cannot do the same pose twice in a row.
5. The leader then goes around and corrects their poses, or can be playful in trying to get them to laugh or off-balance, etc.

Progressions
1. Use a different set of poses, for example yoga poses such as warrior, eagle, mountain and tree.
2. Change tempo and style of music.

What's My Name, Mr Miyagi?

Share
Three or more people, where one person is the nominated leader.

Objective
To let inhibitions go and break through your limitations; to increase positive energy in the room; establishes team building by working in a group and creating communication; to engage mental arithmetic.

Requirements
None.

Time
Ten minutes.

Set up
Someone volunteers or is chosen to be Mr Miyagi who then stands facing the wall. The rest of the group stand on the opposite side of the room.

Tasks
1. All players (except Mr Miyagi) call out, 'What's my name, Mr Miyagi?'
2. Mr Miyagi calls a name, for example 'Martin San'. The players then take six steps (as there are six letters in the name 'Martin') closer to Mr Miyagi.
3. The players repeat from step one, until they either 'tag' Mr Miyagi or Mr Miyagi calls out 'Daniel San'. Then Mr Miyagi has to tag one player while they try to run back to their side without being tagged. The person tagged by Mr Miyagi replaces him in the next game.

Progressions
1. Instead of taking normal steps, the players must use martial movement to advance closer to Mr Miyagi.
2. Tagged players join Mr Miyagi's team until one winner is left.
3. The players do not call out anything, and take quiet steps towards Mr Miyagi. Mr Miyagi can turn around at any time, and the players then have to freeze. If he see's someone move he calls out 'Daniel San' and tries to tag someone, or alternatively someone tags Mr Miyagi before he turns around and shouts 'Daniel San' and everyone runs back to their wall before Mr Miyagi tags them.

Inner Stillness

The second stage of Stillness is 'Inner Stillness'. This includes activities to create stillness internally, within your inner self.

Zen World

Think
By yourself.

Objective
Become aware, accepting and mindful of the external world around us by activating our sensory acuity.

Requirements
Fifteen different food items (ensure that you check participants allergies before giving them any food items).

Time
Fifteen minutes.

Set up
Sit up tall, comfortably and securely in your chair or on the floor.

Tasks
(X = five, four, three, two and one.)

Exercise 1 — Sight

1. Look around, and name 'X' different objects (starting at five). Notice the object's colour, size and shape.
2. Subtract one from the last count, and repeat the previous step until you reach one.

Exercise 2 — Sight and Touch

1. Look at, name and touch 'X' different objects (starting at five). Notice the object's colour, size, shape, weight, temperature and texture.
2. Subtract one from the last count, and repeat the previous step until you reach one.

Exercise 3 — Sight, Touch, Taste and Smell

1. Look at, name, touch, taste and smell 'X' different objects (starting at five). Notice the object's colour, size, shape, weight, temperature, texture, taste and smell.
2. Subtract one from the last count, and repeat the previous step until you reach one.

Exercise 4 — Hearing

Close your eyes and listen for 'X' different sounds (starting at five). Subtract one from the last count, and repeat the previous step until you reach one.

Feed Your Mind

Pair
Two or more people, where one person is the nominated leader.

Objective
To become aware, accepting and mindful of the external world around us by activating our inner sensory acuity.

Requirements
Sultanas, raisins, fruit, biscuits or candy (ensure that you check participants allergies before giving them any food items).

Time
Fifteen minutes.

Set up
Sit up tall, comfortably and securely in your chair or on the floor.

Tasks

1. The leader presents the plate of food items covered with a cloth.
2. The leader then asks the participants to get to a place of mindfulness.
3. The leader uncovers the plate, and asks the participants whether they notice if they are salivating, and whether the salivation has started to increase as they look at the plate.
4. Choose one item in your mind.
5. Switch on your awareness as you experience moving your arm in slow motion towards the plate to pick up your selected item, placing it between your fingers as you hold it still.
6. Imagine you are an alien, and have never seen that food item before... you start to examine it with your senses.
7. Look at it and appreciate its colours, size and shape.
8. Feel the weight, temperature and texture in between your fingers.
9. Bring the item to your nose and smell its aroma.
10. Bring the item close to your ear and gently squeeze it; listen to any sounds it makes.
11. Notice any wandering thoughts in your mind, (like 'what am I doing?'), and just let the thought be. Bring your focus back onto the item.
12. In slow motion, bring the item to your mouth. Notice if your mouth begins to water as your hand knows exactly where to move the item to.
13. Take a bite of the item if it's too big to place the whole item into your mouth, but do not chew it yet.
14. Feel it on your tongue and notice its weight, temperature, texture and taste. Notice the sensations it creates in you.

15. When you are ready, bite into it and notice which side of the mouth it's in. Does it release any flavours?
16. Gradually start chewing, and notice the consistency is starting to change until you feel the desire to swallow.
17. Notice how the food passes down your throat and into your gullet on its way to your stomach.
18. Notice how you are feeling now… happy… relaxed…

Progressions

1. Try with a drink.

Laser Body Scan

Think

By yourself.

Objective

Simply to notice your body in discomfort or pain. It is not to make you relax or relieve stress, though this may be a side-benefit. Also, to show awareness and observation of thoughts, mind chatter and/or noise.

Requirements

None.

Time

Ten minutes.

Set up

Sit up tall, comfortably and securely in your chair or on the floor, or alternatively lie down with your back flat on the floor.

Tasks

1. Imagine you have a laser that is going to scan your body from the top of your head to the tips of your toes.
2. Starting with the top of your head, start the laser scan. Notice if there are any feelings of pain, discomfort, tension or tightness. Notice what you notice and leave it as it is, not judging it as good or bad; let it just be.
3. Gradually move the laser scanner down to your throat. Notice if there are any feelings of pain, discomfort, tension or tightness. Notice what you notice and leave it as it is, not judging it as good or bad; let it just be.
4. Gradually move the laser scanner down to your shoulders. Notice if there are any feelings of pain, discomfort, tension or tightness. Notice what you notice and leave it as it is, not judging it as good or bad; let it just be.

5. Gradually move the laser scanner down to your upper arms. Notice if there are any feelings of pain, discomfort, tension or tightness. Notice what you notice and leave it as it is, not judging it as good or bad; let it **just be**. Notice any thoughts wandering in your mind; just let them float around freely and easily.
6. Gradually move the laser scanner down to your lower arms. Notice if there are any feelings of pain, discomfort, tension or tightness. Notice what you notice and leave it as it is, not judging it as good or bad; let it **just be**.
7. Gradually move the laser scanner down to your hands. Notice if there are any feelings of pain, discomfort, tension or tightness. Notice what you notice and leave it as it is, not judging it as good or bad; let it **just be**.
8. Gradually move the laser scanner down to your chest. Notice if there are any feelings of pain, discomfort, tension or tightness. Notice what you notice and leave it as it is, not judging it as good or bad; let it **just be**.
9. Gradually move the laser scanner down to your upper back. Notice if there are any feelings of pain, discomfort, tension or tightness. Notice what you notice and leave it as it is, not judging it as good or bad; let it **just be**.
10. Gradually move the laser scanner down to your stomach. Notice if there are any feelings of pain, discomfort, tension or tightness. Notice what you notice and leave it as it is, not judging it as good or bad; let it **just be**.
11. Gradually move the laser scanner down to your lower back. Notice if there are any feelings of pain, discomfort, tension or tightness. Notice what you notice and leave it as it is, not judging it as good or bad; let it **just be**.
12. Gradually move the laser scanner down to your pelvis. Notice if there are any feelings of pain, discomfort, tension or tightness. Notice what you notice and leave it as it is, not judging it as good or bad; let it **just be**.
13. Gradually move the laser scanner down to your upper legs. Notice if there are any feelings of pain, discomfort, tension or tightness. Notice what you notice and leave it as it is, not judging it as good or bad; let it **just be**.
14. Gradually move the laser scanner down to your lower legs. Notice if there are any feelings of pain, discomfort, tension or tightness. Notice what you notice and leave it as it is, not judging it as good or bad; let it **just be**.
15. Gradually move the laser scanner down to your feet. Notice if there are any feelings of pain, discomfort, tension or tightness. Notice what you notice and leave it as it is, not judging it as good or bad; let it **just be**.

<u>Progression</u>

1. Focus on one area of your body that you do not like in front of a mirror.
2. Focus on one area of your body that is in pain or discomfort.

Zen Breathing

Think
By yourself.

Objective
Simply to notice your breathing, not to relax or relieve stress, though this may be a side-benefit. Also, to show awareness and observation of thoughts, mind chatter and/or noise.

Requirements
None.

Time
Five minutes.

Set up
Sit up tall, comfortably and securely in your chair with both feet flat on the floor and hands in your lap.

Tasks

1. Breathing is an unconscious process. We all do it all the time, and it is the life-force that keeps us alive and kicking — also called 'Chi' energy. Focus all your attention on your breathing.
2. Start to notice where the in-breath enters the body. Through your nose? Through your mouth?
3. Start to notice how the in-breath travels from entry into your lungs. Just notice what you're noticing, and let any wandering thoughts **just be** as you focus on your breath.
4. Start to notice if your in-breath is warm or cold.
5. Start to notice where your out-breath leaves the body. Through your nose? Through your mouth?
6. Start to notice how your lungs and diaphragm relax to let the in-breath enter.
7. Start to notice the rate of your breath. Is it slow or fast? Just notice what you're noticing, and let any wandering thoughts **just be** as you focus on your breath.
8. Start to notice the depth of your breath. Is it deep or shallow?
9. Start to notice how your stomach or rib cage expands on your in-breath.
10. Start to notice on your out-breath, how your diaphragm contracts to expel the air out of your lungs, and how your stomach or rib cage contracts.

Progressions

1. Lay down with your eyes closed.
2. Take shoes off and do this in a park or garden in which is safe to walk barefoot.

Alternate Nostril Breathing

Think
By yourself.

Objective
Simply to notice your breathing, not to relax or relieve stress, though this may be a side-benefit. To show an awareness and observation of thoughts, mind chatter and/or noise.

Requirements
None.

Time
Five minutes.

Set up
Ensure that all the participants have clear nose and sinuses — blow your nose if need be. Sit up tall, comfortably and securely in your chair and gently seal your lips. Place your left hand on your left thigh, and raise your right hand up to your face with your palm facing towards your face. Place your middle and index fingers in the middle of your eyebrows.

Tasks

1. Breathe gently whilst relaxing your neck and shoulders.
2. Close your right nostril by pressing it with your thumb whilst inhaling and exhaling, using your left nostril as normal, five times.
3. Now release your thumb and close your left nostril with your little finger whilst inhaling and exhaling, using your right nostril as normal, five times.
4. Notice when you breathe, how refreshed and energised you feel
5. Next you are going to alternate the in-breath on the left nostril by closing the right nostril with your thumb and releasing the little finger
6. Take an out-breath on the right nostril by releasing the thumb and pressing the little finger closing the left nostrils. Repeat five times
7. Release both fingers and bring your right hand to rest on your lap, palms facing upwards, breathing normally through both nostrils.
8. Do you notice any change in your mind, balance or energy levels?

Zen Thinking

Think
By yourself.

Objective
To identify that thoughts are not facts. To understanding that thoughts, when repeated for prolonged periods of time, become beliefs. To start to think about thinking (meta-cognition) to move away from accepting thoughts as facts.

Requirements
None.

Time
Ten minutes.

Set up
Sit up tall, comfortably and securely in your chair or on the floor.

Tasks
1. *'A thought is not a fact — a thought is just a thought'* — Jon Kabat-Zinn.
   - For example, 'I am bad', 'nobody gets me', or even, 'I am the best'.
   - Do you have any such thoughts?
2. Identifying that thoughts are not facts.
3. Understanding that thoughts, when repeated for prolonged periods of time, become beliefs.
4. Start to think about thinking (meta-cognition) to move away from accepting thoughts as facts.
   - Start with mindfulness breathing.
   - Notice what you're noticing, and just let any wandering thoughts just be, as you breathe.
   - Notice the wandering thoughts in your mind, and accept these without judging them as good or bad, positive or negative.
   - If you are struggling to find thoughts in your mind now, then think about that... that is a thought which you can allow yourself to think about now.
   - Thoughts are like leaves falling on a flowing river. Just as one leaf falls it drifts away downstream, and another leaf falls, only for that to drift away downstream too, and so on.
   - Buddhist monks like to think of thoughts as pages written on water. Just as you notice one thought, it is replaced by another; the thoughts come and go, continuously flowing.
   - Now bring yourself back in the room, fully aware, switched on and energetic.

Progressions
1. Do this activity in a park or garden in a safe place near running water like a fountain or gentle stream.

Zen Walking

Think
By yourself.

Objective
Simple awareness and observation of thoughts, mind chatter and/or noise.

Requirements
None.

Time
Ten minutes.

Set up
Ensure that the room is safe to take a dozen steps before you have to turn. Take shoes off and play this game in a park or garden that is safe to walk on barefoot.

Tasks
1. Standing still, notice your body — **still**.
2. **Feel the connection** between your feet and the ground.
3. Become aware of the environment around you, noticing what you see, hear, feel, smell, taste and any other sensations.
4. Just notice what you're noticing, and let any wandering thoughts **just be** as you focus on your environment.
5. Notice where your arms are, by your sides, in front of you, or behind you?
6. Notice your breath moving in and out of your body. Just notice what you're noticing, and let any wandering thoughts **just be** as you focus on your breathing.
7. As you begin to **lift** your right leg, notice how you shift your weight onto your left leg as you move it smoothly forward whilst placing it gently on the ground.
8. As you begin to **lift** your left leg, notice how you shift your weight onto your right leg as you move it smoothly forward whilst placing it gently on the ground.
9. Paying close attention to the soles of your feet as you continue walking mindfully. Notice how each part of your sole touches the ground from the heel to the toe.
10. Notice how your body shifts its weight as you walk one step at a time... **lifting**, moving, landing.
11. When you need to turn, do it with fluidity, keeping your awareness on your motion of turning as you start to walk back to where you started.
12. Just notice what you're noticing, and let any wandering thoughts **just be** as you focus on your walking... **lifting**, moving, landing.
13. As you walk, notice your rhythm of motion... **lifting**, moving, landing..

14. As you move, notice where your head, neck, shoulders, arms, torso, hips and legs are as **you move forward one step at a time**
15. Notice your breathing. Notice if it has synchronised with your motion of walking and just let it be.
16. As you walk, just notice what you're noticing, and let any wandering thoughts **just be** as you focus on each motion one at a time.
17. **Keep on moving forwards.**
18. When you return to your starting position next, stand **still** noticing all your sensations in your breathing, body and mind.
19. Notice the **stillness** when the motion comes to a stand.

Sixth Sense

Think
By yourself.

Objective
Simply to notice what you're feeling, hearing, seeing, saying, tasting and smelling at that moment, with a gentle, non-judgmental acceptance and curiosity. To understand that we have been taught to think that there are good and bad thoughts, feelings and emotions, and in reality, they are just what they are.

Requirements
None.

Time
Ten minutes.

Set up
Sit up tall and comfortably, securely in your chair or lay comfortably on the floor.

Tasks
1. Start with mindful breathing.
2. Notice what feelings or emotions that you are experiencing right now.
3. If you can label the feelings and emotions, then that is OK. If you can't, then **just be** aware of what they are.
4. Notice where the feeling or emotion is located in your body
   - For example your gut, heart, or head.
5. Notice if the feeling or emotion is moving... Is it:
   - Rising up and out?
   - Dropping down and out?
   - Circling clockwise?
   - Circling anti-clockwise?
6. Notice how the feelings and emotions make you feel.
   - For example, harmony or anxiety.

7. Notice if there are any emotions that come with the feelings, and just be aware of them with non-judgement.
   - There are no good feelings or emotions.
   - There are no bad feelings or emotions.
8. As you sit **still**, notice whether the thoughts, feelings and emotions are moving about, and the physical sensations.
9. Notice what you're noticing, and just let any wandering thoughts **just be** as you focus on your breathing now.

Outer Stillness

The third stage of Stillness is Outer Stillness. This includes activities to create stillness externally, i.e. they still the outside world.

Ninja Walking

Share

Three or more people.

Objective

To allow you to switch off your critical faculty with a fun game. This requires stillness in motion. It establishes team building by working in a group and creating non-verbal communication. Furthermore, the movement activates your body to improve motor skills such as agility, balance and coordination.

Requirements

A scroll or cone (aka 'Dragon Scroll') and a water gun.

Time

Ten minutes.

Set up

Ensure that the room is safe to take a dozen steps from the edge of the room to the centre. Mark off an area called 'The Dungeon'. Remove your shoes if the ground is safe to walk with bare feet. Someone volunteers or is chosen to be 'The Guard' and stands blindfolded in the middle of the room with the 'Dragon Scroll' next to him/her on the floor. The rest of the group stand still on the edges of the room.

Tasks

1. The rest of the group have to try to steal the 'Dragon Scroll' without getting caught by moving as stealthily as possible so that 'The Guard' cannot catch them;
2. If 'The Guard' tags anyone that comes close, then they are sent to 'The Dungeon' (i.e. they are out-of-the-game), and must go sit quietly in the area marked as 'The Dungeon'.

Progressions

1. Take shoes off and play this game in a park or garden which is safe to walk on barefoot;
2. The guard has a water gun, and can shoot at potential thieves. When the thieves get shot, they are sent to 'The Dungeon'.

Phasic Vision

Share

Three or more people.

Objective

To allow you to switch off your critical faculty with a fun game. To create a state of alertness and awareness. To establish team building by working in a group and creating non-verbal communication. The movement activates your body to improve motor skills such as agility, balance and coordination. It requires stillness in motion.

Requirements

None.

Time

Ten minutes.

Set up

Someone volunteers or is chosen to be 'The Chosen One' and stands in the middle of the room. The rest of the group form a semi-circle in the visual field in front of 'The Chosen One'.

Tasks

1. 'The Chosen One' enables their Phasic Vision by bringing their arms up in front them at shoulder level, with the palms facing each other. 'The Chosen One' looks ahead at one fixed point at someone's chest height. As they wiggle their fingers, they start to spread their arms to the sides until they can just about see the wiggling fingers on the edge of their peripheral vision. Once the phasic vision is enabled, then they can drop their arms and relax whilst maintaining the state of alertness and awareness created.
2. The rest of the group are required to make small movements one at a time by communicating stealthily with one another to coordinate their efforts.
3. 'The Chosen One' is required to detect any motion made by the group and point to it as quickly as possible.

Progressions

1. The movements from the rest of the group are not coordinated, hence can occur in any randomised order;
2. 'The Chosen One' has a water gun, and can shoot anyone that moves, who are then eliminated from the game when shot.

Empty Your Teacup

Think
By yourself.

Objective
To switch off mind chatter and noise. To anchor points of stillness in pauses of breath. When the mind becomes quiet, you simply exist, without body, without mind, without breath.

Requirements
None.

Time
Ten minutes.

Set up
Sit up tall, comfortably and securely in your chair with both feet flat on the floor and your hands placed on your laps, palms open facing the ceiling like teacups.

Tasks

1. Gently open your mouth, and touch the roof of your mouth with your tongue behind the front teeth.
2. Feel free to close your eyes.
3. Notice your breathing.
4. Notice how your lungs work with comfort and ease as you inhale and exhale.
5. Notice how the cool air touches the inside of the nostrils or mouth as you breathe in.
6. Notice how the warmer air touches the inside of your nostrils or mouth.
7. Now imagine that you are sitting in your nostril and watching the waves of your in-breath, out-breath, in-breath, out-breath, in-breath, out-breath, whilst your lungs just do their job easily and effortlessly as you sit there inside the nostril, noticing what you notice.
8. Repeat this for a few minutes. Keep watching your in-breath, out-breath, in-breath, out-breath, in-breath, out-breath…
9. Now jump on the wave of air on the in-breath as you start surfing the wave entering into the nose, surfing into the back of the throat, surfing down the trachea, surfing through the lungs, surfing through the bloodstream, surfing in and out of the heart and surfing into your abdomen, where you will experience a natural pause.
10. Where **everything is still**, without body, without mind, without breath. **It is just you in the moment**, like an empty teacup, surrounded by tranquillity and peace;
11. And then there is another wave which surges you forward as you continue surfing out of the abdomen, surf through the bloodstream, surf through the lungs, surf up the trachea, surf through the nose and out of the body coming to a natural pause 10cm in front of the nostrils;

12. Where **everything is still,** without body, without mind, without breath. **It is just you in the moment,** like an empty teacup, surrounded by tranquillity and peace…
13. And you know that between every breath you take, there is a natural pause…
14. And every time you pause, there is a moment where **everything is still,** tranquil and peaceful, like an empty teacup.
15. You know where **stillness exists now,** don't you? That's right.
16. When you are ready, focus your attention onto your body sitting securely, comfortably, effortlessly in your chair.
17. Bring that **feeling of stillness,** tranquillity and peace back into the room with the pause of each breath, as you gently open your eyes — alive, invigorated, energetic.

Progressions

1. Take shoes off and sit down in a park or garden that is safe and clean to sit in.

Visualisation

Think

By yourself.

Objective

To use visualisation for relaxation and create a resource, a 'happy place' anchor.

Requirements

None.

Time

Ten minutes.

Set up

Sit up tall, comfortably and securely in your chair, with both feet flat on the floor and your hands placed in your lap.

Tasks

1. Gently close your eyes.
2. Blank the picture in your mind now.
3. Imagine a place where you feel comfortable, safe, relaxed… your 'happy place'. This place may be a beach, park, or even your own home.
4. Now your 'happy place' starts to appear in front of you — vivid, loud and clear.
5. Now look to your left. What can you see?
6. What sounds can you hear around you?

7. Take a deep breath in. What do you smell?
8. Now take a walk around your 'happy place', looking, touching, feeling things as you explore. How does your 'happy place' make you feel?
9. Keeping your eyes closed, place your hand over your eyes.
10. Gently open your eyes.
11. Then slowly spread your fingers apart, letting light in.
12. When you are ready, bring the 'happy place' with you as you slowly remove your hand.

Progressions
1. Draw your 'happy place' after doing visualisation.

The Hunting Game

Think
By yourself.

Objective
Get participants into a state of stillness by creating a state of high alertness and awareness, without thinking.

Requirements
None.

Time
Ten minutes.

Set up
Ensure that the room is safe to walk around. Remove your shoes if the ground is safe to walk with bare feet.

Tasks
1. Imagine this room is a jungle, and you are hunting for a really rare fruit that only grows in your special jungle.
2. Imagine there are trees, shrubs, flowers, roots, and mud.
3. Imagine the sun is streaking through the trees, reflecting off the beautiful flowers and leaves.
4. To be a good hunter, you must be on high alert…
5. You must be stealth — move slowly and quietly so no animal or insect can hear you.
6. You must walk slowly and stealthily between the trees, shrubs, flowers, roots and mud, so as not to disturb other animals and avoiding stepping on the beautiful plants.
7. As you listen out for every sound.
8. As you look out for the slightest movement in the jungle.

9. As you feel your way around the jungle.
10. You walk stealthily and carefully with every step, because there is slippery mud, streams and even crags and ridges that you carefully avoid.
11. And there in the distance you see a deer. It has stopped frozen still looking at you. Then it comfortably decides that **you are a friendly human** and continues hopping along **doing your own thing**;
12. And then you notice a beautiful butterfly. You notice what colour, pattern, size and shape its wings have. You notice how it **flutters elegantly**, like it's **playing joyfully** in the fresh jungle air to the songs of the birds in the trees;
13. Let your imagination go wild, literally here... take several minutes.
14. Have you found the rare fruit yet?
15. Aaah there it is. You see the fruit in the distance, and you walk over to it stealthily.
16. Notice the fruit is hanging off a branch of a tree, or is it a bush.
17. Notice the colour, size, shape of the fruit.
18. You decide to pick the fruit, and start reaching for it. You notice your arm reaching out in front of you as your hand grabs the fruit.
19. Notice the texture, temperature and weight of the fruit as you grab it and yank it off the branch. The whole branch shakes.
20. Notice the fruit in your hand; how amazing it looks. Notice how you have started to salivate as you draw the fruit towards your mouth.
21. Notice how the fruit feels when you put it against your lips, and when you open your mouth to take the first bite;
22. You take a bite, and notice the texture of the fruit. Notice how it tastes. Notice how juicy it is.

<u>Progression</u>

1. Practice mindful breathing first;
2. Take shoes off and play this game in a park or garden, which is safe to walk on barefoot.

The Zen Zone

Think
By yourself.

Objective
Simply to notice your breathing, not to relax or relieve stress, though this may be a side-benefit.

Requirements
None.

Time
Ten minutes.

Set up
Sit up tall and comfortably, securely in your chair.

Tasks
1. Gently close your eyes.
2. Notice how your body rests against the chair.
3. Your feet firmly on the floor, the backs of your legs maybe touching the front of the chair, your buttocks resting on the chair, your back resting against the backrest, your shoulders and neck relaxed.
4. Notice where your arms are resting — by your sides, in your lap, or on the armrests.
5. Notice what your hands are touching — the armrests, your lap, each other, the chair or just simply the air around you.
6. Notice your head sitting on your shoulders effortlessly and easily.
7. Notice the sounds around you. Move your focus from one sound to another.
8. Notice any smells around you. Is there more than one smell?
9. Notice your breathing. Simple, natural, effortless and easy. Life is easy…
10. Notice your in-breath and out-breath moving in and out of your body.
11. Notice the movement the breathing creates in your body as your chest or abdomen rises and falls.
12. Notice the temperature of the air coming in and out of your body — cool and warm.
13. Just notice what you're noticing. That's right!
14. Now gently open your eyes when you are ready to do so.

Progressions
1. Expand awareness to feelings, sounds, tension, tightness, etc.

Eagle Eye

Think
By yourself.

Objective
To become still by focussing on an unusual object.

Requirements
Paper and a pencil (and keep a pencil sharpener and eraser to hand).

Time
Twenty minutes.

Set up
Sit up tall and comfortably, securely in your chair at a desk. You will need a paper and sharp pencil.

Tasks
1. Choose a safe object to draw — for example, an empty teacup or empty bowl.
2. The aim of the activity is to notice details about the object and draw them in your picture.
3. The more details you notice and draw, the better, even if your picture is not exactly the same.
4. When you finish the first picture, redraw it a second time.
5. Look for any differences between your first and second pictures.
6. Notice what you notice. Which picture is more accurate? What was it like to become aware of an object that you wouldn't usually study?

Progressions
1. Use colour pencils, felt tips, paints, etc.
2. Use a PC or tablet computer to draw the pictures.

Rising Bubbles

Think
By yourself.

Objective
To create awareness of thoughts, and let go with a gentle, non-judgmental acceptance and curiosity.

Requirements
None.

Time
Five minutes.

Set up
Sit up tall and comfortably, securely in your chair.

Tasks
The instructor reads the following script to the participants, and allows it to take affect:

1. Sit securely in your chair, comfortable, effortless and easily.
2. Gently close your eyes.
3. Now imagine beautiful bubbles start to rise up in front of you.
4. Each bubble contains a thought, feeling, emotion or perception
5. As you see the next bubble rise up, notice what's in it
6. Notice the thought, feeling, emotion or perception in it
7. Just let the bubble rise further and further away from you until that thought, feeling, emotion or perception floats away out of sight, out of mind, easily and effortlessly... That's right
8. Now do the same on the next bubble you notice rising up
9. Repeat this process until all the bubbles are empty inside and slowly float away.

Progressions
1. Use a bubble machine.

Direct Relaxation

The fourth and final stage of Stillness is Direct Relaxation. These include activities to create a state of relaxation using direct relaxation exercises.

Yin and Yang Relaxation

Pair
Another person reads this script to you in a calm and soothing voice.

Objective
To relax the body and mind.

Requirements
None.

Time
Ten minutes.

Set up
Lay down comfortably on your back, flat on the floor, with your arms by your sides and your palms facing up to the ceiling.

Tasks
1. Gently close your eyes as you deepen your relaxation.
2. As you lay there on the floor, feel your body pressing against the floor.
3. Now, starting from your head, press it into the ground — press, press, press.
4. Keep pressing your head into the floor, and moving down to your neck, press it into the ground as well, press, press, press;
5. Keep pressing the head and neck into the floor. Then, moving down to your shoulders, press them into the ground as well — press, press, press.
6. Keep pressing the head, neck and shoulders into the floor. Then, moving down to your upper arms, press them into the ground as well — press, press, press.
7. Keep pressing the head, neck, shoulders and upper arms into the floor. Then, moving down to your forearms, press them into the ground as well — press, press, press.
8. Keep pressing the head, neck, shoulders, upper arms and forearms into the floor. Then, moving down to your hands, press them into the ground as well — press, press, press.
9. Keep pressing the head, neck, shoulders, upper arms, forearms and hands into the floor. Then, moving to your upper back, press it into the ground as well — press, press, press.
10. Keep pressing the head, neck, shoulders, upper arms, forearms, hands and upper back into the floor. Then, moving to your lower back, press it into the ground as well — press, press, press.

11. Keep pressing the head, neck, shoulders, upper arms, forearms, hands, upper back and lower back into the floor. Then, moving to your hips, press them into the ground as well — press, press, press.
12. Keep pressing the head, neck, shoulders, upper arms, forearms, hands, upper back, lower back and hips into the floor. Then, moving to your upper legs, press them into the ground as well — press, press, press.
13. Keep pressing the head, neck, shoulders, upper arms, forearms, hands, upper back, lower back, hips and upper legs into the floor. Then, moving to your lower legs, press them into the ground as well — press, press, press.
14. Keep pressing the head, neck, shoulders, upper arms, forearms, hands, upper back, lower back, hips, upper legs and lower legs into the floor. Then, moving to your heels, press them into the ground as well — press, press, press.
15. Pressing everything into the ground — press, press, press.
16. Now **stop pressing** and **relax all your muscles now!**
17. Wait for six to heaven minutes.
18. In a moment, I am going to count back from ten to one. You will come back to full awareness, feeling energetic and switched on one tenth on each count. Ten, nine, eight, feeling more aware, seven, six, five, feeling energy flowing through every cell of your body, four, three, two, fully switched on, aware and energetic, and one, back in the room. Open your eyes. Roll onto your side and push yourself up to a seated position on the floor.

Progressions

1. Play some soothing music to help you relax.
2. Play this game in a park or garden that is safe and clean to stretch out upon.

Stealth Ninjas

Share
Three or more people, where one person is the nominated leader and takes everyone through the steps of this direct relaxation exercise.

Objective
To relax the body and mind and to teach stillness in motion.

Requirements
None.

Time
Ten minutes.

Set up
Sitting comfortably on the floor, in a position where you can get up and down safely.

Tasks
1. We are now going to be stealth ninjas…
2. Close your eyes as you sit there comfortably.
3. The leader will say, 'In a moment, I will call someone's name. When you hear your name, then come over stealthily and sit next to me.'
4. The leader will then stealthily walk to the other side of the room and wait for a minute or so in silence.
5. The leader then softly whispers a participant's name.
6. The named participant gets up and stealthily walks over to the leader and sits next to him/her.
7. The leader calls the name of each participant in the group one-by-one until the whole group is reunited at the other side of the room.
8. Enjoy a few minutes of silence together.

Progressions
1. See 'Ninja Walking' activity.
2. Take shoes off and play this game in a park or garden that is safe to walk on barefoot.

Zen Silence

Think
By yourself.

Objective
Relax the body and mind.

Requirements
None.

Time
Two minutes.

Set up
Sit up tall, comfortably and securely in your chair, with both feet flat on the floor and both hands resting comfortably in your lap.

Tasks

1. Start with mindful breathing.
2. Gently close your eyes.
3. Sit in comfort and ease in absolute stillness.
4. Wait for one minute.

Progressions

1. Take your shoes off and play this game in a park or garden that is safe to walk on barefoot.

Settle Down

A bell rings.

As you listen to the sound of the bell fading, notice how the grains of the sand in the jar containing the muddied water **start to settle.**

Notice how the coloured sand starts to **fall calmly** to the bottom of the jar of water, as **you settle down.**

Notice how the jar of water **starts to become clear now.**

Notice how the **thoughts and feelings rest** at the bottom of the jar of water.

Notice how clear, calm and crisp your pure water from your mind is.

Take a Step Back to See the Big Picture

Question

If you were to **Change the Way Society, Work and Politics Dictate Our Daily Lives**, then what changes would you make? Take fifteen minutes to brainstorm some ideas how you would create positive change in the world.

This requires some 'Divergent Thinking'. Have you ever considered the following...?

Give Everyone a Base Salary

Denmark is a perfect example of a country which gives all its needy residents a base salary, so everyone is effectively salaried one way or another.

Denmark follows a **societal model** in which **the state assumes primary responsibility for the welfare of its citizens**. This responsibility (in theory) is comprehensive; all aspects of welfare are considered to be universally applied to people living and working in Denmark, since receiving the benefits of the welfare state is deemed as the **citizens' basic right**. In this model, the state implements pension schemes, supports maternity and paternity leave, provides benefits for the unemployed and supports those living with disabilities.

The maximum unemployment benefit in Denmark in 2013 was 17,355Kr per month, which is approximately £1,900 per month, which is a reasonable amount to live comfortably in Denmark.

Countries with a generous welfare system such as Denmark impose income taxes up to 60% along with other social taxes. The VAT amounts to 25%. These **taxes**, however, **are redistributed by the state to the needy** such as the unemployed. This type of welfare system is usually referred to as **the Nordic Model.**

For more information on Denmark's welfare systems, please check out:
www.MartialMindPower.com/Resources

Standard of Living

Crime and safety levels in a country are usually good indicators of the standard of living in any given country. On this basis, the Danes have a better standard of living than do we in the UK and USA. Check out the statistics, they speak for themselves:

%	Crime Index	Safety Index
Denmark	25.71	74.29
UK	42.01	57.99
USA	50.01	49.99

Table 3: Crime and safety indices for Denmark, UK and USA by Numbeo in 2015.

For more information, please check out crime and safety indices for other countries at:
www.MartialMindPower.com/Resources

Now, ask yourself the question, why is it that the Danes have less people in unemployment when they could comfortably live off the state?

The secret lies in what the Danes create. They are famous for the following inventions:

1. Magnetic Storage. Valdemar Poulsen (1869-1942) created the telegraphone or wire recorder in 1898, which was the forerunner of magnetic tape storage.
2. The Loudspeaker. On Christmas Eve 1915, an expectant crowd of 75,000 people stood in front of the City Hall in San Francisco to watch the Danish inventor Peter L. Jensen (1886-1962) demonstrate the world's first loudspeaker. Cheers erupted as the singing voice of a well-known opera diva of the day filled the airwaves, and resonated over a distance of one and a half kilometres.
3. The Dry Cell. In the 1880's Wilhelm Hellesen (1836-1892) put wheat flour into an electrolyte to create the world's first dry cell. He was exporting to fifty countries by the 1890s.
4. Insulin. Though August Krogh (1874-1949) did not discover insulin, he improved it, and was awarded the Nobel Prize in Physiology or Medicine in 1920 for the discovery of the capillary regulatory mechanism in skeletal muscle.
5. The Ostomy Bag. In 1953, Danish nurse Elise Sørensen invented the ostomy bag, a simple but effective device.
6. The Lego Brick. Lego became famous for holding together firmly while also being easy to separate.
7. Carlsberg Yeast. Microbiologist Emil Christian Hansen was employed in the Carlsberg Laboratory in the Copenhagen suburb of Valby in 1877. He was involved in the invention of Brewer's Yeast, used to produce lager beer.

Happy Index

In The Legatum Institute's 2013 Prosperity Index report, Denmark was ranked second place as the Happiest Place to Live for the past four consecutive years, and fell to sixth place in 2013, far ahead of the United Kingdom which lay in a measly sixteenth place and the United States which ranked at eleventh.

Denmark also placed:

- Second in Entrepreneurship and Opportunity.
- Third in Social Capital.
- Ninth in Personal Freedom.

Overall Prosperity Rank	Country	Economy	Entrepreneurship & Opportunity	Governance	Education	Health	Safety & Security	Personal Freedom	Social Capital
1	Norway	1	6	12	4	5	6	2	1
2	Switzerland	2	4	1	27	3	11	15	8
3	Canada	4	16	8	3	11	7	1	6
4	Sweden	6	1	4	14	12	3	4	10
5	New Zealand	17	15	2	1	20	15	5	2
6	Denmark	23	2	3	18	14	8	9	3
7	Australia	10	11	7	2	17	16	3	4
8	Finland	26	3	5	6	16	4	17	7
9	Netherlands	20	8	10	12	7	17	14	5
10	Luxembourg	14	5	6	46	1	10	7	17
11	United States	24	13	11	5	2	31	16	9
12	Ireland	33	14	14	11	15	5	8	11
13	Iceland	41	7	18	13	13	2	6	13
14	Germany	9	18	17	15	4	21	12	15
15	Austria	15	17	15	17	9	14	19	14
16	United Kingdom	28	9	9	30	19	22	13	12
17	Belgium	25	24	16	16	10	20	18	21
18	Singapore	3	12	13	37	18	13	53	34
19	Hong Kong	18	10	23	43	30	1	24	28
20	France	22	21	19	19	8	30	21	42
21	Japan	5	25	21	21	6	25	48	23
22	Taiwan	16	22	33	10	25	9	31	30
23	Spain	44	29	26	8	24	27	23	27

Table 4: The Legatum Institute's 2013 prosperity index.

Check out The Legatum Institute's Prosperity Index at www.MartialMindPower.com/Resources

Destroy the Current 'Busyness' Politico-Socio-Economic System

This seems like a far-fetched concept, though this has already been done by countries like Denmark to remarkable effect, having established one of the highest qualities of life, with low crime, high safety, and a high happiness for its citizens, as discussed in the previous section.

The key to implementing this effectively was to establish a simple tax regime, and use those tax proceeds to help improve the quality of life for its citizens, and ultimately making this mechanism self-perpetuating so as to not rely on the governments for any funding.

Another brilliant example of a simple low tax regime has been witnessed in Hong Kong. Whilst under British rule, Hong Kong was resurrected from the slums. Hong Kong is now one of the most prosperous cities in the world, having re-invented itself in particular over the past fifty years. This was achieved by the abolition of the complex tax preceding it, and the introduction of a simple low tax regime. The question is, why hasn't this system been implemented in the UK since it was conceptualised and implemented by the British in the first instance.

Mr Iliffe previously worked in Hong Kong from 1986 to 1991, and returned in 2011 after twelve years in Ottawa, Canada. He believes the SAR's (now called the Special Administrative Region of China after Hong Kong was granted back to China in 1997) simple, flat, low-tax regime is the foundation of its renowned economic dynamism. Even China realises this is too good to change, and has maintained it so far.

Mr Iliffe says, 'Hong Kong keeps it very simple. There's no capital gains tax, there's no dividend tax, there's no tax on interest and you are only taxed on income earned in Hong Kong — not overseas. The system here makes people more entrepreneurial. Maximum personal tax is 15%, but there are lots of allowances to get it lower, and corporate tax is set at 16.5% — so people are not spending half their time trying to avoid or evade. You have money in your pocket and you do things with it. You invest. You buy shares or you start second businesses.'

The idea of establishing a simple tax regime across the board also implies that the more you earn through creativity, innovation and entrepreneurship, the more you keep, as opposed to feeling penalised for doing better, as it seems is the consensus in the UK and USA with a very complex layered and scaled taxation regime.

For more information on Hong Kong's tax regime, check out www.MartialMindPower.com/Resources

Educate, Inspire and Empower People for Creative Freeflow

If you would like to learn more about finding your flow, then go to the chapter, 'Be Like Water'.

In political economics, entrepreneurship is the process of identifying and starting a business venture, sourcing and organising the required resources and taking both the risks and rewards associated with the venture.

Like the terms 'strategy' and 'business model', the word 'entrepreneurship' is elastic. For some, it refers to venture capital-backed start-ups and their kin; for others, any small business. For some, 'corporate entrepreneurship' is a rallying cry; for others, an oxymoron.

The definition used by the Harvard Business School (HBS), formulated by Professor Howard Stevenson, the godfather of entrepreneurship studies at HBS goes like this:

Entrepreneurship is the pursuit of opportunity beyond resources controlled.

- 'Pursuit' implies a singular, relentless focus and urgency seldom seen in most companies.
- 'Opportunity' implies an offering that is novel in one or more of four ways (which are not mutually exclusive). These are:

1. By pioneering a truly innovative product.
2. By devising a new business model.

3. By **creating** a better or cheaper version of an existing product.
4. By **targeting** an existing product to new sets of customers.

- **'Beyond resources controlled'** implies resource constraints. At a new venture's outset, its founders control only their own human, social and financial capital. Eventually, high-potential ventures must mobilise more resources than they control personally for production facilities, distribution channels, working capital, and so forth.
- As with any entrepreneurial venture, there are risks, which include:

1. **Demand risk** relates to prospective customers' willingness to adopt the solution envisioned by the entrepreneur.
2. **Technology risk** is high when engineering or scientific breakthroughs are required to bring a solution to fruition.
3. **Execution risk** relates to the entrepreneurs ability to attract employees and partners who can implement the ventures plans.
4. **Financing risk** relates to whether external capital will be available on reasonable terms.

The entrepreneur's task is therefore to manage this uncertainty, while recognising that certain risks cannot be influenced by their actions.

Arthur C. Clarke came up with the idea of satellite communications, and he quoted:

'The goal of the future is full UNemployment, so we can play.
That's why we have to destroy the present politico-economic system.'

Arthur came up with the satellite communications idea between scuba diving and playing pinball games, whilst writing a book called *Childhood's End.*

Calm After the Storm

Over the muddied lake, almost as if by a miracle, the relentless rainstorm started to slow down.

As the clouds started to part, the warm sun started to streak through.

The sun caressed my face, with a soothing warm feeling.

As the clouds dissolved away into the blue skies, and the winds died down, you can see clearly now across the landscape.

The lake started to glisten as the sun reflected off of it, and it was like I'd discovered a million jewels.

I could see the depths of the bottom of the deep clear blue lake clearly now.

I felt enveloped with an overwhelming feeling of harmony and happiness as I stood there in that moment in time, enjoy the present of nature.

Conclusion

I cannot say if the world would turn to ruin if you take on these divergent ideas. On the other hand, some would say that it does not need your help, as the current politico-socio-economic framework seems to be doing a jolly good job of that already, so anything would be an improvement.

All I can say is, there are places like Denmark and Hong Kong that showcase some of these divergent ideas in practice, reaping some amazing results for its citizens in the process.

Their formula is one based on creativity and innovation, born out of freeflow of ideas, inspired through dreams and a playful heart.

'To live your dream, you must dream.

To dream, you must relax.

To relax, you must learn the art of stillness.'

I hope I have been able to help you to start seeing, hearing and feeling how to:

- Switch OFF the noise in your mind.
- Stop being 'busy being busy'.
- Practice the art of stillness.
- Take a step back to see the big picture using Divergent Thinking.
- Live in the now.
- Connect to Mother Nature, yourself and humanity.

...over the course of this amazing **Stillness** stage of your self-mastery journey, so you can liberate yourself and align yourself for success in all areas of your life.

And that brings us to the end of the **Stillness** stage of your self-mastery journey. Before you embark on **BEING STILL and MOVING TO SUCCESS**, please answer the following:

Question

1. Do you understand how to **Still Your Mind**? (Yes or No)
2. Do you understand how to **Switch OFF the Noise** in your head? (Yes or No)
3. Do you know how to **Stop Being 'Busy Being Busy'**? (Yes or No)
4. Do you know how to step back to **See the Big Picture Now**? (Yes or No)
5. Do you have a heightened **Sense Of Clarity Now**? (Yes or No)
6. Do you understand how to **Connect to Nature, Humanity and Yourself?** (Yes or No)
7. Do you know how to **Find Inner Peace and Harmony** for your emotional management? (Yes or No)
8. Do you understand how to **Enjoy Living in the Present** moment? (Yes or No)

9. Do you understand how to **Achieve Inner Harmony and Happiness**? (Yes or No)
10. Are you **Primed for Success**? (Yes or No)
11. Are you ready to **Switch OFF to Switch ON**? (Yes or No)

My friend, I would like to deeply thank you for giving me the chance to take you through this **Master Your Life** journey, and remember:

'BE STILL and
MOVE TO SUCCESS!'

2

Empty your teacup

Empty Your Teacup

STAGE 2 — YELLOW BELT

Master Your Mind

What's the Problem?

So, who is this stage of your self-mastery journey aimed at?

- People who have closed minds and reject new ideas and thoughts readily.
- People who are too proud and egotistical.
- People who are stubborn and inflexible.
- People who are control freaks and like things a certain way.
- People who think they are better than others.
- People who talk a lot but do not listen.
- People who probably don't have as many friends as they think they do.
- People who judge others and always have an opinion they feel the need to share.

Objective

Outcomes and Results Question
What outcome(s) and result(s) do you expect to get when you Empty Your Teacup? Take ten minutes to list down all the positive changes you would like to see, hear and feel.

'Emptying your teacup' is not about teacups or drinking tea. It is another matter entirely. It demands that we understand what our teacup is, and what is in our teacup. It's about opening your mind to new possibilities.

Without getting caught up with what kind of tea you're tasting.

Without overfilling your teacup.

Without spilling your tea.

And at the same time, ensuring that the teacup is empty to be useful to be refilled

Examples Question
Can you think of any Examples when you have had a Closed-Mind, and did it cause you any problems? Take ten minutes to make a list of failings you experienced when you were closed-minded. What was the outcome of the situation? How did you feel afterwards?

Be honest with yourself here. Do you sometimes find yourself:

- Closed off to other people's ideas?
- Feeling that your ideas and thoughts are better than others?
- Having a lot of pride in yourself?
- Feeling stubborn and not wanting to budge for anyone?
- Eager to be in control?
- Wanting things done your way?
- Judging others often?
- Having an opinion on most things?
- Liking to be heard and make your point?
- Talking more than you listen?
- Thinking you have more friends than you really do?

If you have answered 'yes' to any of the above, then you're in for an AMAZING TEA PARTY.

Empty Your Teacup is based on Bruce Lee's martial philosophy:

'The usefulness of the teacup
is in its emptiness.'

It is also inspired by Chris Kent's amazing book called *Personal Liberation*. Check out www.PersonalLiberation.com for more information.

This stage of your self-mastery journey will help you to:

Belt	Pillars of Luck	Chapter	Success Goals
2. Yellow	Possibility	**'Empty your teacup'** Master your mind	• Open your mind. • Remove obstacles that prevent you from achieving success • Enjoy new experiences, learn and grow • Open the door to success!

This stage is broken down into nine key substages as follows:

1. Story.
2. Moral.
3. Function.
4. Analogy.
5. Problems.
6. Big Idea.
7. How To.
8. Recognition.
9. Avoidance.

Let's OPEN THE DOOR TO SUCCESS!

Warm Up

Let's jump right in and start warming up by answering the following questions:

Question
What do you think **Empty Your Teacup** means? Take five minutes to define.

Question
What does the **Teacup** mean to you? Take five minutes to define.

Question
What does the **Tea** signify to you? Take five minutes to define.

Question
Why is the teacup only **Useful When It Is Empty**? Take five minutes to define.

Question
Would you like to learn how to **Open the Door to Success**? (Yes or No)

If answered 'yes' to the last question, then you're in the right place, so let's TASTE SOME NEW TEA!

Story

I earned a Bachelors Honours degree in Computer Science/Software Engineering.

A few years after leaving university and working within several IT roles, I got a job heading the Trading Systems for an Equities Trading Floor for a major investment bank in the City of London. As the head, I often got called in to deal with senior traders exhibiting system performance problems, usually where systems were running too slow to trade effectively.

After further investigation, it usually transpired that the computer's *'memory was full'.* After cleaning up the computer's memory, the trading systems performance was restored back to normal.

So what's the big deal? Well the moral of the story can be explained with another story.

Moral

A Zen story, which Bruce Lee quite famously quoted, goes as follows…

'A learned man once went to a Zen master to inquire about Zen. As the Zen master talked, the learned man would frequently interrupt him with remarks like, "Oh yes, we have that too", "we do it this way", and so forth.

Finally, the Zen master stopped talking and began to serve tea to the learned man; however, he kept on pouring and the teacup overflowed.

"Enough! No more can go into the cup!" the learned man interrupted.

"Indeed, I see," answered the Zen master. "If you do not first empty your cup, how can you taste my cup of tea?"'

Bruce Lee went on to quote:

'The usefulness of the teacup
is in its emptiness.'

In the case of the computer system, *'The usefulness of the computer memory is in its emptiness.'*

Function

<u>Question</u>
What is the main **Function** of the teacup and the computer memory?
Take five minutes to define.

In summary: the function of the teacup lies in its ability to hold liquid, and the function of the computer lies in its ability to store data. The contents of which are not really important at this stage.

Analogy

The same goes for our mind. It's the ability of our brain to absorb knowledge that makes it useful, not the quantity of how much information we try and pour into it. In much the same way that we cannot pour more tea into a teacup that is already full, or more data into a computer memory which is already full, we cannot accommodate new knowledge if our brain is already full or mind closed.

Problems

Question
So, what problems can we experience with a full mind? Take five minutes to list down as many problems as you can think of.

In summary, the problems we can experience with a full mind include:

- Being closed off from learning new knowledge.
- Bring prevented from experiencing new things.
- Being prevented from growing as a person to achieve your personal liberation and self-actualisation.
- Being prevented from being more successful.

The Big Idea

Question
So what do you think is the big idea behind this philosophy? Take five minutes to see if you can figure out where I am going with this.

In summary, it's simply to *'Empty your teacup so you can taste new tea.'*

How To

Question
So how can you 'Empty Your Teacup'? Take five minutes to make a list.

In summary, by emptying your teacup you can:

- Unlearn previously taught lessons, for example classical lines-of-thought in favour of more simple, direct, and non-classical ones; and
- Remove any pre-conceived notions, speculations, opinions, prejudices, stereotypes, and other limiting thoughts.

Having worked in Trading Systems since 1997, the biggest challenge I have encountered is managing change. Why? Simply because people are set in their comfort zones and naturally avoid putting themselves in adverse situations. But that is where all the growing happens!

I can give you an example of one of my traders that worked for a boutique stockbroker firm on Broadway, just off Wall Street in Manhattan. I had implemented a state-of-the-art trading system on their trading desk, and this trader refused to use it. Having spoken to him to ascertain why, he said, without hesitation, 'I do not know how to use computers. I'd rather leave the firm.' That was his ego speaking.

I retained that trader in the end, but it took me four weeks of training and handholding, teaching him the basics from how to use a computer mouse to using a state-of-the-art, real-time trading system.

That is essentially four weeks of getting him to empty his teacup and getting him to taste my tea.

Recognition

Question

So how can you recognise a full teacup? Take five minutes to make a list.

I'm sure everyone's met a 'know-it-all'.

A 'know-it-all' or 'know-all' is a person who obnoxiously purports an expansive comprehension of a topic and/or situation when in reality, their comprehension may be inaccurate or limited. This display may or may not be directly expressed.

To identify a full teacup, then, look out for people who (and this includes assessing yourself so you're not the culprit too):

- Go on and on about themselves.
- Repeat how much they know and what they've done.
- People that talk more, and listen less — or not at all.
- People who do not acknowledge anyone else's viewpoint on a subject.
- People not interested in seeking any further advice.
- People who have their mind set in their own ways.
- People who have the answer to everything.

...this is referred to as 'Full Teacup Syndrome.'

Avoidance

<u>Question</u>
So how can you avoid the 'Full Teacup Syndrome'? Take five minutes to make a list.

Cultivate the mind using Zen philosophy, by 'adopting a beginner's mind'.

Zen priest, Daisetz Suzuki, wrote:

> *'The mind of a beginner is empty, free of the habits of the expert,*
> *ready to accept, to doubt, and open to all possibilities.*
> *It's the kind of mind which can see things as they are and*
> *recognise the original nature of everything.'*

People often listen with their minds but restrict opportunities with their experiences or lack thereof.

Start with a clean slate by emptying your mind of any form of preconceived notions, ideas, concepts, stereotypes, opinions, prejudices, etc. that may impede your ability to acquire new knowledge and experiences, limiting your successes. Let your mind be free, like that of an innocent child.

Worksheet

We are now going to tackle the Empty Your Teacup worksheet, which is available on www.MartialMindPower.com/Resources, to get you thinking about the application of the things we learnt about earlier.

As part of this worksheet, we are going to attempt to empty up to three teacups by asking yourself two key questions, which you'll find on the worksheet when you go there now. Enjoy.

Thinking Differently

Eddie was a boy who had failed throughout his school years. He appeared a threat to his teachers. He would not conform. He seemed to have potential, but in his teachers' eyes he seemed to go out of his way to be 'difficult'. He was a born mismatched. A misfit in the miseducation system.

He left school at fifteen without grades or qualifications. He applied for a job in a warehouse. Being a government-run warehouse, there had to be a government-approved interview, conducted by a government-approved interviewer. And the interviewer, like the teachers, expected the right answer to the government-approved questions.

'OK,' said the interviewer, *'first, a general knowledge question. How many days of the week begin with the letter T?'*

Even the interviewer was surprised by the time it took Eddie to answer. Finally, Eddie said, *'Two.'*

'Correct,' said the interviewer. *'By the way, what are they?'*

'Today and tomorrow,' Eddie replied.

'OK,' said the interviewer, thinking, *I'll fix you, wise guy. 'Here's a mathematics question. How many seconds are there in a year?'*

Quick as a flash Eddie replied, *'Twelve.'*

'Twelve?' echoed the interviewer with incredulity. *'How the heck did you get that answer?'*

'Well that's easy,' said Eddie. *'There's January second, February second, March second, April…'*

'OK, OK. Here's a spelling question. How many D's are there in "Rudolph the red-nosed reindeer"?'

Again there was a long silence. Eddie seemed engaged in some complicated internal computation, nodding his head rhythmically. Finally, he said, *'A hundred and three.'*

'A hundred and three? A hundred and three?! Where did you get that answer from?'

'Da da da da da da dah. Dah da da da dah dah dah. Dah da…'

Conclusion

This brings us to the conclusion of the Empty Your Teacup stage:

'The usefulness of the teacup
is in its' emptiness,' Bruce Lee.

In other words:

'Empty your teacup
so you can taste new tea,' Lak Loi.

It is, in essence, 'brainwashing' or 'cerebral cleansing' — that is, cleansing the mind of stale ideas, information and experiences that have already been learnt, abided by and absorbed, so you can move on.

This is crucial to make way for new knowledge to enter your mind, body and soul, and to help you to learn new knowledge, reprogram old unresourceful ideas, thoughts and behaviours with new resourceful ones, so you can experience new things, towards your own personal liberation and self-actualisation and achieve your success goals.

After all, there are many flavours of tea to be tasted.

In this stage, we looked at:

- What is the teacup?
- What is in our teacup?
- How to recognise a full teacup.
- How to empty our teacups.

And that brings us to the end of the Empty Your Teacup stage of your self-mastery journey. Before you embark on TASTING SUCCESS, please answer the following:

Question

1. Do you understand how to Open Your Mind? (Yes or No)
2. Do you understand how to Remove Obstacles that prevent you from achieving success? (Yes or No)
3. Are you ready to Enjoy New Experiences, learn and grow? (Yes or No)
4. Are you ready to Open the Door to Success? (Yes or No)

My friend, I would like to deeply thank you for giving me the chance to take you through this Master Your Life journey, and remember:

'EMPTY YOUR TEACUP,
SO YOU CAN TASTE SUCCESS!'

3

Possess an eagle eye

Possess an Eagle Eye

STAGE 3 — ORANGE BELT

Master Your Alertness and Awareness

What's the Problem?

So, who is this **Possess an Eagle Eye** stage of your self-mastery journey aimed at?

- People who feel blinkered and cannot see the wood for the trees, or are stuck in a blind rut.
- People who do not feel they are 'with it' and are walking around half asleep aimlessly in a zombified state.
- People who feel behind their game, disempowered and have lost faith in themselves.
- People who have lost their direction because they cannot see which way to go.

Objective

Outcomes and Results Question
What outcome(s) and result(s) do you expect to get when you **Possess an Eagle Eye**? Take ten minutes to list down all the positive changes you would like to see, hear and feel.

Looking is one thing. Seeing is another matter entirely. Possessing the eye of an eagle demands that YOU ARE AWAKE, ALERT AND AWARE.

Without being caught up in a gaze or hardened FOCUS.

Without looking hard, trying to SEE THE ANSWERS.

Without being switched off.

All with the softness of seeing and BEing SWITCHED ON.

Examples Question
Can you think of any examples when you have looked really hard to find answers but could not **see them**, and how did it make you **feel?** Take ten minutes to make a list of things you have failed at seeing, what was the outcome of the scenario, and how did you **feel afterwards.**

Do you sometimes find yourself:

- Feeling blinkered?
- Feeling unable to see the wood for the trees?
- Trying too hard looking for answers, but getting nowhere?
- Feeling like you're walking in the dark?
- Feeling like a zombie and de-sensitised to what's going on around you?
- Feeling aimless and disoriented?
- Feeling like you're falling behind everyone, and losing faith?
- Feeling lost and directionless, unable to find a way out?

If you have answered 'yes' to any of the above, then you're in for an EYE-OPENER! Possess an Eagle Eye is based on Bruce Lee's martial philosophy:

'Possess the eye of an eagle,
the cunning of a fox,
the agility and alertness of a cat, with
the courage, aggressiveness and fierceness of a panther,
the striking power of a cobra and
the resistance of a mongoose.'

This stage of your self-mastery journey will help you to:

Belt	Pillars of Luck	Chapter	Success Goals
3. Orange	Perception	**'Possess an eagle eye'** Master your alertness and awareness	• Open your eyes and switch yourself ON • Start to see new opportunities and ways • Create a state of alertness and awareness • Get on top of your game • Stay ahead of the curve • Control and direct your own life • Swoop in and take the new opportunities • Soar to success!

This stage is broken down into six key substages as follows:

1. OODA Loop.
2. Step 1 — Observe.
3. Step 2 — Orient.
4. Step 3 — Decide.
5. Step 4 — Action.
6. Step 5 — Repeat OODA Loop.

Are you ready to FLY and SOAR TO SUCCESS?

Warm Up

Let's jump right in and start warming up by answering the following questions:

Question
What do you think **'Possess an Eagle Eye'** means? Take five minutes to define.

Question
Do you know what an **OODA Loop** is? (Yes or No)

Question
Do you know what is the **Significance of the OODA Loop** to you? Take five minutes to describe.

Question
How do you think **Possessing an Eagle Eye** Will Help You? Take five minutes to answer and describe how.

Question
Would you like to learn how to **Soar to Success**? (Yes or No)

If you answered 'yes' to the last question, then you're in the right place, so let's SOAR TO SUCCESS!

The Ugly Man

I had been in the Italian seaside town for almost a week, working all day and free to do as I pleased in the evening. Unfortunately, it was February. Fortunately, this gave me time to indulge a passion of mine: Italian food. Unfortunately, it was hard to locate good restaurants out of season. Fortunately, on the last day somebody mentioned the *Z Bass* restaurant.

Standing outside the glass door, I knew it was going to be a good choice. It was full. Only one table was vacant. Opening the door was like stepping into a world of pleasure and sensation. First was the rich smell of fish stew, *zuppe di pesce*, the house speciality. Then the vibrant chatter of Italians enjoying themselves. And, of course, the waiters with brightly striped waistcoats holding aloft steaming platters, smiling, shouting to each other and behaving as if they were born to wait in a way that seems unique to Italian waiters.

I sat down at my table and ordered. Across from my small table, a much larger table was occupied by twelve men, six each side. Perhaps they were relatives, or workmates. At any rate, they were celebrating something and were well into their meal of *zuppe di pesce*.

The man sitting opposite me, against the wall, caught my attention. He was ugly. His face was deformed, stretched and misshapen, ravaged by some disease. He seemed like an elephant-man, and was certainly the ugliest man I had ever seen. I knew I shouldn't stare, but in a way that a tongue seeks incessantly a missing tooth, my eyes kept wandering back.

OODA Loop

What Is an OODA Loop?

We are going to start off talking about something called an OODA Loop. OODA stands for:

1. Observe,
2. Orient,
3. Decide and
4. Act.

Conceptualised by a US Air Force military strategist called Colonel John Boyd, his objective was to apply the OODA Loop concept to strategic military operations to stay ahead of the opponent in order to intercept them to incapacitate the opponent.

Here is a diagram of the OODA Loop decision cycle:

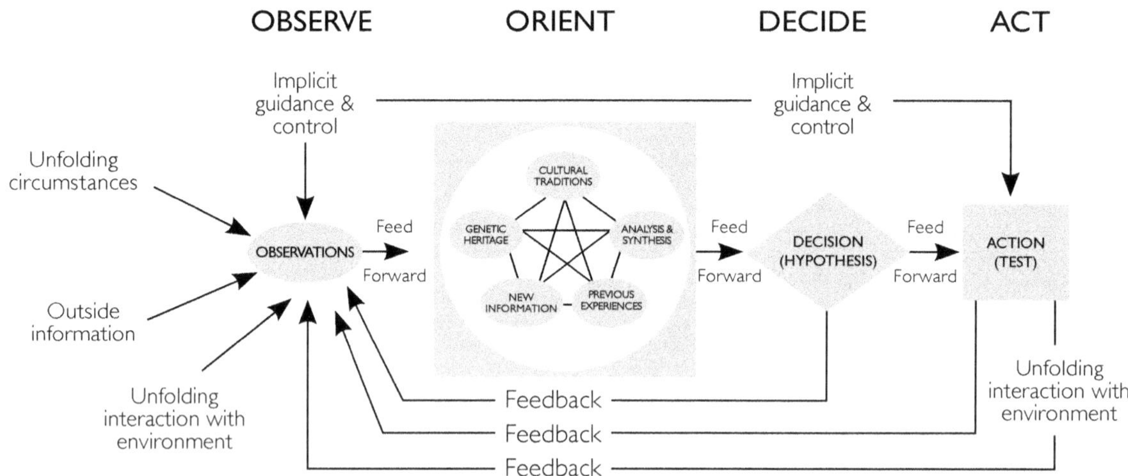

Figure 6: Diagram of a decision cycle known as the Boyd cycle, or the OODA loop.

Overview

The theory behind John Boyd's OODA Loop is that decision-making takes place in a recurring cycle of Observe, Orient, Decide, Act. The idea is to use a tactic or strategy to draw a desired reaction from your opponent. Bruce called this *'Attack By Drawing'* or *'ABD'.*

When the opponent starts to respond by engaging their OODA Loop decision-cycle, you exploit it by *'intercepting'* their OODA Loop with an advantageous counter-attack if the desired response is given — else you need to change tact rapidly to 'stay ahead'. John Boyd emphasised that you should maintain many OODA Loops in process at any one time in your opponent.

In order to be successful, then, we have to operate at a faster rhythm than our opponent to generate rapid changes in conditions that prevent your opponent from adapting and/or reacting to those changes, in order to suppress and destroy their awareness. Whilst they are in this state of confusion, we intercept their rhythm or OODA Loop with a counter-attack. Bruce Lee called this *'Broken Rhythm'.* Please refer to the Stay Ahead chapter for more information on rhythm and broken rhythm.

The ultimate effects of this activity should be: to make you appear unpredictable to your adversary whilst simultaneously clarifying their intentions; to create a sense of disorder and confusion among our adversaries as they struggle to predict what we are trying to do; and to keep them in a constant state of 'playing catch-up'. Bruce Lee called this 'staying ahead'. However, this all starts with seeing first effectively, and Bruce Lee sums this up beautifully when he said:

'Speed of perception is somewhat affected by the distribution of the observer's attention — fewer separate voices, faster action.'

Question

Before I continue, what movie is playing in your mind as I described the OODA Loop? Say the first movie that came into your mind.

Though the OODA Loop was designed for strategic military purposes, it has been adapted for business and I see no reason why you cannot apply it in the workplace, home, school/college, etc.

We are going to have a look at a combative application, so you can understand how the OODA Loop works from the 'inside'.

Progressive Indirect Attack Drill

1. Get a partner.
2. For safety, put some boxing gloves on, gum shields and a face guard, and do this drill in a state of relaxation and fluidity with seventy percent speed and fifty percent power.
3. Your partner will stand in a fighting stance, awaiting to defend your attack only.
4. You will start attacking on your partner's mid-line by aiming a punch from your lead hand to your partner's abdomen.
5. As soon as your partner starts to move his hand to defend his midline against your attack, you will re-direct your attack by changing the punch into a backfist and aiming it to your partner's high-line, aiming it towards his head instead whilst continuing to progress forwards toward the target.
6. Take three minutes each way, and explore different redirections of an attack using the same weapon whilst maintaining forward progressive movement.

I hope you have a better experience of the OODA Loop at work, and how to exploit it by intercepting it whilst it's in motion. This will allow you to create a state of disarray in your adversary and allow you to stay ahead.

Applicability of OODA loop

A tactical-level example can be found on the football pitch, where a player takes possession of the ball and must get past an opponent who is taller or faster. A straight dribble or pass is unlikely to succeed. Instead, the player may engage in a rapid and elaborate series of body movements designed to befuddle the opponent and deny him the ability to take advantage of his superior size or speed.

At a basic level of play, this may be merely a series of fakes & feints, with the hope that the opponent will make a mistake or an opening will occur, but practice and mental focus may allow one to accelerate tempo, get inside the opponent's OODA loop and take control of the situation. In this way, one can cause the opponent to move in a particular way, and generate an advantage rather than merely react to an accident. Taking control of the situation is key. It is not enough to speed through OODA faster — that results in flailing.

The same cycle operates over a longer timescale in a competitive business landscape, and the same logic applies. Decision makers gather information (observe), form hypotheses about customer activity and the intentions of competitors (orient), make decisions and act on them. The cycle is repeated continuously. The aggressive and conscious application of the process gives a business advantage over a competitor who is merely reacting to conditions as they occur, or has poor awareness of the situation. OODA Loops often get stuck at the 'D' stage; no action is taken, allowing the competition to gain the upper hand or resources to be wasted. This is especially common in business, where teams of people are working the OODA Loop.

We are now going to start exploring each step of the OODA Loop in more detail.

Question
Are you READY?

Step 1 — Observe

What Does Observe Mean?

Observe is a verb that means to notice or perceive (something) and register it as being significant; or to watch (someone or something) carefully and attentively.

In order to increase your observation capacity, Bruce Lee spoke about creating a state of

'Relaxed Alertness.'

It is a state of being relaxed, but not too relaxed that you're falling asleep or jellylike. At the same time, it is a state of being alert, but not too alert that you are strained or stressed.

So, to prepare us for the physical part of this Possess an Eagle Eye stage, we are going to prepare ourselves by first getting relaxed, then enabling our alertness.

Relaxation

For the relaxation part, we are going to start with some 'Haa Breathing'. This is a relaxation breathing method, developed by the Kahunas (priests) in Hawaii. They used to practice it for up to eight hours a day to help them focus their mind's eye first.

<u>Haa Breathing Technique</u>

When Haa Breathing, ensure that you:

1. Breathe in through the nose and fill your belly with air (not the chest) for two seconds;
2. Then breathe out through the mouth whilst making a 'Haa' sound for six seconds.

<u>Haa Breathing Drill</u>

1. Dim the lights or switch them off.
2. Sit comfortably in your chair, with both feet firmly on the floor and your hands comfortably sitting in your lap.
3. Close your eyes.
4. Relax each part of your body from toe to head.
5. Start Haa Breathing.
6. Visualise your 'happy place' whilst Haa Breathing; see, hear and feel all the senses in your 'happy place'.
7. After five minutes, countdown from ten to one in your mind and come back wide awake and alert into the room. Take another five minutes to relax yourself.

Peripheral Vision

Now that we are all relaxed, we are going to switch our alertness on. To do this we are going to switch our peripheral vision ON. Our peripheral vision creates a 'learning trance state', also called the 'shaman state'.

Question
Have you seen a **Bruce Lee movie?** (Yes or No)

Can you describe how **Bruce Lee's eyes** look when he is Kung Fu fighting? Take two minutes to describe.

Before we switch our peripheral vision ON, we need to understand visual perception.

Visual Perception

Visual Perception is your ability to process and create an internal representation of your external environment in the presence of visible light, using your visual sense, i.e. your eyes.

We often call this vision or eyesight, and the collective physiological components are known as the 'Visual System'.

Visual System

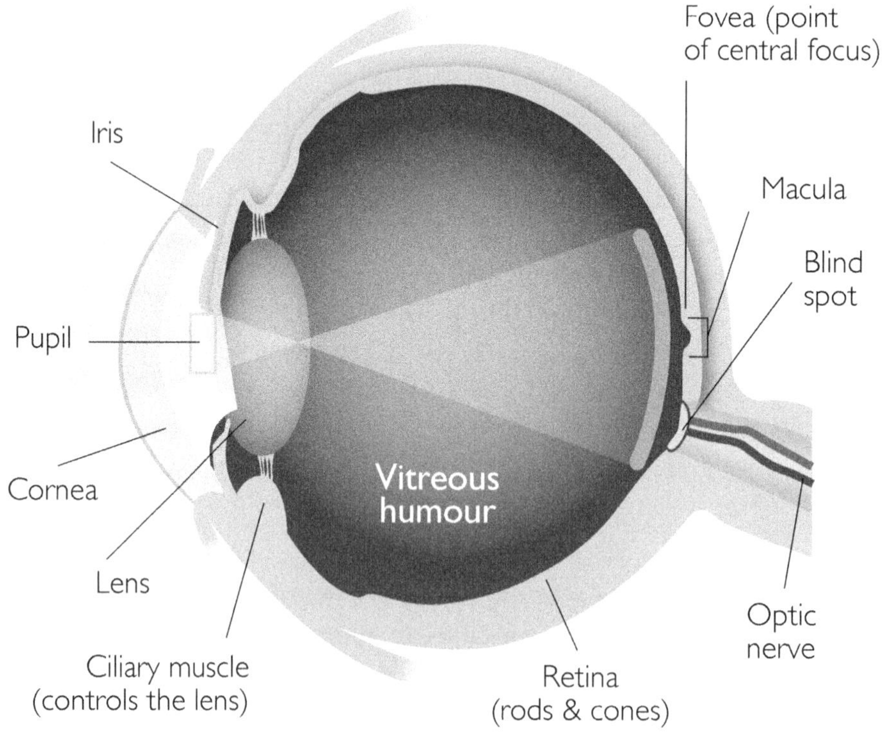

Figure 7: An illustration of a human eye.

Animal eyes work in much the same way as human eyes. So in order to possess an eagle eye, we are going to talk briefly about how the eyes work, how our visual system works.

The eye simply allows you to create an internal representation of your external environment.

Seeing starts with the lens of the eye, which focuses an image of its surrounding environment within immediate view onto a photo-receptive cell membrane in the back of the eye called the retina.

The retina detects photons of light and transduces the light patterns into neural signals, which are then sent to different parts of the brain for processing.

The main difference between a human's eye and an eagle's eye is simply that the neural signals are routed and processed by different parts of the brain.

Peripheral Vision (Tiger Eye)

So, peripheral vision is the vision that occurs outside of the centre of gaze.

There are three types of peripheral vision, which are:

1. Far peripheral — edges of field of view.
2. Mid peripheral — middle of field of view.
3. Near peripheral or para central — adjacent to centre of gaze.

When you lose peripheral vision and retain the para central vision, it is known as 'tunnel vision'.

When you lose the para central vision and retain the far and near peripheral vision it is known as a 'central scotoma'.

We are going to explore these further shortly.

Due to there being a greater density of photo-receptor cells in the centre of the retina, human peripheral vision tends to be weaker than animals such as eagles. This limits the ability of the human eye to distinguish colours, shapes and motion as effectively.

At night, our para central vision is quite weak when there is a lack of light. However, our mid and far peripheral vision operate better than usual. In fact, pilots are taught to use peripheral vision to scan for aircraft at night.

On that basis, it would be safe to assume that Bruce Lee was striving to have superior vision than his fellow human adversary by modelling his vision on an eagle.

Peripheral Activation Drill

1. Stand tall and still.
2. Fixate your eyes on an object in the distance at eye level.
3. Do not move your head whilst you do this.
4. Extend your arms out straight in front of you at shoulder level with your palms facing towards each other like clapping your hands.
5. Wiggle your fingers.
6. Then slowly spread open both arms to the side whilst being aware of the wiggling fingers.
7. Stop when the hands and wiggling fingers are about to go out of view – you may have to stop one hand before the other.
8. Take two minutes to do this drill thoroughly.

Congratulations, your peripheral vision is now switched on. I want you to Stay Switched ON throughout the rest of this book, as the most effective learning happens when in a peripheral state.

But before we move on, we are going to do a peripheral vision reaction drill, to test the sensitivity of our peripheral vision.

Peripheral Vision Reaction Drill

1. Get into a group of five people.
2. Give each person a number from one to five.
3. Ask number one to be the trainee and stand in the middle in a fighting stance.
4. Ask the rest of the trainers to make a semi-circle in front of their peripheral field of view.
5. Ask the trainee to Switch their Peripheral Vision ON if they have switched it off.
6. Then ask each trainer to stand in a fighting stance.
7. Each trainer will then execute a strike, starting with slight movement (e.g. hand opens then closes), gradually moving in to more exaggerated movements (e.g. punches and kicks).
8. The trainee in the middle has to point to any motion he detects without moving his head, eyes or body whilst remaining in his fighting stance.
9. Rotate every minute.
10. Ensure you have two goes each in turn to practice this drill.

Visual Field

I am also introducing you to the notion of a 'Visual Field', as I will be referring to it later.

Firstly, the 'field of view' is not the same as the 'visual field'.

The 'field of view' comprises the external environment, which you can see around you, which is projected onto your retina.

The visual system processes the information received from the field of view and computes this into an internal representation and output called the visual field.

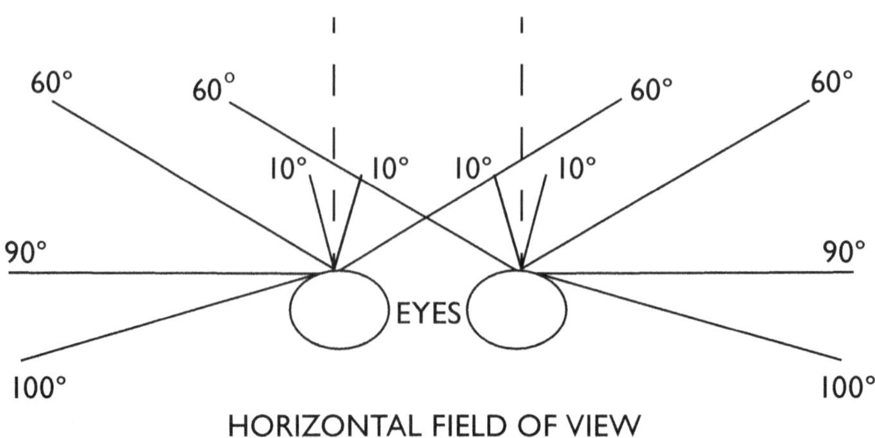

HORIZONTAL FIELD OF VIEW

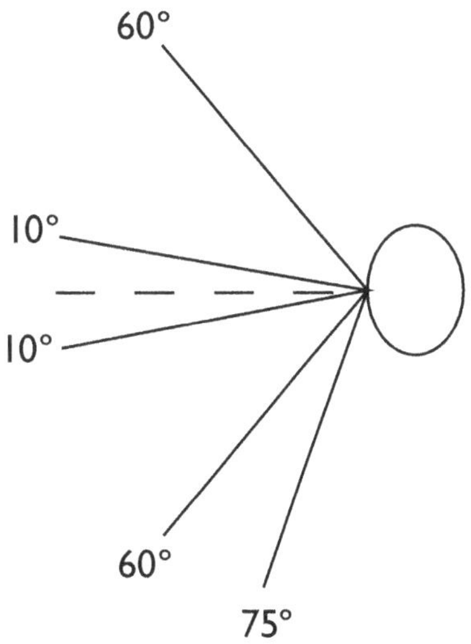

Figure 8: An aerial and side plan of a human field of view.

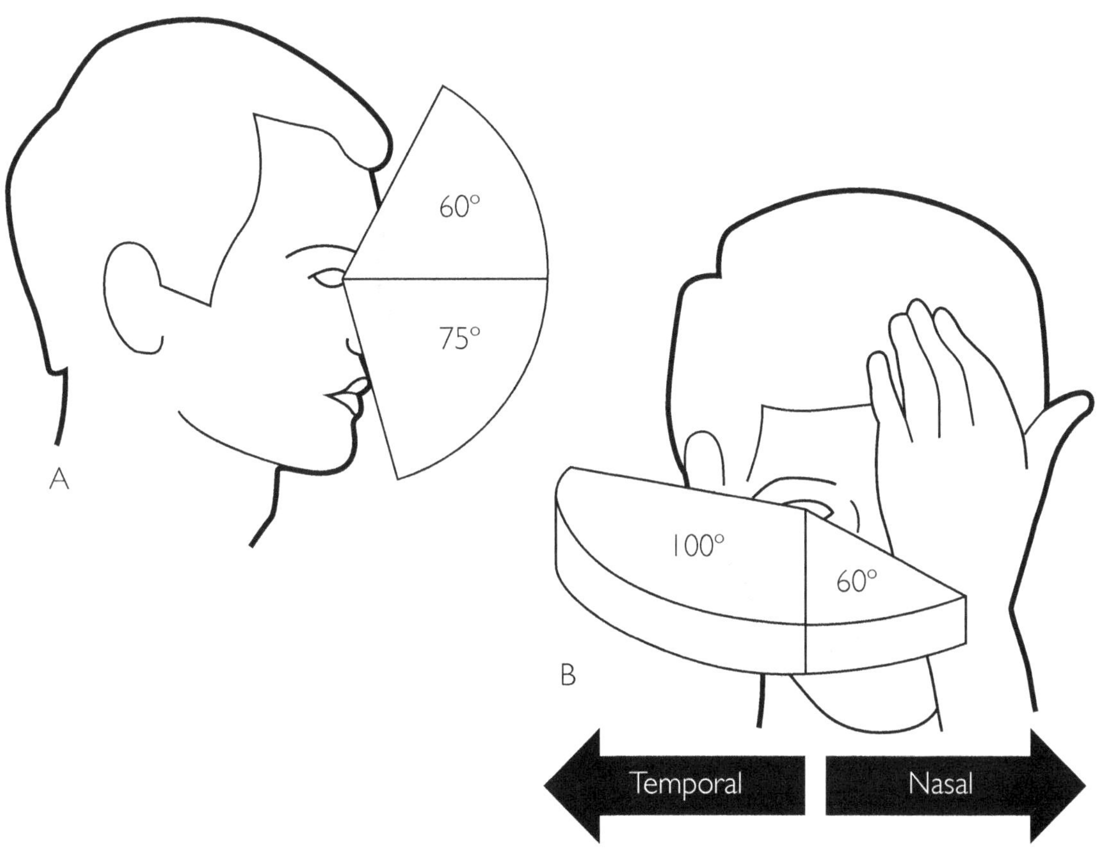

Figure 9: Another perspective of the aerial and side plan of a human field of view.

Empty Field Myopia

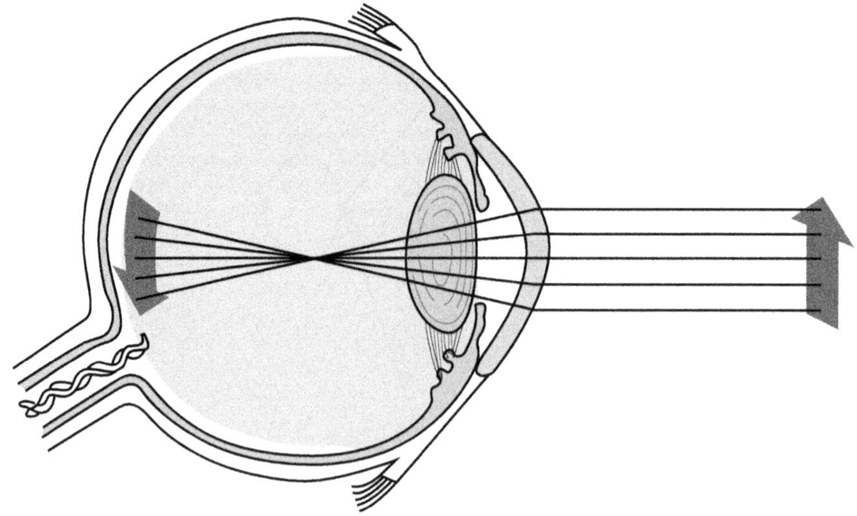

Distant image: lens is flattened

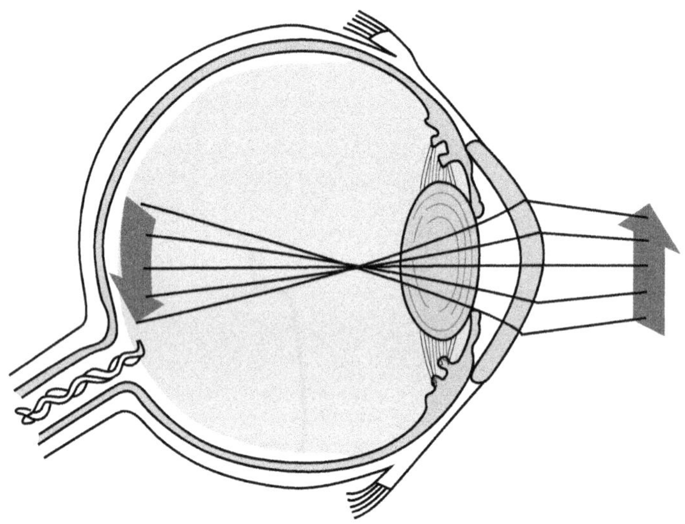

Close image: lens is rounded

Figure 10: Image of a human eye and its lens shape focussing on close and distant objects.

I want to start looking at a something called 'myopia', which is also commonly known as 'near-sightedness'. This is where objects near appear fine, but objects further away appear blurry.

The symptoms of empty field myopia (also known as 'empty space myopia') is that the eyes automatically focus on average eighty centimetres ahead. The detection of objects outside of this limited field is delayed, and determining the size or range of anything entering within it is problematic.

Martial artists can exploit this limitation by allowing the vision to relax between strikes. When there is a lack of stimulation, where there is no preparation or telegraphy of an incoming strike, the lens shifts to a resting state, making the near-sighted person vulnerable to get hit.

This problem is quite common for pilots. There have also been cases where aircraft which appear as dots in the sky suddenly disappear because there is a lack of stimulation, and the field of view is perceived as empty, so the eye goes back to its resting state.

Figure 11: Aircraft with low level of contrast against featureless background.

Martial artists can adapt this feature of the human eye by keeping the body and weapons static outside the eighty centimetre range momentarily, forcing your opponent's eye to come to its momentary resting state, allowing you to take advantage with an explosive attack.

Gate Drill

1. Pair up with a person.
2. One person will be the trainer, who will stand tall and put on a pair of goggles, raising his gates (hands on either side of face to block an incoming attack to the eyes with palms facing each other).
3. The other person will be the trainee, who will stand at a range whereby he can touch the trainer's goggles with his fingertips with one of his arms fully extended, without moving his feet or body.
4. The object of the drill is for the trainee to try and touch the trainer's goggles before the trainer blocks by parrying the trainee's hand out of the way;
5. Please try this with a near-sighted and normal sighted person. Take three minutes to practice this drill each way.

Since the average person's eyes have an average resting field of view range of eighty centimetres, we are all susceptible to this phenomenon. Therefore, it would be beneficial to understand how we can defend against this weakness.

Question
Do you have any ideas on how we can defend against Empty Space Myopia? Take two minutes to make a list.

Here is a list to summarise how to prevent your eyes going into the Empty Field Myopia, or resting, state:

1. Frequently focus on distant objects such as objects furthest in your field of view.
2. On the same note, frequently focus on closer objects such as your adversary.
3. Use motion to keep the field of view changing, to provide constant stimulation to your visual system.
4. Use your peripheral vision to detect slight movements in your aggressors' actions.

Blind Spot

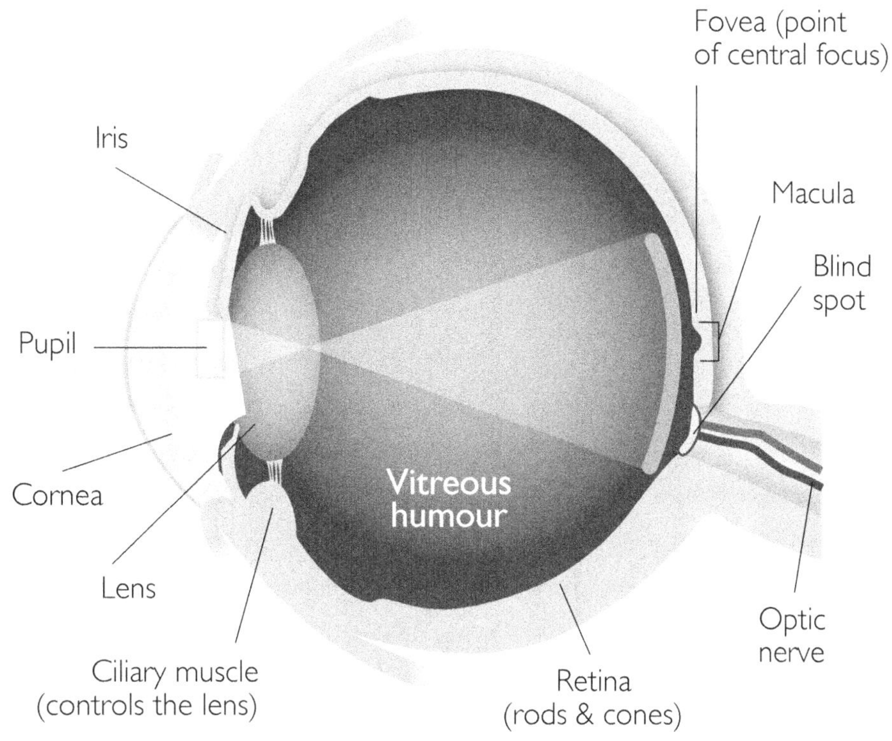

Figure 12: Illustration of a human eye, and its blind spot (on bottom-right).

A blind spot, also known as a scotoma, is an obstruction in the visual field, where there is a lack of light detecting photo-receptor cells on the retina. This is because this is the point where the optic nerve passes through the optic disc, creating a break in the retina, which results in part of the visual field being missing.

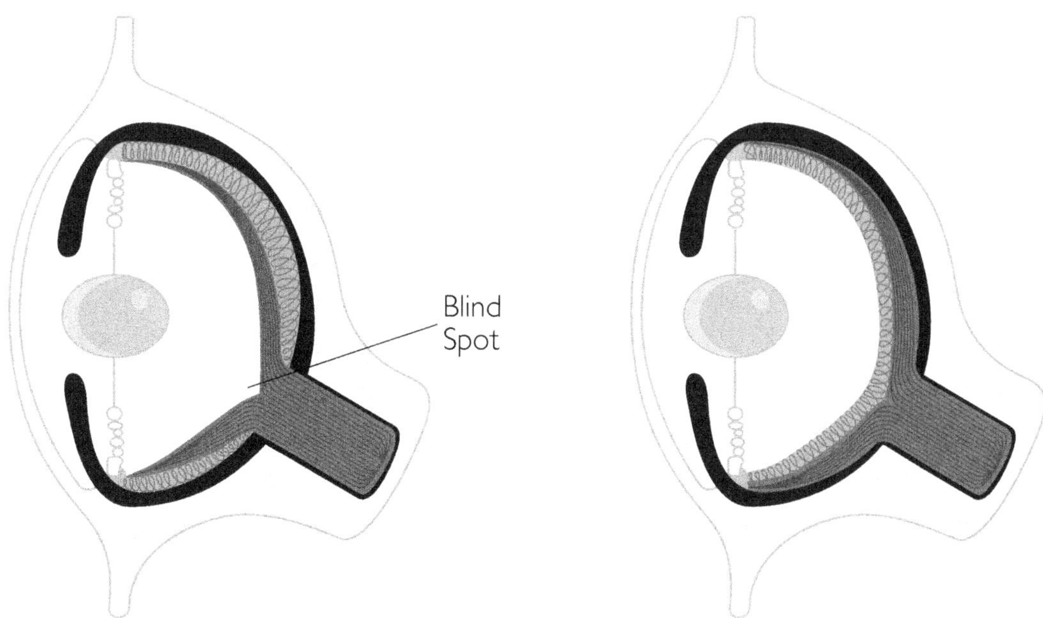

Figure 13: Illustration of a human eye showing blind spot (left) versus a cephalopod eye, e.g. octopus (right) with no blind spot.

Cephalopod eyes, such as octopus eyes, do not have blind spots. So, trying to do a non-telegraphic strike on an octopus won't work (sorry, that was a martial artist joke if there ever was one).

The blind spot is located about 12–15° temporal and 1.5° below the horizontal and is roughly 7.5° high and 5.5° wide.

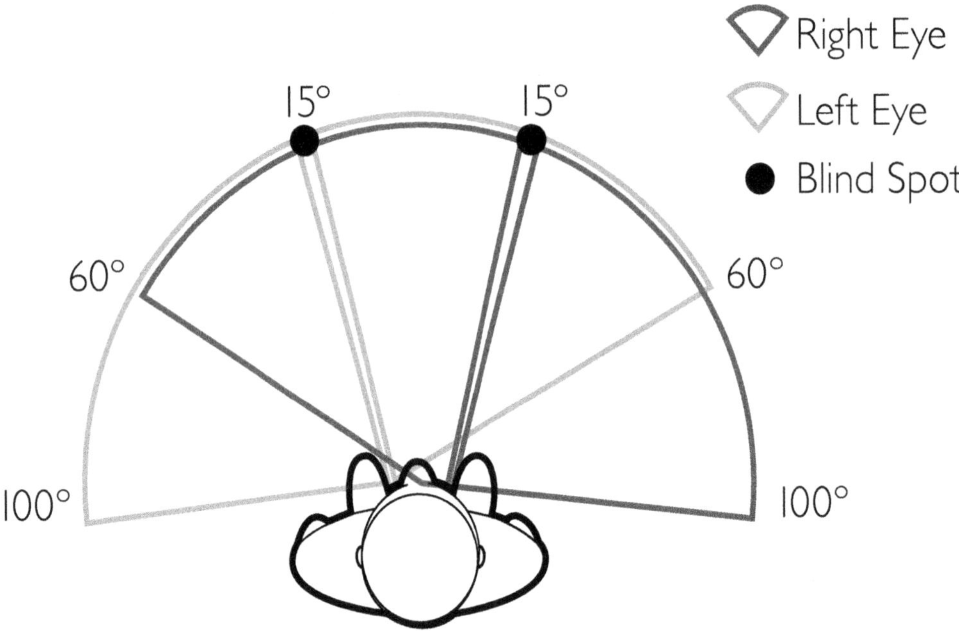

Figure 14: Illustration of the human eye's blind spots.

This blind spot may just well be the basis on which Bruce Lee's non-telegraphic Hammer Principle was developed to deceive the opponent's eyes by going under their peripheral vision, causing their eyes to relax to the incoming attack, impairing their judgement to defend against it effectively. As Bruce Lee said:

'A strike should be felt and not seen.'

Blind Spot Test

1. Get a blank piece of paper.
2. Draw a star on the left and a round circle on the right, the size of a hole-punch hole, one full index finger's width apart.
3. Hold up the piece of paper at arm's length at eye level.
4. Cover your right eye and focus your left eye on the circle on the right.
5. Bring the paper closer to your face slowly, and you'll notice there is a point at which the star on the left will disappear.
6. Repeat on the other side.
7. Take ten minutes to find your blind spots on each eye.

Hammer Principle Demonstration
Please visit our website on www.MartialMindPower.com/Resources to see Bruce Lee's Hammer Principle demonstration, which shows how Bruce exploited his foe's blind spot to attack them effectively on this line.

Hammer Principle Drill

1. Pair up with a person.
2. One person will be the trainer, who will stand in a fighting stance and put on a pair of goggles.
3. The trainee will stand outside the fighting measure (i.e. a distance from which he has to take half a step before he can strike his opponent).
4. Then the trainee has to try and touch the trainer's goggles using the Hammer Principle.
5. Take three minutes to practice this drill each way.

Averted Vision (Eagle Eye)

Averted Vision is a technique that employs peripheral vision to view faint objects such as fast incoming strikes. It works by looking off the line rather than directly at the object, while continuing to concentrate on the object itself.

Astronomers popularly use this technique, and there is even some evidence that the technique has been around since Aristotle's time.

To avoid the blind spot getting in the way, it is advisable to look on the nasal side or the 'inside'. So, for right-eyed observers it is best to shift to the right, and for left-eye observers it is best to shift to the left. In the extended version of *Enter the Dragon*, Bruce said:

'Never take your eyes off your opponent,
even when you bow.'

If you remember, earlier I asked you what did Bruce Lee's eyes look like when he was in the fighting zone… well they looked like he was looking off the line of attack and staring into the ether with wide eyes, whereas in fact he was using his eagle eye, or averted vision, to capture every little movement, as discussed so far.

You are now going to activate your eagle eye with the following drills. Enjoy.

Figure 15: Bruce Lee using his eagle eye, or averted vision.
Photo from Enter the Dragon, Concord Production Inc. and Warner Bros

Visual Focus Principle (VFP) Drill

1. Get into pairs.
2. The trainer stands tall and still.
3. The trainee stands tall and still opposite the trainer.
4. The trainee focuses on the trainer's mid-line, an imaginary line running horizontally across the trainer's chest/nipples.
5. The trainee can see the trainer's whole body without moving his head. Take three minutes to practice this drill each way.

Phasic Motion Drill

1. Get into pairs.
2. The trainer stands tall and still.
3. The trainee stands tall and still opposite trainer.
4. The trainee focuses on the trainer's mid-line, an imaginary line running horizontally across the trainer's chest.
5. The trainer slightly moves one part of his body at a time.
6. The trainee has to detect any motion and call it out or point at it.
7. Take three minutes to practice this drill each way.

Step 2 — Orient

John Boyd believed that the second step, **Orientation**, was the most important step in the OODA Loop, as he felt it shaped the way we **Observe**, the way we **Decide**, and the way we **Act**.

Orientation utilises the brain's Reticular Activating System (RAS), which is the part of the brain responsible for retrieving information relating to the external sensory information it receives to create an internal representation and meaning out of the information. It processes some twenty million bits of information a second, ignoring the bits it thinks are not important and prioritising the parts that it thinks are important, to create situational awareness.

For example, as you sit here reading this book, there is information that your brain is processing but ignoring and deleting, such as the sounds people and pets are making around you, sounds traffic is making outside, the colour of your wallpaper, and so on.

Awareness drills require you to pick up as much detail as possible, and this section investigates how we can do that effectively.

Eye Movement

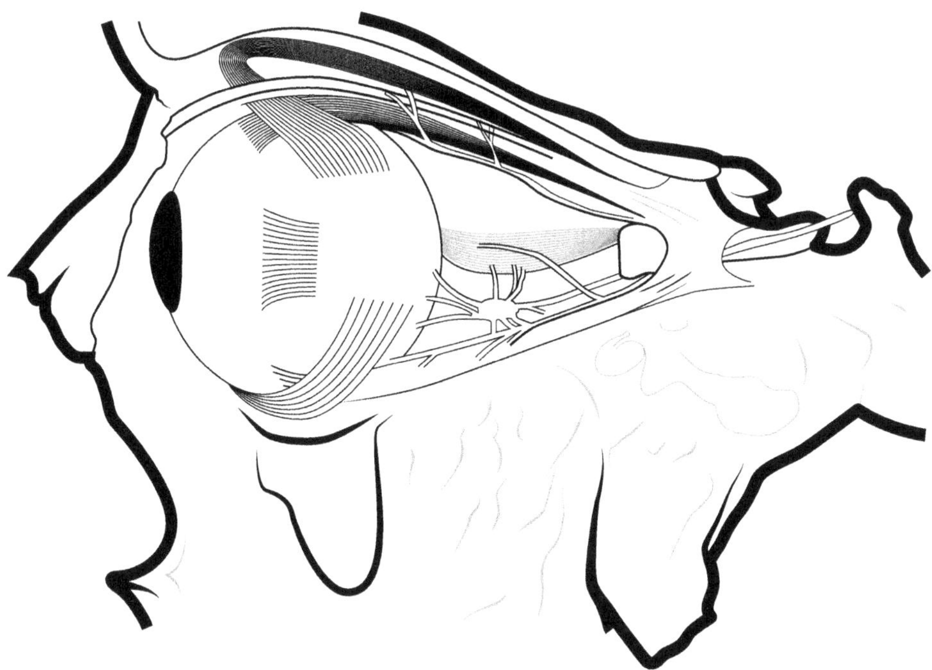

Figure 16: *Illustration of the human eye's skeletomusculature.*

Eye movements (either voluntary or involuntary) allow for the acquisition of data, fixation, and tracking visual stimuli.

There are three types of eye movements that primates and other vertebrates use, which are:

1. Smooth pursuit — used for tracking images of moving objects and making rapid shifts to maintain a smooth image.
2. Vergence shifts — shifting both eyes to ensure the image falls on the same part of the retina of both eyes, which is used for depth perception.
3. Saccades — short rapid eye movements used to scan a visual scene, such as reading a book, where the speed cannot be controlled in-between stops. This is the fastest of the three eye movements.

Eye movements are categorised as:

1. Ductions — eye movement in one eye only.
2. Versions — eye movement in both eyes together.
3. Vergences — eye movement in both eyes in opposite directions.

Yoked Movement vs. Antagonistic Movement

When an object is crossing your field of vision and in turn falling on the retina more than a few degrees per second, the brain cannot process that information fast enough and the image may look blurred. To compensate, the brain engages the eyes to turn two degrees to correct the image.

Yoked Movement vs. Antagonistic Movement Drill

To see a quick demonstration of this fact, try the following experiment.

Hold your hand up, about one foot (thirty centimetres) in front of your nose. Keep your head still, and shake your hand from side to side, slowly at first, and then faster and faster. At first you will be able to see your fingers quite clearly. But as the frequency of shaking passes about 1 Hz, the fingers will start to become blurry.

Now, keep your hand still, and shake your head (up and down or left and right). No matter how fast you shake your head, the image of your fingers remains clear.

This demonstrates how the brain controls eye movements opposite to head motion much better than it can follow a hand movement. When your pursuit system fails to keep up with the moving hand, images slip on the retina and you see a blurred hand.

The brain must point both eyes accurately enough that the object of regard falls on corresponding points of the two retinas to avoid the perception of double vision. In most vertebrates (humans, mammals, reptiles, birds), the movements of different body parts are controlled by striated muscles acting around joints. The movements of the eye are slightly different in that the eyes are not rigidly attached to anything, but are held in the orbit by six extra-ocular muscles.

In a combative situation, this is another good reason to keep on moving to keep your adversary clearly in sight, and to avoid being vulnerable by getting hit.

Perimetry or Campimetry

Perimetry or campimetry relate to how wide your visual field is. We are going to test our perimetry now.

Static Perimetry Test

1. Get into groups of three.
2. Nominate one person as the trainee.
3. Ask the trainee to stand tall and look forwards without moving the head.

4. The other two people in the group face the trainee and start to walk slowly, pausing between each step as they near the perimeter of the visual field, until they are about to vanish from the trainee's visual field.
5. Repeat for all members of the team. Take three minutes each to practice this drill.

We are now going to look at how to access the visual field with economy of motion, moving just the head to keep our perimetry in view with moving objects within it.

Kinetic Perimetry Test

1. Get into groups of three.
2. Nominate one person as the trainee.
3. Ask the trainee to stand in the middle in a fighting stance, able to move their head.
4. The other two people in the group are to circle the trainee as fast/ slow as they like, but moving continuously.
5. The trainee must move his/her head to keep both people in view (when possible) without moving feet or body.
6. Repeat for all members of the team. Take three minutes each to practice this drill.

Vision Span or Perceptual Span

Vision or perceptual span is the vertical and horizontal angle in which the human eye has sharp vision to read text. On average, each human eye spans 100 degrees of arc, most of which is peripheral vision. Six degrees of arc is typical for reading text clearly at a distance of 50 cm from the eyes.

Tunnel Vision

When you lose peripheral vision and retain the para central vision, it is known as Tunnel Vision.

Some typical causes which induce tunnel vision include:

- High acceleration for more than one second.
- G-forces over 4G.
- Wearing glasses, goggles, mask or helmets which constrict the field of view through the lens or window
- Extreme fear or distress, most often in the context of a panic attack or when in a combative situation.
- During periods of high adrenaline production, such as an intense physical fight.
- Intense anger, due to the body being rapidly flooded with adrenaline and oxygen.
- Also if you get bitten by a Black Mamba and other snakes with similar strength venom.

Next, we are going to test our tunnel vision as follows:

Tunnel Vision Group Drill

1. Get a group of ten or more people together.
2. Split the group into two, and make a tunnel with two lines of people facing each other about two metres apart.
3. One volunteer puts on some goggles and stands at the beginning of the tunnel.
4. The leader will indicate to one of the people in the rows to step in/out quickly.
5. The volunteer has to try and call out whenever they detect any motion. Take turns so that everyone has a chance to walk through the tunnel.

Binocular Vision (Snake Eye)

When both eyes are used together, it is known as binocular vision, where *'bini'* is Latin for double, and *'oculus'* is Latin for eye.

The benefits of having binocular vision are:

1. It gives you a spare eye in the event one gets damaged.
2. You have a greater horizontal field of view — one eye equates to 100 degrees, whereas two eyes can give approximately 190 to 200 degrees.

3. It gives you an enhanced ability to detect faint objects.
4. It allows stereopsis, where *'stereo'* meaning solid, and *'opsis'* meaning sight. This gives you the ability to perceive depth, known as 'binocular depth perception' or 'stereoscopic depth perception'.

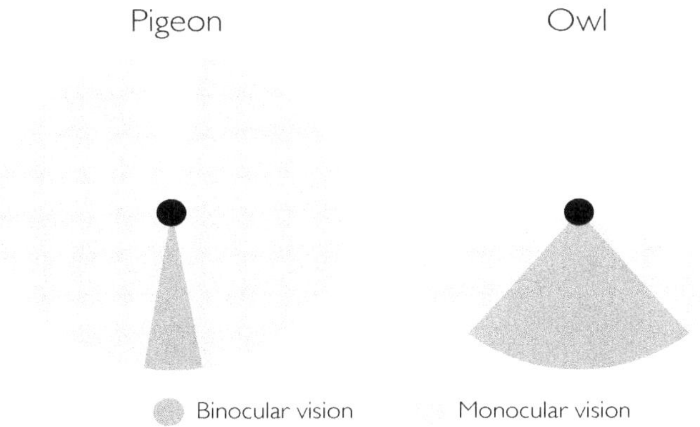

Figure 17: Illustration of the field of view for binocular vision (in a pigeon) vs. monocular vision (in an owl).

Animals that are prey (such as rabbits, buffaloes and antelopes) tend to have a larger binocular field of view where the eyes are usually on the sides of their head.

The hunters however tend to have eyes on the front of their head closer together (such as snakes, eagles and humans), so they have enhanced depth perception for targeting on their prey for hunting and survival.

Occupations which require a high degree of precision to judge distances and demonstrate a high level of stereo acuity, include pilots, surgeons and, of course, martial artists.

Cyclopean Eye

The cyclopean eye is the point at which the field of view of both eyes cross. This is usually slightly off centre, as the eyes are not always 100% symmetrically positioned. In such cases, one eye can become more dominant than the other. This is known as allelotropia, and you can exploit this in combat by playing away from your opponent's dominant eye to gain a perceptual advantage over your adversary.

On the same note, if you are the one with the dominant eye, then you would want to keep your adversary in clear view of the dominant eye.

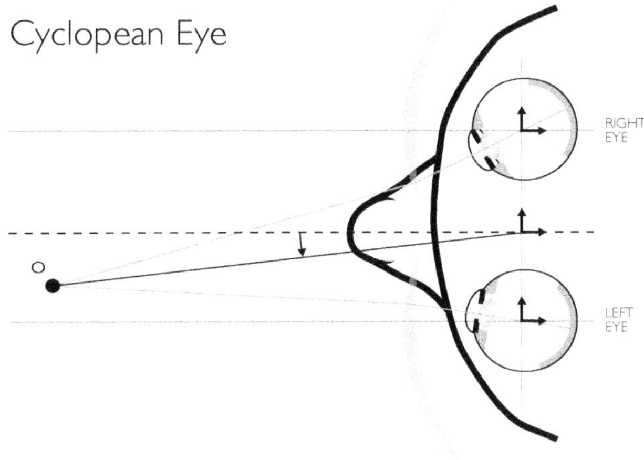

Figure 18: Illustration of the cyclopean eye usually being closer to the dominant eye.

Binocular Rivalry

When very different images are shown to the same retinal regions of the two eyes, perception settles on one for a few moments, then the other, then the first, and so on, for as long as one cares to look. This alternation of perception between the images of the two eyes is called binocular rivalry.

Binocular Rivalry Partner Drill

1. Get into pairs.
2. Partners stand in front of each other in a fighting stance.
3. Move around using footwork only outside the fighting measure.
4. One of the partners will be the trainer, and raise their rear hand by flashing their palm towards the trainee to instil binocular rivalry.
5. If the trainer notices that the trainee is momentarily absent, then they should try and tag the trainee on the chest or shoulder gently.
6. The trainee must try and avoid being tagged. Take three minutes each way to practice this drill.

Step 3 — Decide

The purpose of any decision in combat is to use reasonable force to incapacitate your opponent. Bruce Lee quoted:

'I do not hit,
it hits all by itself.'

With this statement Bruce is talking about something called the 1,000:10,000 rule.

The idea here is if you practice a technique 1,000 times with precision and accuracy, then you will lay down the proprioceptive neuromuscular pathways to coordinate brain and limb in order to perform the technique proficiently upon your conscious instruction.

However, if you practice the technique 10,000 times, then you will programme the technique into your sub-conscious brain so that you will be able to deliver the technique as a reflex response without thinking about it when the need arises, for example blocking an incoming attack when you see one coming. This is what Bruce meant when he spoke about 'it hitting all by itself'.

So, the decision process starts with practicing whatever it is you want to get good at, whether it's martial arts in combat or practising to become a pilot.

The decision process that takes place in a human's mind involves cognitive processes, and the four stages of learning are:

1	Unconscious incompetence	When you don't know that you're not good at something;
2	Conscious incompetence	This is when you are aware that you're not good at something;
3	Conscious competence	This is when you've been working on something and are getting quite good at it and you know it – 1,000 rule; and
4	Unconscious competence	This is when you are good at something but don't even know it any more – 10,000 rule

Bruce Lee referred to this as the three stages, which are:

1	Partiality	Cultivating the tool	Stages 1 and 2 from above
2	Fluidity	Utilising the tool	Stage 3 from above; and
3	Emptiness	Dissolving the tool	Stage 4 from above

Step 4 — Action

Motor Cognition is when 'cognition' or mental processing is embodied in 'motor', i.e. when thought translates into action.

The fundamental unit of the motor cognition paradigm is action, defined as the movements produced to satisfy an intention towards a specific motor goal, or in reaction to a meaningful event in the physical and social environments. One such example may be when someone attacks you, and you defend against it.

Perception-Action Coupling is when you see something and respond with an action, and vice versa. This is the foundation of all fighting exchanges.

Wolfgang Prinz *et. al.* at the Max Planck Institute for Human Cognitive and Brain Sciences in Leipzig theorised that all actions are coded and leave behind a motor pattern, and vice versa. These actions can be accessed and replayed whenever the pattern is detected. This is when your motor responses become reflex — in other words, by the 10,000 rule, you reach the stage of 'emptiness'.

Step 5 — Repeat OODA Loop

Finally, the idea of triggering multiple OODA Loop decision cycles in your opponent is to keep them in a constant state of decision making and disarray. This will allow you to **stay ahead of your opponent and direct your own fight.** So you,

'KEEP MOVING TO

STAY AWAKE, ALERT AND SWITCHED ON!'

The Beautiful Man

I began to notice what the ugly man was doing. He was eating *zuppe di pesce.* He would bring the spoon slowly up to his mouth, his whole face expectant with anticipation. His eyes would shine and then close and he would hold the stew in his mouth, letting it melt and cool slowly. Each spoonful took minutes to savour. He extracted every last taste from each mouthful as if tasting some food reserved for the gods.

He would take three spoonfuls in this way and then put his spoon down. Then he reached over and took a cigarette from the packet in front of him. He lit it in the same deliberate way that he ate the food and then he inhaled each pull deep into the centre of his body. He made cigarette smoking seem an art form, an act more desirable than any other sensual pleasure. It was as if each pull would be the last before the firing squad ended his life, and he wished to extract as much as humanly possible from each last moment.

I began to realise how wrong I had been in my former assessment. This man was not ugly. He was able to do something that is very special, something that I have long desired to do better myself.

This man knew how to live in the present moment, to extract as much experience as possible from the now. Rather than looking at an ugly man, I could **see something else now.** While some people look back to the past for reference, many others worry about what is to come, thinking how to plan and organise their future. These things are of course important. But it takes a special kind of wisdom to appreciate that each present moment is precious, full of experience, and will never come again. Far from being ugly, perhaps this was the most beautiful man I had ever seen. And to this day I thank him for his **present.**

Conclusion

We've looked at the OODA Loop, and its application in combat. We have been focussing specifically on our perceptual skills and abilities with a view to improving them to better ourselves as martial artists in combat, as well as applying these skills to our daily lives. When you start to become more aware and alert when you **engage your eagle eye**, you **start to see things more clearly**, like opportunities you would have otherwise been blind to, and create a new vision of possibilities.

The OODA Loop process and its intelligent application in combat but also in daily life allows you to:

1. Create a state of alertness and awareness.
2. Get on top of your game.
3. Read situations better.
4. Stay ahead of the curve so your opponent is always playing catch up.
5. Control and direct your own life by not being led or played by others.

Most importantly, it helps you SOAR TO SUCCESS!

Bruce Lee famously quoted:

> *'A perceptual speed is the quickness of your eyes to see an opening through the action or inaction of your opponent. Visual awareness is needed to attain greater speed. Vision awareness or keen perceptual speed must be learned through constant practice as it isn't inherited. It should be part of your daily training — just a short, concentrated practice to perceive rapidly. A person who is slow in responding and in delivering can overcome this disadvantage through quick perceiving.'*

And that brings us to the end of the Possess an Eagle Eye stage of your self-mastery journey. Before you embark on SOARING TO SUCCESS, please answer the following:

<u>Questions</u>

1. Do you feel your Eyes Are Wide Open now? (Yes or No)
2. Do you feel more Switched ON now? (Yes or No)
3. Do you think you have better skills to See New Opportunities and ways? (Yes or No)
4. Do you understand how to Switch ON Your Alertness and Awareness? (Yes or No)
5. Do you understand how to Get On Top of Your Game? (Yes or No)
6. Do you understand how to Stay Ahead of The Curve? (Yes or No)
7. Are you ready to control and Direct Your Own Life? (Yes or No)
8. Are you ready to swoop in and Take New Opportunities? (Yes or No)
9. Are you ready to Soar to Success? (Yes or No)

My friend, I would like to thank you deeply for giving me the chance to take you through this Master Your Life journey, and remember:

'DON'T LOOK,
SEE!'

4 Think and become

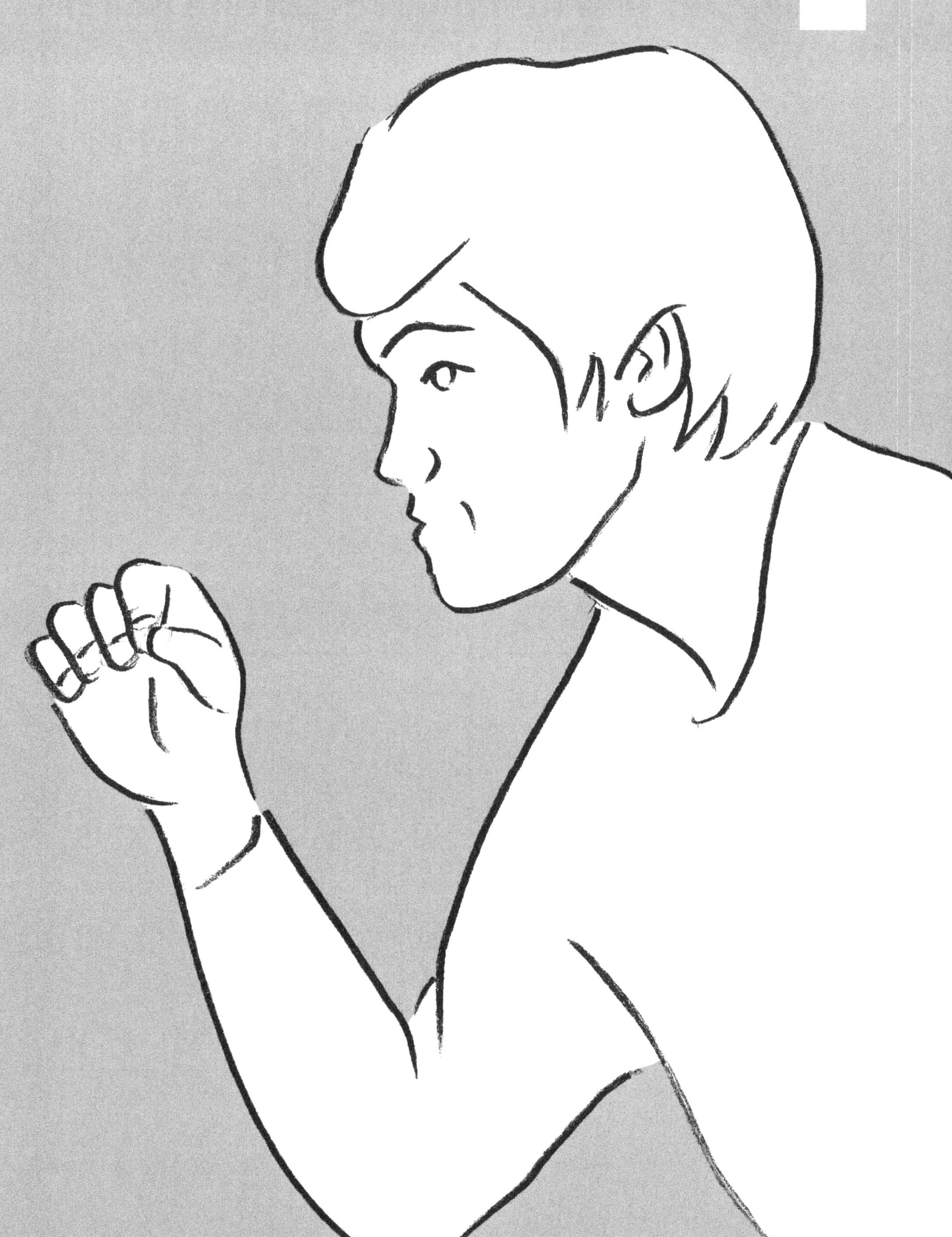

Think and Become

STAGE 4 — GREEN BELT

Master Your Confidence and Self Belief

What's the Problem?

So, who is this Think and Become stage of your self-mastery journey aimed at?

- People who have a volatile temper and get angry easily.
- People who lose their composure and calibration.
- People who lack vision and direction in their life.
- People who are confused and cannot see the wood for the trees.
- People who sabotage themselves.

Objective

Outcomes and Results Question
What outcome(s) and result(s) do you expect to get when you start to Think and Become? Take ten minutes to list down all the positive changes you would like to see, hear and feel.

To think and do is one thing. To think and become is another matter entirely.

To think and become demands the cultivation of your mind to think in a certain way, so you can become the manifestation of your mind.

Without thinking the things you do not want.

Without becoming the things you do not want.

Without losing the faith and belief in the process of becoming.

All with certainty that you are what you think.

Examples Question
Can you think of any examples when you have thought about something you did not want, and it manifested, and how did it cause you to feel? Take ten minutes to make a list.

Do you sometimes find yourself:

- Getting angry quickly when things do not go your way?
- Losing your composure?
- Feeling like you are not calibrated?
- Feeling like your mind is out-of-sync with the outside world, and things are not happening as planned?
- Having a lack of vision?
- Sensing a lack of direction in your life?
- Feeling confused and combobulated?
- Losing self-belief and wanting to give up if you have not already done so?
- Sabotaging yourself because things have not worked out?

If you have answered 'yes' to any of the above, then you're in for an amazing MENTAL SHIFT!

Think and Become is based on Bruce Lee's martial philosophy:

'As you think,
so shall you become.'

It is also inspired by an interview with Anthony Robbins, Frank Kern and John Reese. Check out www.AnthonyRobbins.com for more information.

This stage of your self-mastery journey will help you to:

Belt	Pillars of Luck	Chapter	Success Goals
4. Green	Positivity	**'Think & become'** Master your confidence & self-belief	• Create a sense of calmness • Get clarity so you can see clearly • Have absolute certainty • Tap into your unlimited potential • Take massive action • Get massive results • Get massive belief and confidence • Think success, be success!

This stage is broken down into twenty substages as follows:

1. Calmness.
2. Clarity.
3. What is Success?
4. What Can People Do to Become Successful?
5. How Effective are Business/Personal Development Products?
6. Why Don't Most People Achieve Success with Business?

7. What Do Successful People Do?
8. What is the Difference Between Successful People and Everyone Else?
9. How Do You Create a State Of MUST?
10. How Do You Create a Breakthrough?
11. What is Certainty?
12. How Do You Get into a Mindset of Following Through?
13. The Holy Grail of Certainty.
14. The Secret: Why the Rich Get Richer, and the Poor Get Poorer.
15. The Secret to Getting Rich.
16. Acting 'As If'.
17. 'As If' Experiment.
18. The Secret to Making it Work for You.
19. The Paradox.
20. The Turning Point.

Let's start to THINK SUCCESS, BE SUCCESS!

Warm Up

Let's jump right in and start warming up by answering the following questions:

Question
What do you think 'Think And Become' means? Take five minutes to define.

Question
Do you know What Successful People Do to become successful? (Yes or No)

Question
Do you know why most people do not Achieve Success? Take five minutes to make a list.

Question

Do you know **The Difference Between Unsuccessful And Successful People?** Take five minutes to write a list.

Question

Would you like to know the **Holy Grail Of Success?** (Yes or No)

Question

Do you know the secret why the **Rich Get Richer** and the poor get poorer? Take five minutes to explain.

Question

Would you like to know the **Secret to Getting Rich?** (Yes or No)

Question

Would you like to learn how to **Think Success, Become Success?** (Yes or No)

If you do not know the answer to any of the questions above and are eager to learn, or answered 'yes' to the last question, then you're in the right place, so let's **THINK YOUR WAY TO SUCCESS!**

The Chicken Farmer

There was once a chicken farmer who was a very keen rock climber. One day, climbing a particularly challenging rock face, he came upon a large ledge. On the ledge was a large nest and in the nest, three large eggs. Eagle eggs.

He knew it was distinctly un-ecological, and undoubtedly illegal, but temptation got the better of him and he discreetly put one of the eagle eggs in his rucksack, checking first to make sure the mother eagle wasn't around. Then he continued his climb, drove back to his ranch and put the eagle egg in the hen house.

In the fullness of time the egg hatched and the baby eagling emerged. It looked around and saw the mother hen. *'Mama!'* he squawked.

And so it was that the eagle grew up with his brother and sister chicks. It learned to do all the things that chickens do: clucking and cackling, scratching in the dirt for grits and worms, flapping its wings furiously and flying a few feet into the air before crashing to earth in a pile of dust and feathers. Above all, it believed that it was totally and absolutely a chicken.

JFK at NASA

In the pioneering days of space research, John F. Kennedy was visiting NASA at Cape Canaveral.

He met many great scientists and researchers.

He met men whose great ambition was to conquer space and walk on the surface of the moon.

He met administrators and accountants, and many others whose contribution to the project was immense.

Men and women who had a sense of destiny, purpose and pride.

Introduction

Bruce Lee used martial artistry to self-actualise himself, i.e. to be the best he could possibly be, in his case the best martial artist on and off screen — he wanted to be known as an artist of life, not just a martial artist.

Bruce Lee studied profound philosophers, both past and present. One such philosopher was Dr Napoleon Hill, who wrote the bestseller book *Think and Grow Rich.*

He presented the idea of a 'Chief Definite Aim' as a challenge to his readers in order to make themselves ask themselves, 'In what do I truly believe?' According to Hill, 98% of people had few or no beliefs, and this alone put true success firmly out of their reach.

Bruce wrote the following 'Chief Definite Aim', at which time Bruce would've been twenty-eight years of age and a minor TV star in the USA, having featured in a number of shows which included, most notably, the ill-fated Green Hornet series. With his second child recently born and no financial security to speak of, the clearly determined founder of Jeet Kune Do decided to put his 'Chief Definite Aim' down on paper, as a means to set his SUCCESS GOALS! The rest is history.

Bruce Lee's 'Chief Definite Aim' read as follows:

> *'I, Bruce Lee, will be the first highest paid Oriental superstar in the United States. I will give the most exciting performances and render the best quality in the capacity of an actor. Starting 1970 I will achieve world fame and from then onward till the end of 1980 I will have in my possession $10 million dollars. I will live the way I please and achieve inner harmony and happiness,' Bruce Lee, 1969.*

Bruce Lee died on 20th July 1973 at the young age of thirty-two, two weeks before the release of his blockbuster movie *Enter the Dragon.* After Bruce's untimely passing, *Enter the Dragon* catapulted Bruce Lee into superstardom, not only in the USA, but worldwide. His exciting performances are still revered today as the pinnacle of martial artistry, and Bruce's legend and martial art Jeet Kune Do inspires millions worldwide.

Enter the Dragon grossed over $25 million in the US alone, so it's probably safe to say that the Bruce Lee Estate exceeded $10 million dollars in revenues, smashing Bruce's financial success goal.

As for inner peace and harmony, I personally feel that Bruce's fame and fortune would have bought him unrest on Earth. Chillingly, I feel that his passing dealt him the 'inner harmony and happiness' that he longed, but in another realm — satisfying Bruce's spiritual success goal.

As they say, 'Be careful what you wish for'... On the same token, 'If you don't ask you don't get'. In Hill's own words, *'What the mind can conceive and believe, it can achieve'* - Dr Napoleon Hill, author of *Think and Grow Rich,* the premise upon which the 'Chief Definite Aim' is built. Bruce reframed that powerful philosophy in his own words as:

'As you think,

so shall you become.'

That's what I call Martial Mind Power!

Calmness

As a first step, I'd like you to liberate your mind from the rigmarole of daily life that can sometimes shackle your thinking. Now, please **'Empty Your Teacup'** so you are ready to taste my tea.

We are going to start off with a relaxation drill covered in the **'Stillness'** stage.

Yin and Yang Relaxation

Think
By yourself.

Objective
Relax the body and mind.

Requirements
None.

Time
Ten minutes

Set up
Lay down comfortably on your back with your arms by your sides with your palms facing up to the ceiling.

Task
1. Gently close your eyes as you deepen your relaxation.
2. As you lay there, feel your body pressing against the floor.
3. Now, starting from your head, press it into the ground — press, press, press.
4. Keep pressing the head into the floor. Moving down to your neck, press it into the ground as well — press, press, press.
5. Keep pressing the head and neck into the floor. Moving down to your shoulders, press them into the ground as well — press, press, press.
6. Keep pressing the head, neck and shoulders into the floor. Moving down to your upper arms, press them into the ground as well — press, press, press.
7. Keep pressing the head, neck, shoulders and upper arms into the floor. Moving down to your forearms, press them into the ground as well — press, press, press.
8. Keep pressing the head, neck, shoulders, upper arms and forearms into the floor. Moving down to your hands, press them into the ground as well — press, press, press.
9. Keep pressing the head, neck, shoulders, upper arms, forearms and hands into the floor. Moving to your upper back, press it into the ground as well — press, press, press.

10. Keep pressing the head, neck, shoulders, upper arms, forearms, hands and upper back into the floor. Moving to your lower back, press it into the ground as well — press, press, press.
11. Keep pressing the head, neck, shoulders, upper arms, forearms, hands, upper back and lower back into the floor. Moving to your hips, press them into the ground as well — press, press, press.
12. Keep pressing the head, neck, shoulders, upper arms, forearms, hands, upper back, lower back and hips into the floor. Moving to your upper legs, press them into the ground as well — press, press, press.
13. Keep pressing the head, neck, shoulders, upper arms, forearms, hands, upper back, lower back, hips and upper legs into the floor. Moving to your lower legs, press them into the ground as well — press, press, press.
14. Keep pressing the head, neck, shoulders, upper arms, forearms, hands, upper back, lower back, hips, upper legs and lower legs into the floor. Moving to your heels, press them into the ground as well — press, press, press.
15. Pressing everything into the ground — press, press, press.
16. **Stop pressing** and **Now Relax All Your Muscles!**
17. Wait for a six to heaven minutes
18. In a moment, I am going to count back from ten to one. You will come back to full awareness, feeling energetic and switched on one tenth on each count. Ten, nine, eight, feeling more aware, seven, six, five, feeling energy flowing through every cell of your body, four, three, two, fully switched on, aware and energetic, and one, back in the room and open your eyes. Roll onto your side and push yourself up to a seated position on the floor.

<u>Progressions</u>

1. Play this game in a park or garden which is safe and clean to lie down on.
2. Play some soothing music to help you relax.

Clarity

Now that we have created a state of calmness, let's progress onto create some CLARITY in your thoughts.

<u>Question</u>

Put your hands up if you **Think Negative** things about yourself? (Yes or No)

Question
Please can you write down some **Examples of Your Negative Thoughts?** Take five minutes to make a list.

Based on Bruce's philosophy, 'as you think, so you shall become', it would be a fair assumption that if you're thinking negative things, then you are manifesting a negative reality.

Question
Put your hands up if you would **Like to be More Positive** and therefore successful towards your own desires? (Yes or No)

I would comfortably say that most people would love to be more positive and successful in all areas of their lives.

What is Success?

However, success is relative to the individual. Before we start, let's try and define what success means to you.

Question
What is your **Definition Of Success**, and what would you have to see, feel and hear to know you got it? Take five minutes to define and describe.

What Can People Do to Become Successful?

Question
If you have not achieved your success yet, then **What Are You Doing to Become Successful?** Take five minutes to make a list.

Quite often people mention the use of business and/or personal development products and services.

Question
Did you mention **Martial Arts and Philosophy** as a means of **Personal Development?** (Yes or No)

Question
Would you like to know **What Bruce Lee's Kung Fu** called Jeet Kune Do **Really Is?** (Yes or No)

In Bruce's own words:

'Jeet Kune Do, ultimately, is not a matter of petty technique
but of HIGHLY DEVELOPED PERSONAL SPIRITUALITY and PHYSIQUE.
It is NOT a question of developing what has ALREADY BEEN DEVELOPED
but of RECOVERING what has been LEFT BEHIND.
These things have been WITH US, IN US, ALL THE TIME and have NEVER BEEN LOST or DISTORTED except by our MISGUIDED MANIPULATION OF THEM.
Jeet Kune Do is NOT a matter of technology,
but of SPIRITUAL INSIGHT and TRAINING.'

Jeet Kune Do therefore is a set of personal development skills and tools that can help us raise our game.

Let's look at personal development products and services for a moment.

How Effective Are Business/Personal Development Products?

Question
What percentage of people that Purchased Business and/or Personal Development Products and Services, did Not Take Any Action Within Ninety Days of acquiring them? Take a guess if you do not know (as a percentage).

The answer is... 72.3%.

The largest problem with people who purchase or use business and/or personal development products and services, is that the majority of them DO NOT GET RESULTS!

Question
Why do you think that is? Take five minutes to make a list.

You would think if everyone who bought the business and/or personal development products and services actually used them, then they would be more successful.

But it's not that straightforward in reality. Let us explore this in more detail, with a view to GETting RESULTS and Make JKD work towards your success goals.

Why Don't Most People Achieve Success with Business

It is for the same reason why when a doctor advises a lung cancer patient to stop smoking, 70% of the people carry on smoking.

It's life 101: most won't, but a much smaller percentage will follow through and get results. That'll be the other 30%.

What Do Successful People Do?

Question
How can we Model Success for ourselves? Take five minutes to explain.

One way of understanding how to achieve success, is by studying what successful people do.

Question
Do you think successful people were Already Successful? (Yes or No)

The truth of the matter is that successful people did not start out successfully.

Take Bruce Lee, for example. He was completely broke and had to go back to Hong Kong to jump start his film career. Up until then, Linda Lee, his wife, held more than one job to support Bruce, working at a telephone call centre and a supermarket to support Bruce whilst he painstakingly worked on developing his film career.

On the flip side, did you know that every five generations, someone will make a fortune? And the following generation usually squanders it all in one go. So the cycle of wealth creation and destruction perpetuates.

Frank Kern, a successful Internet Marketing guru, started out with nothing, He built up his business to earn $300 per day. He described his most exciting moment in his business when he hit the $2,500 per day mark, even more vividly than when he made $18 million.

He could have stopped at $300 per day, or even $2,500 per day, but he didn't.

Question
The question is, Why Didn't He Stop? Take a quick guess.

It was not about the money; he wanted to experience the chase and achieve his goals. He wanted the validation that the fear doesn't matter anymore. As Bruce Lee said:

'To understand your fear is the beginning of really seeing.'

He wanted to feel that he's already won. Bruce Lee went on to quote:

'Life's battles don't always go to the stronger or faster man.
But sooner or later the man who wins is the man who thinks he can.'

Then at a higher level, doing more of it, he took it on as a personal challenge. Bruce quoted along these lines:

'Even today, I dare not say that I have reached a state of achievement.
I'm still learning, for learning is boundless.'

Therefore the difference between a successful person and an unsuccessful person is that successful people fear not following through but rather stagnating and staying where they are, hoping for the best with an expectation of something for nothing. It's the fear of missing out on the possibilities that can be.

Frank Kern states:

'You don't have to be at the goal to feel alive,
you just have to make some progress towards your goals.
Buy the product, then open the damn thing up and start using it.
Then just enjoy the journey.'

Bruce Lee supports this point when he says:

'A goal is not always meant to be reached,
it often serves simply as something to aim at.'

What Is the Difference Between Successful People and Everyone Else?

Question
What do you think is the Difference Between Successful People And Everyone Else? Take five minutes to make a list.

Typically, people that have breakthroughs have hit rock bottom before that MUST has hit them as an urgent reality. Bruce Lee said:

'Without frustration you will not discover that
you might be able to do something on your own.
We grow through conflict.'

Most people are not in a MUST situation. Rather, they are in a DESIRE situation.

They have big dreams, but do not have what it takes to push through the wall of DESIRE, a psychological barrier which blocks you from going further.

How Do You Create a State of MUST?

Question
So how do you Get into the State of MUST, where your back is against the wall and you feel like you have no other choice but to Act Now? Take five minutes to explain.

John Reese, the first man to make $1 million using internet marketing, said:

> *'It was not about the money — it was about breaking a barrier of progress. A recognition of what I'm capable of.*
>
> *For someone who is already successful, it is about what tools and skills can I take on which will create more freedom for my life?*
>
> *First, I am going to create a ritual for the next eight weeks, to get into the state to follow through.*
>
> *Second, I am going to create a MUST, not because my back's against the wall, but because I want to master something in life to create freedom. And each week, I'm going to create progress.'*

Tony Robbins, the famous Personal Development guru, started out as a truck driver earning $100 per day, with the dream of earning $3k per month.

Once he reached that target, he said to himself that he now wanted to make $10k per month.

Once he reached that target, he said to himself that he now wanted to make $100k per month, then $1 million, and so on.

One day he was delivering a speech to an audience of 15,000 people, and one of his colleagues approached him during the 'stretch break' and told him that the value of company's stock had reached $400 million.

Question
Guess what he said right after that? Take a quick guess.

His precise words were, *'What's next?'*, and he went right back to where he left off. Tony stated:

'Once you break through,
it becomes a game!'

I say:

'Excitement lives in the chase of the game!'

How Do You Create a Breakthrough?

Question
How do you create a **Breakthrough**? Take five minutes to make a list.

72.3% of the people that are purchasing the business and/or personal development products, have not yet broken through.

To break through, you need to simply **Condition Your Mind.**

<u>Question</u>
How can you **Condition Your Mind?** Take five minutes to describe how.

Ways you can condition your mind include having a role model, anchoring a success story. You can also create a ritual, for Bruce Lee once said:

'What you habitually think
largely determines what you will ultimately become.'

You can then take small steps towards your success goals and gradually build up momentum to ultimately get your mind into peak-state. As Lao Tzu said, 'The journey of a thousand miles begins with one step.'

The most important question is, **WHY IS IT A MUST FOR YOU?**

It has to be something you're **hungry** for. If you're not hungry, then put yourself around people that are hungry, and it'll hit you, and all of a sudden you'll say, 'my life sucks!' That's when you start to do something about it, one step at a time.

At the same time:

'If you spend too much time thinking about a thing, you'll never get it done.
Make at least one definite move daily toward your goal,' Bruce Lee.

I call this the 'Analysis Paralysis Syndrome'. Tony Robbins stated:

'People can change their standard by improving some aspect of their life all the time. When you are absolutely CERTAIN that that result is going to change my life, that's when you're going to do it. CERTAINTY or the most common word is BELIEVE. If you're ABSOLUTELY CERTAIN you can do it, then YOU WILL. If you're absolutely certain you can NOT do it, then YOU WON'T. The middle no-man's land of maybe it will work or maybe it won't, KILLS PEOPLE.'

What Is Certainty?

The definition of 'certainty' according to the Oxford dictionary*: 'A firm conviction (or belief) that something is the case.'*

Michelangelo

Under a hot sun, a little boy is gazing at a young man called Michelangelo, a sculptor who is intently chipping away at a large piece of rock.

'Why are you doing that?' asks the little boy.

'Because,' said Michelangelo, *'there's an angel inside, and he wants to come out.'*

How Do You Get into a Mindset of Following Through?

Question
How do you **Get into a Mindset of Following Through?** Take five minutes to explain.

So how do you get people to follow through on their own?

Use **THE HOLY GRAIL OF CERTAINTY.** It's the difference between why the rich get richer and the poor get poorer.

Question
Would you like to **Know This Secret?** (Yes or No)

The Holy Grail of Certainty

This is the Holy Grail of Certainty:

1.Potential	**2. Action**
4. Belief	**3. Results**

<u>Table 5</u>: *The Holy Grail of Certainty.*

1. Potential

What is your potential?

As an example, Roger Bannister was the first man to run the four minute mile. To do this, he had to cultivate his mind to make a major mental shift to break the four minute barrier in his head.

Bruce said:

'Give me six hours to chop down a tree, and
I will spend the first four sharpening the axe.'

Once Roger Bannister sharpened his mind, he achieved his goal and readily broke the four minute barrier. He created a congruency between his mind and body which made it so.

<u>Question</u>
How Many people do you think **Ran the Four Minute Mile After Roger Bannister?** Take a quick guess.

Thirty-seven people ran the four minute mile within two years of Roger Bannister achieving the goal. Why? Because people were proven it was possible, and Roger Bannister had removed this psychological barrier in everyone's minds.

Abraham Lincoln summed it up by saying:

'That some achieve great success, is proof to all,
that others can achieve it as well.'

Your potential is infinite. All you have to do is to tap into it!

2. Action

People have a belief of their potential, which affects how much action they take.

3. Results

This determines the results people get.

4. Belief

The results reinforce peoples' belief.

The Secret: Why the Rich Get Richer and the Poor Get Poorer

So what's the secret to why the poor get poorer, and the rich get richer. Let's have a look at poor getting poorer first. The poor get poorer because they have unlimited potential but take little action and therefore get limited results. This could be because they have little faith or belief in themselves.

What happens is, if you believe you have very little potential, how much action are you going to take? None! When you pair a little potential with half-hearted action, you get half-hearted results. Then what does that do to your beliefs? You think, *'See, I told you this was a waste of time and it wouldn't work!'* Then you put in even less action and get even worse results, and your belief gets even weaker. It's a vicious cycle that feeds on itself until you're in a poisonous self-fulling downwards spiral of self-sabotage and destruction!

Now let's look at the flip side of the rich getting richer. What if something came along and filled you with absolute certainty and belief; not like *'I can believe'* in a casual way, but when *'you know'* because you *'had to find a way'* and get into a state of must and get that certainty to do something about it now!

If you get yourself into a state of CERTAINTY that this is GOING TO WORK. That YOU ARE GOING TO FIND A WAY! If not, then say to yourself, I WILL MAKE THE WAY; then you tap a lot more potential. When you're certain of your potential, you take MASSIVE ACTION, and when you take MASSIVE ACTION when you really BELIEVE IN SOMETHING, then you get GREAT RESULTS. Then your brain goes, *'See, I knew I could do it!'*

That's exactly how Tony Robbins went from $100 per day, to $1000 per day, to $3000 per day, to $10,000 per day, to $100k, to $1M, to $100M, to $400M.

And then you go on to tap more potential, to tap into more action, get more results and further reinforce your beliefs.

That is why the rich get richer, and the poor get poorer.

So what's the Secret to Getting Rich?

The Secret to Getting Rich

Well it's all in the execution. If you do not believe in what you're doing, the execution is going to be so weak that you will not convince people to buy whatever product you sell or service you provide.

You may get some sales, but probably out of pity. It's like someone selling something door-to-door and saying, *'You don't want one of these, do you, maybe, please...?'* You won't convince anyone to give you their money to be successful.

The question is, how do you **produce CERTAINTY** when the world isn't giving it to you? Well, you **go out and try, and try, and then try some more.**

Bruce quoted:

'Defeat is a state of mind.
No one is ever defeated until defeat has been accepted as a reality.
To me, defeat in anything is merely temporary, and its punishment is
but an urge for me to greater effort achieve my goal.
Defeat simply tells me that something is wrong in my doing;
it is a path leading to success and truth.'

So how do you keep it going without accepting defeat?

You didn't change **YOUR POTENTIAL**, because it **IS ALREADY THERE**, isn't it?

I don't really want to take more action either, because taking action where a belief doesn't exist won't change anything, much like the feeble door-to-door salesman.

You do it by believing that you have achieved the results in your head. It is a state of acting 'AS IF', to make CERTAIN that it had already happened.

When I was a kid, I gravitated towards cars and motorbikes. I knew that I was going to own my dream cars and motorbikes. When I was a kid, I couldn't afford to buy car magazines, so I used to go to the library to read them. My father loved to change his cars every year, and he would often have a copy of AutoTrader lying around. I would go through the sports car section picking the cars that I wanted in my dream car garage. Now I own and drive my dream cars.

There was never any doubt. I just knew it was going to happen because I conditioned myself to believe I was going to get them by acting 'AS IF' I already owned them.

Acting 'As If'

So let's take an example of basketball.

If you normally shoot hoops really well, what happens when a basketball player fails to make the perfect shot? Something's changed, something's interfering with your state. What is it?

A group of psychologists took a group of people, split them into three groups and gave each group a specific exercise to perform for six weeks.

- First group — Do nothing.
- Second group — Practice only.
- Third group — Only allowed to mentally visualise. Practice makes perfect, so these guys see themselves making the perfect shot every time.

At the end of the six weeks, each group was tested in a basketball shoot out. It may be obvious that the people who didn't do anything had the worst results.

Question
What order do you think the three Groups Performed in, with Best first and Worst last? Take three minutes to make a list.

Surprisingly, the mental visualisation group performed the best. It is not just about practise; it is about getting yourself SO CERTAIN so many times so that when you actually DO IT, there is NO HESITATION at all and you do it perfectly every single time! It's having that ABSOLUTE CERTAINTY that makes you TAP YOUR FULL POTENTIAL and take MASSIVE ACTION to GET MASSIVE RESULTS. You become even stronger with REINFORCED BELIEFS, and this is what makes you a star!

Jack Nicholson used to visualise every hit before he took a swing at the ball. He used to visualise the ball landing exactly where he wanted to place it, unlike other golfers who just point in the right direction, then hit and hope for the best.

Question
Guess what the really bad golfers are Focusing on? Take five minutes to explain.

Bruce Lee famously quoted:

'I am not easily discouraged.
I readily visualise myself as overcoming obstacles,
winning out over setbacks,
achieving impossible objectives.'

'As If' Experiment

We are now going to try a little 'As If' experiment.

1. Stand up with your feet together.
2. Put your right index finger straight out in front at shoulder level.
3. Without moving your feet, I just want you to turn comfortably clockwise and notice where you naturally stop, and then come back round to the start point and drop your hand.

Now we are going to try something different:

1. Drop your hand and close your eyes, standing with your feet together.
2. You don't even have to visualise, but **just FEEL**.
3. Imagine that you have put your hand up as before and, treating this like a game, feel yourself rotating twice as far as before.
4. Then repeat it again, and feel yourself rotate three times as far.
5. Then repeat it one more time, and feel yourself rotate all the way to the front.
6. See it and feel it like a game, going further each time, enjoying it!

Only **when you feel good**, I want you to open your eyes, and try it again and see how far you can rotate comfortably and **see how far you can go round. Go all the way round now.**

Question
How much **further** did you go?

On average, people go 25% further round than the first time.

The question is, did you have the potential to go round as far you did the second time, as you did in the first instance? The answer to that is, yes of course you did.

Question
The question is, **'So Why Didn't You?'** Take five minutes to explain.

In short, it's because you did not Believe It.

- We have unconscious beliefs about how far you can turn comfortably;
- We have beliefs in our unconscious that we don't even know exist.

Question

So **What Was Different** between the first and second attempts? Take five minutes to explain.

Here's the difference:

- The potential was there the first time — it has always been there, hasn't it?
- And you took the action and got a result;
- But it was 25 to 50% less than the first time, and the only difference was you decided to **CHANGE YOUR BELIEF SYSTEM!**

Question

How did you **Change Your Belief System**? Take five minutes to explain.

How did we change our belief? We didn't change our potential, or take more action.

I simply got you to **SEE THE RESULT IN ADVANCE**, to take you further! To quote Bruce:

'As you think,
so shall you become!'

Mohammad Ali said that:

'The man who has no imagination has no wings'.

Bruce went on to say:

'Don't fear failure.
Not failure, but low aim is the crime.
In great attempt it is glorious even to fail.'

Or put another way,

'Aim for the stars, and you'll land in the sky.'

I say:

'THINK SUCCESS, BE SUCCESS.'

The Secret to Making It Work for You

That's what I did when I saw myself driving around in my Ferrari. That's what is missing in these people. They are literally not able to SEE IT.

I had certainty that, no matter what, I could see myself driving around in my dream car. I could hear that FI engine revving, I could see myself in the driving seat looking up at the cluster of retro-styled dials on the dash and I could feel the snug leather sports seats. I could feel the leather steering wheel firmly in my hands giving me accurate feedback from the road surface as I carved through the undulating mountain roads, I could feel the heat bellowing from the engine and I could smell the leather in the cabin, enveloping me in my Ferrari experience.

That is what people don't get. The execution is everything when you have absolute certainty, a belief that you can do it, and see the results ahead of time as if they are TRUE NOW.

Question
What difference do you think it makes to **Have Certainty, Self-Belief and Visualise the Results Being True Now?** Take five minutes to explain.

Here's the secret to making it work for you... This shifts people's certainty; people are uncertain they want to succeed at first; they want it, but are in a state of fear. The best way to get over it is to get a big enough reason that you MUST do something about it because you HAVE TO SUCCEED, as there is no other option. You must condition yourself to see it and feel it so often that you JUST DO IT; train your mind so that you can SEE THE RESULTS for real. Create a DAILY RITUAL, then LIVE IT, BREATHE IT!

The Paradox

The paradox people get stuck in is that they feel that the product or service has to prove it works before they start using it, therefore they never start using it.

The problem is, to defend themselves people lower the expectations and become sceptical. When people say *'I am sceptical or pessimistic'*, Tony Robbins says, 'No man, you're gutless!'

It takes no guts to be sceptical, or a critic, or an internet warrior critiquing others behind an anonymous veil.

It takes guts to believe and put something on the line, because if you think someone else is going to do that for you, you might as well forget it now.

The late Steve Jobs summed it beautifully by saying

'Have the courage to follow your heart and intuition.

They somehow already know what you truly want to become.

Everything else is secondary.'

So don't let the fear paralyse you — **get some guts and get over it!** As Bruce Lee said:

'Courage is not the absence of fear.
It is the ability to act in the presence of fear.'

People think that I will be presented with disappointment if I do not succeed. So what?

Question
Can you guess how many times Honda got turned down for funding for his first venture, motorised bicycles? Take a quick guess.

Answer... 1,000 times.

Most common people when hit with failure simply crash and burn, whereas successful people use that energy to drive themselves further. Use that lesson as a driving force. As Bruce said:

'Sorrow is our best educator.
A man can see further from our fears than a telescope.'

The question here is this: are you going to take this thing and make a bunch of excuses and say why it didn't work, or are you going to figure out why it didn't work and find a way to MAKE IT WORK?

It may not happen the first, second, third or hundredth time, but the people that are RELENTLESS WILL SUCCEED. In Japanese, the word for persevere is 'com-bate', which is to fight or combat.

All the money moguls did it with will too. They created it.

Some of you may have heard that 99% of the worlds' money is owned by 1% of the people, because only 1% of the people will condition their mind and body through daily ritual.

Question
Guess what the rest do? Take a quick guess.

The rest just complain about why they haven't got what the money moguls have. There are simply two things in life... a result or a story. Choose one and:

'As you think,
so shall you become.'

The Turning Point

I think the majority of people believe that the 1% are entitled to it, and they are not.

Let me tell you one thing: it's all in the head.

Let me tell you another thing: it can all be changed with some basic reconditioning.

And the beauty of it all is, your life may have sucked for five, ten, fifteen years — but all it takes is one moment of clarity to change your life forever, and that moment is when you decide! When you finally say, no more, I QUIT THE OLD WAY, let's BEGIN THE NEW WAY RIGHT HERE, RIGHT NOW! You can start right now by putting yourself in a state where you get started and start to make progress!

The Cleaner at NASA

Walking through the corridors of Cape Canaveral on his way back to his limousine, John F. Kennedy came across a stooped, grey-haired black man with a bucket in one hand and a mop in the other. It seemed to be quite a redundant question, but the President asked him politely, 'And what do you do here at the Cape?'

Straightening his back, the cleaner looked squarely at the President, and with a strong sense of pride and dignity in his voice replied, *'Sir, I'm doing the same as everybody else. I'm working here to put a man on the moon. That's exactly what I'm doing here.'*

The Majestic Bird in the Sky

One day late in its life, the eagle who thought he was a chicken happened to look up at the sky. High overhead, soaring majestically on the thermal currents, flying effortlessly with scarcely a beat of its powerful golden wings, was an eagle.

'What's that?' said the old eagle in awe to his farmyard neighbour. *'It's magnificent. So much power and grace. Poetry in motion.'*

'That's an eagle,' said the chicken. 'That's the king of the birds. It's a bird of the air. But we are only chickens, we're birds of the earth.'

And so it was that the eagle lived and died a chicken, because that was all it thought it was.

Conclusion

It's not the product, service or the advice that are not effective, it's the people that have purchased them.

Do you possess something like an expensive car, and polish and clean it, admire it, but never use it? Or do you jump in, start it up, rev it up and go for the drive of your life to that special destination you always dreamt of, and **see, hear, feel, and LIVE IT!**

Anybody who wants to succeed must know that it just does not just *happen*, you have to MAKE IT HAPPEN; you've gotta CONDITION YOURSELF; make a MUST; create a RITUAL; live the dream because you HAD TO. You have to make your brain BELIEVE it by SEEING IT over and over again to RAISE YOUR POTENTIAL, making you TAKE MORE ACTION and get MORE RESULTS, which in turn REINFORCE YOUR BELIEFS. This, my friend, is why the rich get richer. The POORER CAN START GETTING RICH too — right now!

I'm going to conclude this Think and Become stage of your self-mastery journey by quoting Tony Robbins:

> *'If you develop the absolute sense of certainty that powerful beliefs provide, then you can get yourself to accomplish virtually anything, including those things that other people are certain are impossible.'*

Robbins went on to say:

> *Make it so today is not like yesterday, and tomorrow will be different forever.*

In this stage, we looked at:

- What is Success?
- What Can People Do to Become Successful?
- How Effective are Business/Personal Development Products?
- Why Don't Most People Achieve Success with Business?
- What Do Successful People Do?
- What is the Difference Between Successful People and Everyone Else?
- How Do You Create a State of MUST?
- How Do You Create a Breakthrough?
- What is Certainty?
- How Do You Get into a Mindset of Following Through?
- The Holy Grail of Certainty.
- The Secret: Why the Rich Get Richer and the Poor Get Poorer.
- The Secret to Getting Rich.
- Acting 'As If'.
- The Secret to Making It Work for You.
- The Paradox.
- The Turning Point.

And that brings us to the end of the **Think and Become** stage of your self-mastery journey. Before you embark on thinking and becoming successful, please answer the following:

Questions

1. Do you have a better **Sense of Calmness** Now? (Yes or No)
2. Can you **See More Clearly Now**, and have a renewed sense of **Clarity?** (Yes or No)
3. Do you have **Absolute Certainty** in your life about one (or more) things? (Yes or No)
4. Do you understand how to **Tap Into Your Unlimited Potential Now?** (Yes or No)
5. Will you **Take Massive Action to Get the Desired Results** you want? (Yes or No)
6. Do you already have an increased sense of **Self Belief and Confidence?** (Yes or No)
7. Are you ready to start to **Think Success**, so you can **Be Success**? (Yes or No)

My friend, I would like to deeply thank you for giving me the chance to take you through this **Master Your Life** journey, and remember:

'THINK SUCCESS,
BE SUCCESS!'

5

Waatah!

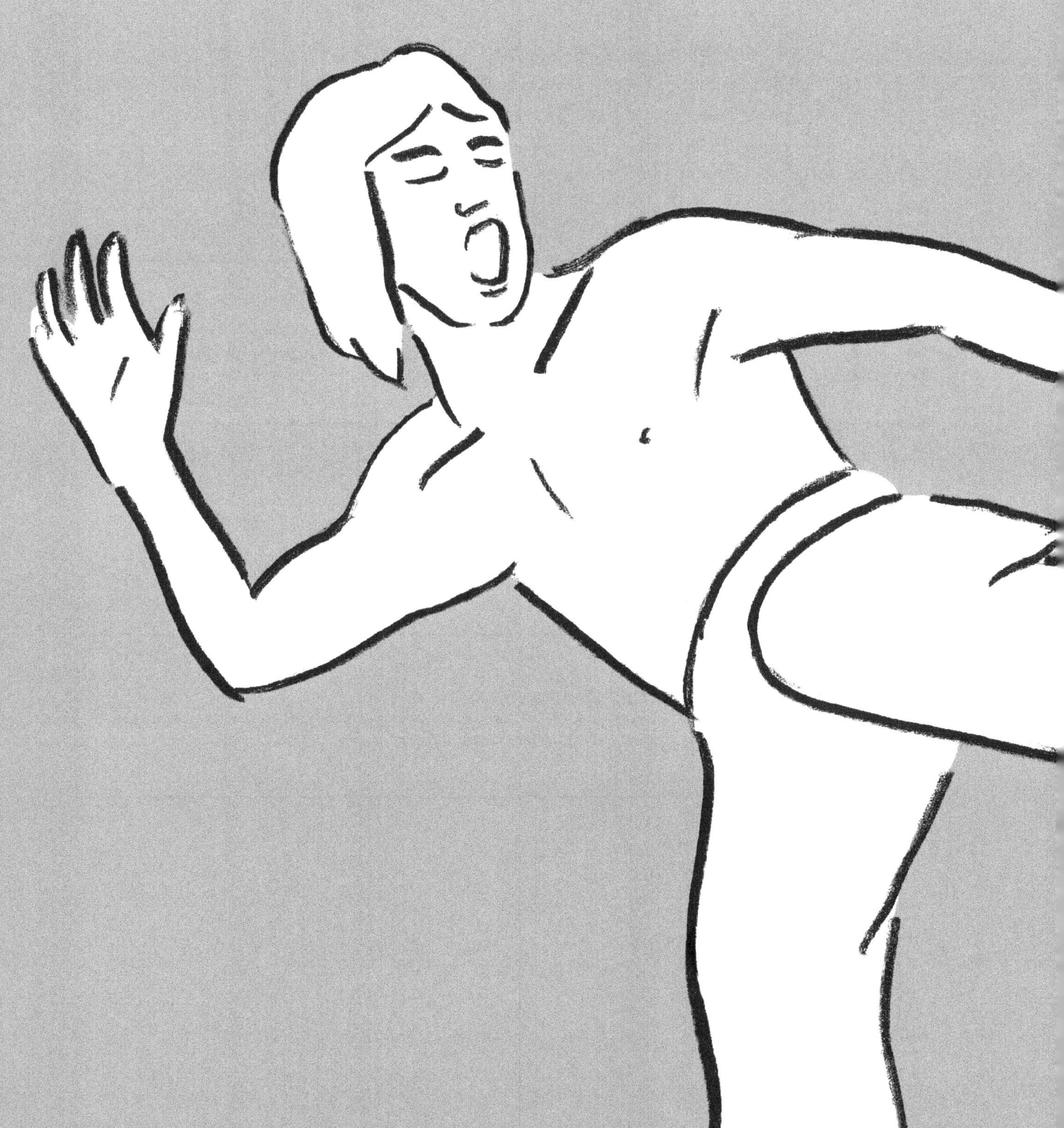

Waatah!

STAGE 5 — BLUE BELT 1

Master Your Fears

What's the Problem?

So, who is this **Waatah!** stage of your self-mastery journey aimed at?

- People who feel anxiety, panic, and fear often and don't know how to deal with it.
- People who freeze or act un-resourcefully when they sense fear.
- People who feel confused and do not understand why they feel scared.
- People who lose control when they experience fear.

Objective

Outcomes and Results Question
What outcome(s) and result(s) do you expect to get when you start to scream Waatah? Take ten minutes to list down all the positive changes you would like to see, hear and feel.

Don Miguel Ruiz said:

'Death is not the biggest fear we have.
Our biggest fear is taking the risk to be alive.
The risk to be alive and express what we really are.'

Examples Question
Can you think of any **Examples** when you felt fear, and what happened? Take ten minutes to make a list.

Do you sometimes find yourself:

- Living in fear?
- Feeling anxiety or panic?
- Not knowing how to deal with fear, anxiety or panic?

- Freezing when you feel scared?
- Acting in an unresourceful way when you sense fear?
- Feeling confused when in fear?
- Unable to understand why you feel scared?
- Losing it when you experience fear?
- Feeling powerless when you get scared?
- Not knowing how to deal with any of these emotions?

If you have answered 'yes' to any of the above, then YOU'RE IN FOR A SCREAM!

WAATAH! is based on Bruce Lee's martial philosophy:

'To understand fear
is the beginning of really seeing.'

It is also based on the works of Geoff Thompson's famous book called *Fear — The Friend of Exceptional People.* Check out www.GeoffThompson.com for more information.

This Waatah! stage of your self-mastery journey will help you to:

Belt	Pillars of Luck	Chapter	Success Goals
5. Blue I	Pluckiness	**'Waatah!!!'** Master your fears	• Learn and understand what fear is • Develop a healthy respect for fear • Accept and recognise your own fears • Understand how to control fear • Conquer your fears • Scream to success!

This stage is broken down into five key substages as follows:

1. What is Fear?
2. How Can You Reprogram Your Fear?
3. How Does Fear Kick In?
4. Physical Reactions to Adrenaline.
5. How to Control Fear... Adrenaline Control.

So you can SCREAM TO SUCCESS — WAATAH!

Warm Up

Let's jump right in and start warming up by answering the following questions:

Question
Do you know what **Fear Is**? Take five minutes to define.

Question
Do you know how to **Reprogram Your Fear?** (Yes or No)

Question
Would you like to **Learn How to Reprogram Your Fear?** (Yes or No)

Question
Do you know how **Fear Kicks In?** (Yes or No)

If No, then would you like to learn? (Yes or No)

Question
Do you know the signs of the **Physical Reactions to Adrenaline?** (Yes or No)

If no, then would you like to learn? (Yes or No)

Question
Would you like to learn how to **Control Fear?** (Yes or No)

If you do not know the answer to any of the questions above and are eager to learn, or answered 'yes' to the last question, then you're in the right place, so let's start learning how to FACE YOUR FEARS!

The Caged Bird

The bird in the cage had lived there for a very long time. Often it would look through the bars of the cage, out of the window to the meadows and trees beyond. It could see other birds flying free in the open air and often it would wonder how it would be to feel free in the open air; how it would be to feel the sun on its back, the wind in its feathers, to swoop and soar and snatch mosquitos in flight.

When the bird thought of these things it could feel its heart beating with excitement. It would sit taller on its perch and breathe deep into its bird belly, sensing the thrill of possibility.

Sometimes another bird would land on the window sill, resting from its travels, and look inside at the caged bird. The traveller would put its head on one side, as if quizzically asking itself how such a thing could be. A bird in a cage. Unimaginable.

And it was at these times that the caged bird felt most miserable. Its little shoulders slumped, it felt a lump in its throat and heaviness in its heart.

Introduction

Abraham Maslow once quoted:

> *'We are generally afraid to become that which we can glimpse in our perfect moments; under the most perfect conditions, under conditions of greatest courage, we enjoy and even thrill to the god-like possibilities we see in ourselves at such peak moments, and yet simultaneously shiver with weakness, awe and fear before the same possibilities.'*

Bruce Lee famously quoted:

'To understand fear,
is the beginning of really seeing.'

What Is Fear?

Mike Tyson's trainer, Cus Damatio stated:

'The coward and the hero both feel the same feelings of fear,
the only difference between the two is that
the hero handles the feelings and
the coward does not.'

When the brain senses danger, it triggers something called an adrenaline response, where adrenaline causes your body to dump energy by means of glucose and fats instantly into your blood-stream for instant speed, power and anaesthesia to help the individual under threat to fight, flight or freeze. It is like a human turbo-boost!

There are two types of accelerators in the body, which are:

1. Positive Body Accelerator

   This is action.

2. Negative Body Accelerator

   This is panic, fear or anxiety. When you experience panic, fear or anxiety, excess adrenalin is triggered but not used and often overwhelms the individual, causing them to freeze — mainly because they do not understand how to cope with the adrenaline sensation.

   Pent-up aggression is another term for excess adrenalin circulating in your body; if not used this can turn into depression over a prolonged period of time, leading to a downward spiral of fear and adrenalin. This is extremely exhausting for the mind and body and can lead to confusion, depression, and physical and mental illness.

Fear is often referred to by the acronym:

F — False
E — Evidence
A — Appearing
R — Real

In this Martial Mind Power section we are going to discover the real truth behind fear.

How Can You Reprogram Your Fear?

To change any behaviour, let's take a look at Prochaska and DiClemete's model of the seven stages of change as follows:

1. Pre-contemplation (The State of Not Even Being Aware You Fear Something)

Many people are embarrassed or even ashamed to admit their shortcomings, so they simply ignore them. It is truly a strong person who can be honest with themselves to admit they have a problem or fear. Even alcoholics cannot help themselves until they admit they have an issue.

Saying you don't feel fear is not human. It is like saying you don't get hungry or thirsty. It is a primitive physiological response we all share as human beings. There is no such thing as being fearless. Even the bravest soldier has trained to master their fear in a positive manner.

The Goldfish Bowl Syndrome

Many people live in what I call their 'Goldfish Bowl', which is our metaphorical comfort zone such as in your job, relationship, house, lifestyle, etc.

The Goldfish Bowl is an interesting place, as people seldom want to venture outside of it because of the following reasons:

1. If you grow, then you'll LOSE YOUR COMFORT ZONE — in fact, your comfort zone is just replaced by a new one again and again.
2. You may face rejection from family and friends — usually from insecure people showing their weaknesses on the way down. As Bruce said, 'Walk on baby.'
3. There's the temptation of not failing by staying where you are — *'if I don't try then I can't fail'*. The act of not trying is failure alone. If you do try, then you've already succeeded, plus you learn more from failures than successes. As they say, 'The man who has not made a mistake has not done anything.'
4. You cannot HANDLE IT — you have to believe you can handle more to grow and prosper, else you will stagnate.
5. Security — another anchor to stagnate and not grow. A Chinese saying goes, *'If you earn two pennies, spend one on food to live, and one on flowers to give you a reason to live.'*
6. The 'when complex' — *'when I've got X then... BLAH BLAH BLAH will happen'* — it's a cop out, as 'when' never comes, and if it does, then it's usually extended with another *'when'*. People fail to live life to its truest potential in fear of risking their security, so they end up unhappy and unfulfilled in a constrictive comfort zone. That's the paradox... these people become insecure in their secure comfort zones because they fear external disruption, e.g. losing your job. I say, *'If you are insecure in your security, then break out.'*

Think Outside the Box
Bruce Lee did not like the idea of thinking outside the box, as it still presented a boundary which you could potentially fall into. Instead, Bruce liked to think of **Being at the Centre of a Circle Without a Circumference.** You can travel in any boundless direction you like. For this exercise, I want you to list all your comfort zones, i.e. identify your goldfish bowl. Take ten minutes to make a list.

2. Contemplation (Be Aware That You Have a Fear and Accept the Feelings of Fear — Only Then Will You Be Able to Cope With Fear)

Some shock usually creates the awareness in this stage.

You often hear words to the extent of *'if only'*. These words simply suggest that you are scared to do something. It is your fears that stop you from achieving your goals, and it is important to conquer them to overcome them.

Sun Tzu called this the *'inner opponent'*. On that basis, it is fair to assume that if you cannot defeat the man on the inside, then you cannot beat the man on the outside.

Bruce Lee once said:

'Defeat is a state of mind.
No one is ever defeated,
until defeat has been accepted as a reality.'

There are three ways to defeat the inner voice:

<u>1. Reject Thoughts</u>

Thoughts are just thoughts, not facts, and many people get caught up in their thoughts.

<u>Drift Away Exercise</u>

Practise this mindfulness exercise to help you to start moving away from accepting thoughts as facts to LIBERATE YOUR MIND as follows. It may help if someone reads this to you in a calm and soothing voice while you sit comfortably and securely in a chair, or lay down comfortably on the floor:

1. Start with mindfulness breathing (see the Zen Breathing exercise in the Stillness chapter).
2. Notice what you're noticing, and let any wandering thoughts JUST BE as you breathe.
3. Notice the wandering thoughts in your mind, and accept these without judging them as good or bad, positive or negative.
4. If you are struggling to find thoughts in your mind now, then think about that… that is a thought which you can allow yourself to think about now.
5. Thoughts are like leaves falling on a flowing river. Just as one leaf falls it floats downstream, and another leaf falls, only for that to float downstream too, and so on.
6. Buddhist monks like to think of thoughts as pages written on water. Just as you notice one thought, it is replaced by another, as the thoughts come and go, continuously flowing.
7. Now bring yourself back in the room, fully aware, switched on and energetic.
8. Take ten to fifteen minutes to become still and detach yourself from your mind and body, become non-judgemental and clear your mind.

2. Counter-Attack Negative Thoughts

According to *The Secret* by Rhonda Byrne, every positive thought is ten times more powerful than a negative one. If indeed this is true, then counter-attack each negative thought with a positive one and see what happens.

Mind Counter-Attack

1. List the most common negative thoughts that come into your mind, and register their intensity from one to ten, ten being the most intense.
2. Now list one counter-attack thought for each negative thought.
3. Step back and read the negative thought followed by the counter-attack thought and ask yourself, is the intensity of the negative thoughts the same, less, or nothing for each one?
4. Take fifteen minutes to do this exercise thoroughly.

3. Create a Mantra

Negative begets negative begets defeat. Positive begets positive begets victory.

My Martial Mantra

Create your own **Martial Mantra (i.e. Warrior Mindset)**. Take fifteen to thirty minutes to do this.

There are several types of obstacles that you'll have to contemplate in order to move on to the next step in pursuit of conquering your fears, which are as follows:

1. **Tangible** — e.g. physical injuries, illnesses and ailments, financial deficiencies, etc.
2. **Intangible** — psychological reasons — too difficult, denial, can't be bothered.
3. **Boredom** — my father-in-law says, *'only boring people get bored'.* I say, 'Only un-stimulated people get bored, so find something that makes you tick.' Boredom is also the lazy person's excuse not to practise — use concentration to dissolve boredom. We will also talk about the 1,000:10,000 rule shortly.
4. **Lack of enjoyment** — nobody enjoys a good thing all the time, or training through sweat and pain all the time. The real enjoyment comes from the results at the end of the journey.
5. **Lack of improvement** — there are three stages of development which are:
   - Partiality (primitive/sharpening the tool);
   - Fluidity (art/utilising the tool); and
   - Emptiness (artlessness/dissolving the tool).
   - At the beginning you're learning something new every day and improvement can be as fast and furious as the metaphorical upwards spiral. As time goes on, the advancement seems to slow down or become un-noticeable, but this is just an illusion. Everyone around you will be seeing your true improvement. It's about working on micro-tweaks for perfection rather than macro-corrections as time goes on.

6. **Silly reasons** — using a silly reason to cover up the true problem. These are the worst and commonplace — everyone does it at some point in time. As they say, *'The presenting problem is never the problem.'*

Face Your Fears
Write up to five fears in a **Fear Pyramid**, with the top of the pyramid being the most intense fear. Take fifteen minutes to make a list.

3. Preparation (Start Doing Something About Conquering Your Fears)

Make a plan. Simply break down your fears in to small manageable chunks, and tackle them one at a time. As they say:

'Fail to plan,
plan to fail.'

Have a game plan and definite achievable success goals. To learn more on this, read the chapters on **'Power Side Forwards'** and **'Stay Ahead'**. Create a roadmap of how you feel, and where you are now, to how you want to feel and where you want to be at the end of the journey.

Well Formed Outcome Pyramid Drill
Pick one fear you want to tackle the most on your fear pyramid, and then list steps on how you can breakdown that fear into small manageable chunks in a well-formed outcome pyramid, with the top level being actions to validate your fear when it has been completely conquered.

For example, here is how someone with a fear of joining a martial arts school broke it down into manageable chunks:

1. Talk to someone in the know.
2. Watch martial arts videos.
3. Go and watch a lesson.
4. Try on some boxing gloves.
5. Go do a trial lesson.
6. Join a martial arts school.

Take fifteen minutes to write down a plan of action to conquer your fear!

Keep telling yourself that if something untoward happens, then YOU'LL HANDLE IT! Geoff Thompson writes:

'In the supermarket of life, the currency is time, dedication, commitment and calculated risk. All

the things are in there for anyone who is willing to pay the price. If you're not, you'll always be a window shopper…

The real goal is the journey and the character you develop during that year of commitment and dedication.'

Sun Tzu said:

'Before you wage war,

you should first count the costs.'

I call it calculated risk. Beware you don't get caught up in something I call 'Analysis-Paralysis', just get on with it as in the next step.

To help you on your way, use the art of visualisation, another powerful tool covered in the 'Power Side Forwards' and 'Stay Ahead' chapters.

As the boxing legend Muhammed Ali said:

'Champions aren't made in gyms.

Champions are made from something they have deep inside them…

A desire, a dream, a vision.

They have to have the skill, and the will.

But the will must be stronger than the skill.'

4. Action (You Are Here and Now, Being the Change. Strengthening Your Mind and Body to Heal)

Some people believe this can only happen on New Year's Day and for a few weeks or days after that. This is false. As they say,

'If you do the same thing, then you will get the same result.

To get a different result, you must do something different now.'

Today is your New You Day! You only get out of life what you put into it. I like to say,

'Where your focus goes, energy flows —

and it will expand!'

Bruce Lee famously quoted:

'If you want to learn to swim, jump in the water.

On dry land no frame of mind is going to help you.'

To quote Nike, 'Just do it!' A wise person once said, *'Risk is the cavernous hole that lies between those that dream and those that DO.'* So the best way to conquer your fears is:

1. To face it — I call it ARP therapy:

   A — Accept.

   R — Recognise.

   P — (Re-)Program feeling of fear with positive responses and well-formed outcomes.
2. To control your cut out switch — people have a low threshold, and their brains cut out at the slightest bit of stress/pain leaving us short of our ends desires.
3. Extend cut-out switch threshold level — simply master your inner opponent to stretch your threshold so you can reach your full potential.
4. Push through the pain barrier — adopt a *'who dares wins'* attitude.
5. Adrenal exposure — extend the cut-out threshold limit by training in an adrenalised state.
6. Indomitable spirit — adopt an *'anything is possible'* attitude and switch your *'fighting spirit'* on.

In Bruce's own words...

'Knowing is not enough,
you must apply,
Willing is not enough,
you must do.'

To act you can:

1. Model someone who has already successfully travelled that path;
2. Read inspirational and empowering books, audio and videos;
3. Elicit council from someone who is already in the place you are heading;
4. Surround yourself with like-minded people — you become the company you keep;
5. Complete what you started — have **stickability.**

Someone once said:

'The real power is not making others do what you want.
It is making yourself do what you want.
The hardest fight has not been with an exterior thing
it has been with myself.'

I Can Handle It Drill

Look at your fear pyramid, and **Visualise Your Fears**. Go through each fear one at a time, and **tell yourself, 'I CAN HANDLE IT!'** Take ten to fifteen minutes to get into your fear state, and face your fear **WITH POSITIVE INTENT.**

5. Maintenance (Keep Programming New Healthy Habits)

It is a lot easier to maintain momentum once you've started. As Dr Napoleon Hill quoted:

'Whatever the mind can conceive and believe, it can achieve.'

I am a firm believer that there are no failures, only lessons. The fact that you tried, makes you a SUCCESS! So keep on doing it!

As they say, practice makes perfect. In Bruce's own words:

'I do not fear the man that has practised 10,000 kicks once.
I fear the man that has practised 1 kick 10,000 times.'

In Kung Fu I call this the 1,000:10,000 rule. Practise a technique 1,000 times, and you will become a good technician, i.e. you'll get the technique if practised with accuracy and precision. Practise the technique 10,000 times and it will become a subconscious response or natural reflex, i.e. you will be able to do it without thinking; you'll become a practitioner, an expert.

To motivate yourself, give yourself rewards and incentives to keep doing what you're doing until it becomes a habit even if you don't like it at first. Ali himself said:

'I hated every minute of training, but I said
Suffer now and live the rest of your life as a champion.'

However, be careful — you may start to like the feeling of fear or adrenaline, and become an adrenaline junkie to 'keep getting the buzz'. When it's a well-formed outcome, then that can only be a good thing! To make that happen, keep on moving.

Ali said:

'Float like a butterfly,
sting like a bee,
the hands can't hit
what the eyes can't see.'

In Bruce's own words:

'Be like water.'

To learn more about how to 'be like water', check out the **Be Like Water** chapter. Remember, nothing of value ever came without a fight. You're a warrior, so BRING IT ON! As they say:

'At the top of the mountain is the ultimate goal of complete self-control.
On the journey you will have developed an iron will and an indomitable spirit, because you've overthrown all your hurdles and pitfalls.'

You will gain enlightenment along the way, whilst cultivating yourself mentally, admitting and recognising your weaknesses in order to confront and overcome them.

6. Relapse (Falling Off the Bandwagon)

It's OK to fall off the bandwagon, you just need to learn how to JUMP BACK ON. Simple! To do that, avoid negative people — in particular stay away from those people who you left behind because they refuse to grow with you. It's OK to do that. As Confucious said:

'Our greatest glory is not in never falling
but in rising every time we fall.'

A stumble or a fall is yet another learning experience which develops real character. Sylvester Stallone in Rocky famously quoted:

'Life is not about how hard a hit you can give.
It's about how many you can take and still keep moving forward.'

7. Termination (Fear Reprogrammed as a New Healthy Habit)

Enjoy a better you, a better life!

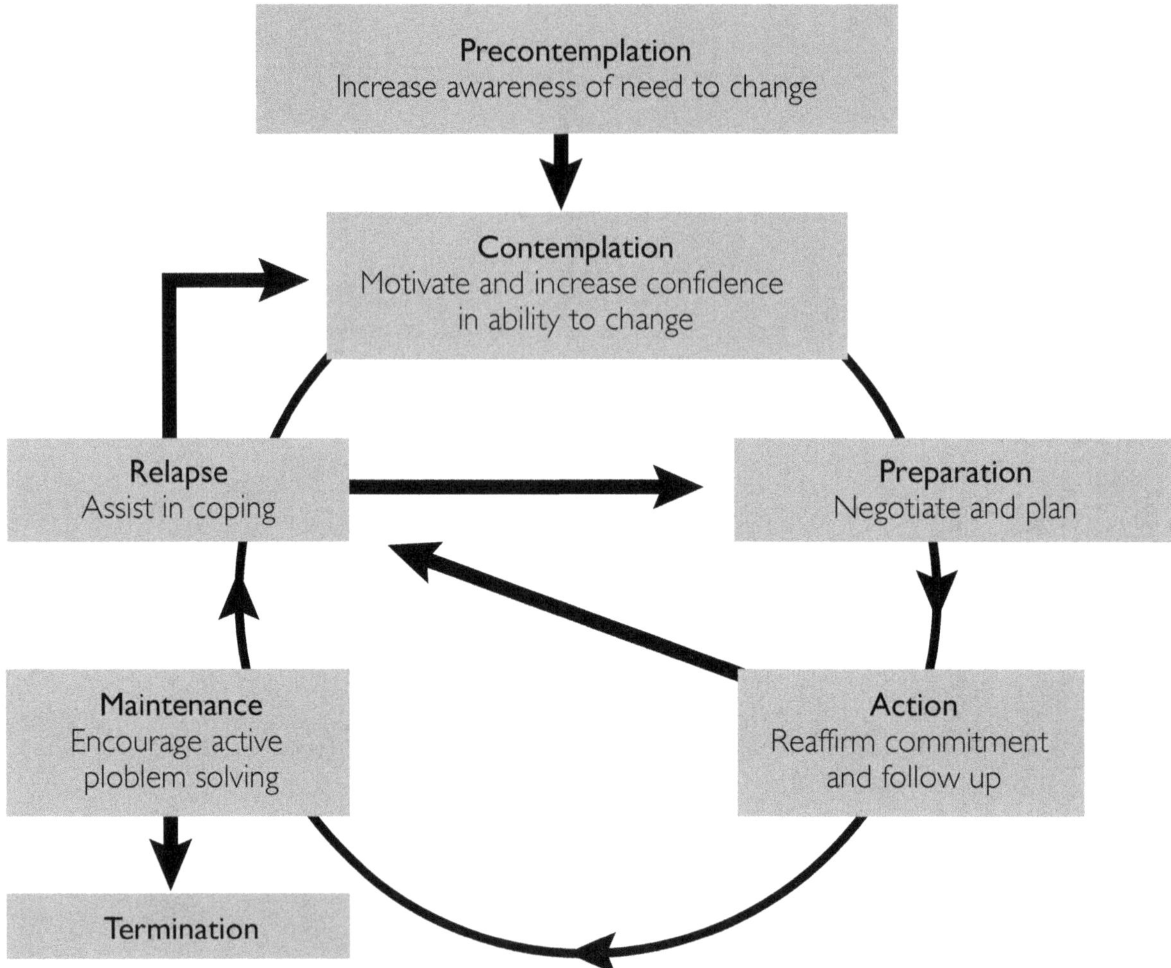

Figure 19: Prochaska and DiCelemente's 'Seven Stages of Change' model.

How Does Fear Kick In?

There are nine ways in which fear kicks-in, and they are as follows. The exercises allow you to sense what each type of fear feels like, so you can acclimatise yourself to it so you can manage fear efficiently.

1. Anticipation of Confrontation

This is the fear of something frightening about to happen.

Slow adrenalin release over a long-period of time. It has been said that 95% of all the things we fear never happen, therefore 95% of the time we are worrying about nothing. It's your mind, it's your body, so **Master Your Life** by **Mastering Your Mind**. That's why I call it **Martial Mind Power.**

Anticipation of Confrontation Drill

To sense what the fear of anticipation of a confrontation feels like, split up into a small group on one side as the rowdy group, and one person on own on the other posing as the victim, then:

1. The victim pretends to walk on one side of the road at night — put lights down in the room.
2. The rowdy group acts like drunks on opposite side of the road, being quite rowdy amongst themselves, not necessarily shouting any abuse at the victim. Take turns for one minute each.

2. Fear of Consequence

This is the fear of that consequence in #1 above materialising.

Fear of Consequence Drill

To sense what the fear of a consequence actually happening feels like, find a partner and one will be the killer, the other the deceased, then:

1. The deceased lies on back, hold up focus pads for the trainee to power strike with jabs and crosses continuously for one minute, then pretends to be dead.
2. The killer pretends they're beating the living daylights out of an attacker, and when they're done, feel the sense the impending doom of that thought that they may have killed that person.
3. Swap it over.

Another fear of consequence is that of losing friends as you 'walk on'. As they say, you find out who your true friends are when you hit rock bottom or when you reach the top. There are several causes for this, such as:

A. Envy.
B. Fear.
C. Insecurity.
D. Resentment.
E. Disorientation.
F. Anger.

Part of practice is using crutches to help you expand, just as part of succeeding is letting go of the crutches so that you can complete the process.

In short, tell your family and friends that you love them and need them as much as ever before, and want them to be an integral part of your life. Tell them their reluctance to let you fly and soar to success is preventing your personal growth and causing resentment in you for them. Tell them that you want to take them with you on this exciting new journey.

In Bruce's own words:

'Walk on.'

3. Pre-Confrontation Fear

Pre-Confrontation Fear Drill

To sense what the pre-confrontation fear feels like, split up into a small group on one side as the attackers, and one person on their own on the other posing as the victim, then:

1. The victim stands in the middle.
2. The attackers assault the victim by pushing him around. The victim is not allowed to react/respond.
3. Take turns for one minute each.

Face the Fear Drill

To sense what the pre-confrontation fear feels like, split up into a small group on one side as the attackers, and one person on own on the other posing as the victim, then:

1. The victim stands in the middle.
2. The attackers assault the victim by punching slowly starting outside fighting measure one at a time — victim evades attack by slipping, ducking bobbing, weaving, evading using footwork, etc. (using the OODA Loop process — see 'Possess an Eagle Eye' for more information on the OODA Loop).
3. Victim relaxes and is aware of the adrenaline flowing in their body — get used to it.
4. Take turns for one minute each.

This is the fear induced by the adrenaline dump due to a situation erupting out-of-control.

Typical fear symptoms include panic and self-pity. To overcome fear, the big idea is to simply to RELAX, ACCEPT IT, FEEL IT FLOWING through you; CHALLENGE IT and RISE ABOVE IT.

Once anxiety, depression and paranoia creep in, your judgement will be impaired, so stop them in their tracks before they get beyond your control.

Detach yourself from thoughts that start running scenarios which may trigger more adrenalin to take you over with fear, and tell yourself, whatever happens, keep telling yourself, 'I CAN HANDLE IT.'

Relaxation Drill

To sense what pre-confrontation fear actually feels like, find a partner and one will be the attacker, the other the victim, then:

1. Attacker shouts at the victim aggressively.
2. Victim relaxes using diaphragmatic breathing whilst observing and orienting oneself, and telling yourself, 'I CAN HANDLE IT!'
3. Take turns for three minutes each.

4. In-Confrontation Fear

This is when things are still not going to plan, then another danger or threat may be triggered releasing more adrenalin in the midst of the confrontation itself.

It's All Kicking Off Drill

To sense what the in-confrontation fear feels like, split up into a small group on one side as the attackers, and one person on own on the other posing as the victim, then:

1. The attackers shout at victim aggressively.
2. The attackers start pushing victim around one-by-one.
3. The attackers start slapping victim with focus pads on body to simulate hits, then the attackers hold the focus pads up ready for the victim to strike back.
4. The victim remains relaxed and fights back by hitting pads and using footwork, maintaining the fighting measure to control the fight.
5. Take turns for one minute each.

5. Secondary Adrenaline

Before, during or after a confrontation, the brain may trigger a second turbo-boost of adrenalin usually misread as fear.

Have you ever been out on the town, and seen a fight kick off and just then it all quietens down, and all of a sudden one of the people involved decides they are going to go back and have another swing at the other party, and it all kicks off again. It could be several minutes before a secondary adrenaline dump. That is the secondary adrenalin hit doing its thing. USE YOUR SELF-CONTROL to manage it.

6. Post Confrontation Fear (or the Aftermath)

This is when the brain's backup fighting mechanism continues to slowly release adrenalin after a confrontation has happened just in case any danger or threats re-appear.

Secondary Adrenaline Drill

To sense what the pre-contemplation fear feels like, split up into a small group on one side as the attackers, and one person on own on the other posing as the victim. To make this work, you have to believe this situation is real and take it extremely seriously as follows:

1. Repeat the 'It's All Kicking Off Drill' as above.
2. Then the attackers sit in a circle, and the victim sits in the middle of the 'circle of intimidation', and the victim has to listen to his/her body for any feelings to rise up to re-confront the attackers again, i.e. the second adrenaline dump. This could take a few minutes. When the feeling hits the victim, just stand up and let everyone know.
3. Take it in turns until everyone has had a go.

7. Adrenal Combo

Working and/or living in a stress-related environment is an example of an adrenal combo, where multiple things are inducing fear and therefore a physiological adrenaline response in your mind and body.

Stress Drill

List all the **Stressful Things** in your work or life? Take five minutes to make a list.

8. The Duck Syndrome

A duck may seem calm whilst it glides on the water, but beneath the surface it may be flapping its feet. Often in life, you put on a cool and calm personality on the outside, only to be found flapping on the inside, in your mind.

Duck Syndrome Drill

List things in your work or life in which you **Put On a Brave Face**, but underneath you are flapping your feet in fear and desperation? Take five minutes to make a list.

9. Jonah Complex

This is the fear of achieving your success itself. Abraham Maslow stated:

> *'We are generally afraid to become that which we can glimpse in our most perfect moments, under the most perfect conditions, under conditions of greatest courage we enjoy and even thrill to the godlike possibilities we see in ourselves at such peak moments, and yet simultaneously shiver with weakness, awe and fear before the same possibilities.'*

This can often lead to self-sabotage if not managed effectively.

Jonah Complex Exercise

1. List your success goals.
2. List all your fears of becoming successful in a spider diagram.
3. List how your successes will affect your ecology (in all areas of your life), positive or negative... family & friends, romance, physical, mental, spiritual, financial, social and career/vocational.
4. Make sure you take fifteen to twenty minutes and do this exercise thoroughly.

Physical Reactions to Adrenaline

There are several natural bodily reactions to adrenaline, which are as follows:

1. Pre-flight shakes.
2. Dry mouth.
3. Voice quiver.
4. Tunnel vision.
5. Sweaty palms and forehead.
6. Nausea.
7. Bowel & bladder loosening.

Then there are more severe reactions to adrenaline, like the ones described below:

8. Yellow fever — feelings of helplessness and abject terror, extreme feeling of depression and foreboding, tears, lack of appetite are common place. It's a bit like asking you to hold a glass of water with your arm stretched out straight in front of you. It feels absolutely fine for fifteen to thirty seconds. Sixty to ninety seconds later it is still bearable, though the glass of water may start feeling heavy now. Three to five minutes later and the glass of water feels like a 30kg weight! It is amazing how something so insignificant can become such a burden, until eventually you have to LEARN HOW TO LET GO. So here's how to let go… You can try crying the fear away. Crying often makes you feel a lot lighter, so if you feel the need to cry, then just do it. Don't try and be macho about it and punish and kill yourself on the inside by letting it build up. You can eat healthily. This can allow the mind and body to recuperate from the exhaustion caused by fear. You can also try to relax and meditate; get plenty of rest, meditate and allow your mind and body to relax.
9. Time distortion — time can appear to stand still. Ever heard the statement, 'It all seemed to happen so fast' or 'everything seemed to be in slow motion'. That is because when you are in an adrenalised state, your brain speeds up and it seems as if things are moving slower, but in fact you are processing a vastly greater amount of information in the same amount of time than usual.
10. Restless nights — slow release of adrenaline will keep you up at night, because all that energy in your bloodstream is not being used up. Some remedies that can help you get a better night's sleep are as follows...You can EXERCISE REGULARLY, RELAX, AND MEDITATE, OR READ a calming, inspiring and empowering book before going to bed. After a short while, you'll start to feel drowsy and sleepy and will have a great night's sleep. If you wake up with the dread of fear in the morning, that's OK. FACE IT, ACCEPT IT, and WASH AWAY THE FEAR down-stream, and notice how it drifts away.

Accept the feelings of fear without latching onto them, like thoughts embodied as leaves, falling onto a stream, drifting away one leaf after another.

Haa Breathing

Practice the 'haa breathing' technique used by the Hawaiian Kahunas, to relax your mind.

1. Sit safely and comfortably.
2. Feel free to close your eyes.
3. Inhale through the nose, filling your belly up with air in two seconds.

4. Breathe out through the mouth for 6 seconds, whilst making a *'haa'* sound.
5. Continue until you are in a deep state of relaxation.

Take fifteen minutes to *'haa'* breathe, and decide to let go of your fears as simply thoughts drifting away.

11. A loss of appetite results in dramatic weight-loss. Eat healthily to allow the mind and body to recuperate from the exhaustion caused by fear. If you owned a Ferrari, then you wouldn't put cheap fuel in it. You will want to put in the super nitro plus hyper-performance fuel. Treat your body like a Ferrari. Look after it: TAKE VITAMINS; AVOID PROCESSED FOODS and CONSUME ORGANIC FOOD; EAT IN MODERATION — try practicing the Zone Diet, which is eating 30% protein, 30% fat, and 40% carbohydrates — or the Paleo Diet, i.e. eating like a caveman, as our bodies have not adjusted to modern GM processed foods; DRINK PLENTY OF WATER, five to six glasses per day, which includes water in food and beverages.
12. Increased heart rate — learn to relax. Please refer to the 'Stillness' chapter for more relaxing exercises and drills in addition to *'haa'* breathing.
13. Depression — the result of a tired mind.

Occupy Yourself

Let the mind rest by occupying yourself and DO SOMETHING EXCITING. Dance, sports and martial arts are an excellent way to occupy yourself and get healthy and fit in the process. Slowly, the mind will regain its strength too. As Franklin Roosevelt said:

'The only thing we have to fear,
is fear itself.'

How to Control Fear? Adrenaline Control

In the gap between confrontation and action, adrenaline can be controlled with diaphragmatic breathing (deep controlled breathing through the nose into the belly) to trigger the parasympathetic system, which slows the release of adrenalin and acts like the 'brakes of fear'.

Practise these exercises to help you control fear.

So What Drill

Think of a fear that is threatening you, then get into the habit of countering those thoughts with the following sayings:

1. 'So what?'
2. 'If it happens, it happens, and if it does, I'll deal with it. I don't care.'
3. 'Just do it, I can deal with that all day long.'
4. Take five minutes to get into a fear state and respond by saying, **'SO WHAT?'**

Divided Mind Drill

1. Think of one fun thing you really enjoy doing right now.
2. Think of one of your fears.
3. Now think of that fun thing.
4. Try and bring back the feeling of your fear. Is it the same as before, less or has it gone all together?
5. Take five minutes and divide your mind, and make the fear fade away.

Kiai Drill

You are going to learn how to switch adrenaline on and off:

1. Project a high pitched scream to turn adrenaline on.
2. Project a low pitched exhalation to turn adrenaline off.
3. Take five minutes to explore how you feel when you go from high to low pitch, and low to high pitch.

Warrior Face Drill

With a partner, one of you will be the trainer, and the other the trainee.

1. The trainee picks an anchor, for example, pushing your thumb against your longest finger's tip together.

2. The trainer asks the trainee how they want to feel (e.g. like a brave warrior), and makes a list of empowering thoughts.
3. The trainer encourages the trainee to get in to their warrior mode by reading the list of empowering feelings. Just before their emotion peaks, they then apply the anchor.
4. The trainer tests the anchor by asking the trainee to recover the fear state, and then asks them has it lessened, gone altogether or stayed the same?
5. Take five minutes to get your warrior face on.

Face Your Fears Drill

Split up into a small group on one side as the group, and one person on own on the other as the individual, then:

1. The individual writes up to five fears onto post-it notes, and then visualises these fears.
2. The group holds kicking shields in a line with the post-it notes stuck to them.
3. The individual then faces the fears written on the post-it notes stuck on the kicking shields, and visualises them staring right back at them.
4. Take five minutes to get into the fear state and just face your fears.

Well-Formed Outcomes Drill

Split up into a small group on one side as the group, and one person on own on the other as the individual, then:

1. The individual writes up to five fears onto post-it notes, and visualise these fears.
2. The group holds kicking shields in a line with post-it notes stuck to them.
3. The individual faces the fears written on the post-it notes stuck on the kicking shields, and visualises them staring right back at them.
4. The individual comes up with well-formed outcomes they would like to achieve when they tackle their fears head-on.
5. Take five minutes to visualise what the outcome will be once you conquer your fears now.

Don't Push Me Drill

Split up into a small group on one side as the group, and one person on own on the other as the individual, then:

1. The individual writes up to five fears onto post-it notes, and visualises these fears.
2. The group holds kicking shields in a line with post-it notes stuck to them.
3. The group pushes the individual around with kicking shields, and you are not allowed to react, just maintain footing whilst noticing your fears pushing you around.
4. Take five minutes and just get used to your fears pushing you around without bothering you anymore.

Break Through Fears

Split up into a small group on one side as the group, and one person on own on the other as the individual, then:

1. The individual writes up-to five fears on individual post-it notes, and up to five well-formed outcomes on one post-it note and visualises them.
2. The group holds kicking shields in a line with the fear post-it notes stuck to them, and sticks the well-formed outcome post-it on the wall behind the line of kicking shields.
3. The individual uses 'kiai' to get into warrior mode and recall resource 'warrior mode' anchor set earlier.
4. The individual strikes through each fear with any strike of your choice to get to the well-formed outcome, realising the feelings of having achieved the end result.
5. Take five minutes to get into warrior state and break through your fears.

Progression

1. Use martial arts boards, write your one fear on one board, and break through them... literally and metaphorically!

The ultimate adrenaline rush is when you are fighting. To understand that, join a reputable martial arts school like www.JKDLondon.com, and build up to controlled and freestyle sparring under safe guidance.

Flight to Freedom

One day, the owner of the caged bird accidentally left the door of the cage open. The bird looked through the door. It saw the birds swooping and soaring outside, the sun on their backs and the wind in their feathers, and it felt a stirring inside. The caged bird noticed that the window was open, and its heart beat even faster.

It considered its options.

It was still considering them at sunset when the owner returned and closed the door of the cage.

The bird, for whatever reasons, valued security over freedom.

Conclusion

The mission of this **Waatah!** stage of your self-mastery journey today was to help you to learn and understand what fear is, develop a healthy respect for fear, accept and recognise your own fears, understand how to control fear and conquer your fears so you can **SCREAM TO SUCCESS!**

In this stage of your self-mastery journey we looked at:

1. What is fear?
2. How can you reprogram your fear?
3. How does fear kick in?
4. Physical reactions to adrenaline.
5. How to control fear… adrenaline control?
6. So you can conquer your fears.

And that brings us to the end of the **Waatah!** stage of your self-mastery journey. Before you embark on **SCREAMING TO SUCCESS**, please answer the following:

Questions

1. Do you **Understand Fear?** (Yes or No)
2. Have you developed a healthy **Respect for Fear?** (Yes or No)
3. Do you **Accept and Recognise Your Own Fears** better now? (Yes or No)
4. Do you understand how to **Control Fear** now? (Yes or No)
5. Have you **Conquered Your Fear(s)?** (Yes or No)
6. Are you ready to **Scream to Success?** (Yes or No)

My friend, I would like to deeply thank you for giving me the chance to take you through this **Master Your Life** journey, and remember:

'CONQUER YOUR FEARS and
SCREAM TO SUCCESS — WAATAH!'

6

Honestly express yourself

Honestly Express Yourself

STAGE 6 — BLUE BELT 2

Master Your Communication and Influencing

What's the Problem?

So, who is this Honestly Express Yourself stage of your self-mastery journey aimed at?

- People who struggle to communicate with others effectively.
- People who get frustrated and angry because they cannot express themselves effectively.
- People who cannot get the message of their communication across effectively.
- People who cannot say what they want, feel and think.
- People who feel the need to lie to get people to do what they want.
- People who cannot persuade or influence other people to see their point of view.
- People who want to improve their 'people skills'.

Objective

Outcomes and Results Question
What outcome(s) and result(s) do you expect to get when you start to Honestly Express Yourself? Take ten minutes to list down all the positive changes you would like to see, hear and feel.

Expressing yourself is one thing. *Honestly* expressing yourself is another matter entirely. Honest self-expression demands that we express our own thoughts and feelings without conforming to styles, methods and systems expected by others. Without fear of not being understood, accepted or approved by others. Without compromising our values, beliefs or souls to satisfy others. All with being connected to our authentic self with honesty and integrity.

Examples Question
Can you think of any examples when you have Expressed Yourself Dishonestly? How did it make you feel? What was the outcome of the conversation?

Take ten minutes to make a list.

Do you sometimes find yourself:

- Worrying that you will offend someone if you say the message you want to communicate to them?
- Fearful of creating a conflict and confrontation?
- Holding back?
- Diluting your message?
- Not saying what you mean?
- Creating a lack of trust and confidence?
- Creating confusion in yourself and others?

If you have answered 'yes' to any of the above, then you're in for an EXPRESS RIDE.

Honestly Express Yourself is based on Bruce Lee's martial philosophy:

> *'Knowledge in martial arts actually means self-knowledge.*
>
> *A martial artist has to take responsibility for himself and accept the consequences of his own doing. The understanding of JKD is through personal feeling from movement to movement in the mirror of the relationship and not through a process of isolation.*
>
> *To be is to be related. To isolate is death.*
>
> *To me, ultimately, martial arts means honestly expressing yourself. Now, it is very difficult to do. It has always been very easy for me to put on a show and be cocky, and be flooded with a cocky feeling and feel pretty cool and all that. I can make all kinds of phoney things. Blinded by it. Or I can show some really fancy movement.*
>
> *But to experience oneself honestly, not lying to oneself, and to express myself honestly, now that, my friend, is very hard to do.'*

Bruce went on to summarise:

'Always be yourself,
express yourself,
have faith in yourself;
do not go out and look for a successful personality and duplicate it.'

This chapter is also inspired and based on the works of:

- John Demartini's 'Determination Process Questionnaire' www.DrDemartini.com
- David Key, my Sifu in NLP and hypnotherapy www.Auspicium.co.uk
- David's Sifu, Tad James www.NLPCoaching.com
- Jerry Clark's famous audiobook called *The Magic of Influence* www.ClubRhino.com
- Sukhi Wahiwala's famous course called *The Art of Selling Without Selling* and guest speaker at the 'Honestly Express Yourself' experiential event www.SukhiWahiwala.com

This stage of your self-mastery journey will help you to:

Belt	Pillars of Luck	Chapter	Success Goals
6. Blue 2	Poise Projection	**'Honestly express yourself'** Master your communi-cation and influencing skills	• Learn the art of how to express yourself with honesty and integrity • Know yourself • Develop tools and skills to communicate effectively with poise, confidence, and act 'as-if' • Learn how to invest in emotional content • Make it your own • So you can win friends, influence people and enrich relationships with your family, friends, loved ones and colleagues • Express your way to success!

This stage is broken down into four key substages as follows:

1. Know Yourself.
2. Develop a Strong Foundation.
3. Invest in What You Do with 'Emotional Content'.
4. Make It Your Own.

To quote Bruce Lee on expression from deep within:

'An artists' expression is his soul made apparent, his schooling, as well as his 'cool' being exhibited. Behind every motion, the music of his soul is made visible.'

Bruce goes on to explain simplicity and effectiveness of expression as:

'To me, the extraordinary aspect of martial arts lies in its simplicity.
The easy way is also the right way, and martial arts is nothing at all special;
The closer to the true way of martial arts, the less wastage of expression there is.'

Are you ready to EXPRESS YOUR WAY TO SUCCESS?

Warm Up

Let's jump right in and start warming up by answering the following questions…

Question
Do you know what **Honestly Express Yourself** means? Take five minutes to define.

Question
Do you really **Know Yourself?** (Yes or No)

If not, then would you like to understand yourself better? (Yes or No)

Question
Do you know how to **Develop a Strong Foundation** for honest self-expression? (Yes or No)

If you do, then please take five minutes to describe how.

Question
Would you like to learn how to ask questions to **Influence and Persuade People?** (Yes or No)

Question
Do you know what **Emotional Content** means? (Yes or No)

If you don't, then would you like to learn? (Yes or No)

Question
Would you like to jump on the **Express Train to Success?** (Yes or No)

If you do not know the answer to any of the questions above and are eager to learn, or answered 'yes' to the last question, then you're in the right place, so let's JUMP ON THE EXPRESS TRAIN.

Riches to Rags

The quarryman's work was hard. He had worked all day in the quarry from dawn to dusk. His hands were hard and callused. His back was bent, and his face was weathered and lined.

He was not happy. He said, *'This is no life. Why is it my fate to be a quarryman? Why can't I be someone who has more wealth than I do? If only I were rich, then I'd be happy.'*

An angel appeared and said, *'What would have to happen for you to know you were rich and happy?'*

'That's easy. If I was rich I'd live in the city, in a beautiful apartment on the top floor. I'd be able to see the sky. I'd have a four-poster bed with cool black silk sheets, and I'd sleep all day. Then I'd be happy.'

'You are rich,' said the angel, waving her magic wand. The quarryman became rich, and he lived in the city in an apartment on the top floor. He slept all day in a four-poster bed with cool black silk sheets. And he was happy.

One day he was disturbed by a commotion in the streets below. He sprang out of bed and ran to the window. Looking down, he saw a graceful golden carriage. In front were horses and behind were soldiers. It was the king. And the people who thronged the street were cheering and bowing.

The rich man instantly knew unhappiness. *'I'm not happy. The king has more power than I do. If only I was a king, then I'd be happy.'*

And the angel appeared and said, *'You are a king!'* And he became a king. And he was happy. He felt his power and he felt his might. He loved the way people paid him homage, the way his servants obeyed him and the way he had power to decide whether others should live or die. He was happy.

Know Yourself

To know yourself, there are three key aspects of your being that you need to be in touch with. They are as follows:

- Mental.
- Physical.
- Emotional.

We are going to look at each one individually in more detail below. To start with, let's explore our *mental* beings.

Mental

Dr John Demartini quotes:

> *'The space and time in your innermost dominant thought determines your outermost tangible reality.'*

Demartini talks about the following thirteen key points, which reveal your values, which are born and realised from your mind, i.e. your 'mental' being:

1. Space.
2. Time.
3. Energy.
4. Money.
5. Order.
6. Focus.
7. Thoughts.
8. Vision.
9. Internal dialogue.
10. Social.
11. Inspiration.
12. Goals.
13. Learning.

Question
To help you better understand yourself in these thirteen key areas, please refer to www.MartialMindPower.com/Resources for the Dr John Demartini's *'Determination Process Questionnaire'* so you can *'Know Yourself, Be Yourself'*.

Take sixty minutes to answer all the questions thoroughly for the best results.If you do, then please take five minutes to describe how.

Question
Did you discover something new about yourself, and what was it?

Take five minutes to highlight your insights.

Physical

The physical aspect is to understand your body, what it is saying, doing and creating in you. That is congruency and rapport, and is explained as follows.

Congruency

Firstly, we must talk about congruency.

Congruence is the state achieved by coming together, the state of agreement. The word comes from the Latin '*congruō*', meaning *'I meet together, I agree'*.

In order to express yourself effectively, you must have congruency between your mind and your body, what you are saying, doing and creating in you.

Question
For example, if I hold my head down staring at the floor while I shake my head side-to-side, and say, *'Yes, I'm really excited to go to work on a Monday morning'*, would you believe me? (Yes or No)

What does my communication come across as?

- How does it look to you?
- How does it sound to you?
- How does it feel to you?
- Is it clear?

Take two minutes to quickly answer these questions.

Firstly, does it look like I am being honest to myself? (Yes or No)

Secondly, what level of confidence and trust do I install in the person I am communicating with?

Take five minutes to analyse this behaviour and list down everything it says and feels like to you.

That's right. My body, what I am saying, doing and creating in me, is incongruent with the message, hence it is confusing, insincere and creates distrust and a lack of confidence with my communicating recipients.

So, later in this chapter we are going to take a brief look at Rapport and Body Language.

Rapport

The Oxford Dictionary's definition of rapport is:

A close and harmonious relationship in which the people or groups concerned understand each other's feelings or ideas and communicate well.

So, rapport is about having a trusting, responsive interaction between people, regardless of whether they like each other or not.

The basis of all rapport is built on a win-win situation, and we are going to look at some powerful techniques on how to do this.

However, if you try to utilise rapport-building techniques for your own selfish benefit only, you could risk losing trust completely. Is it worth it? Can you do something about it? We are going to explore this shortly.

Question
So what is communication made of? Take five minutes to make a list.

Albert Mehrabian, Professor Emeritus of Psychology, UCLA, claims that human communication is comprised of:

- Sender—encoder.
- Message.
- Medium.
- Channel.
- Receiver—decoder.
- Feedback.

We are going to explore communication further in the next section (Develop a Strong Foundation) on building rapport.

'When people are like each other,
they also tend to like each other.'

Emotional

Next you are going to explore your emotional being, so you can understand the emotions you are creating, to manage your emotional state effectively.

Emotional Management

Everyone experiences negative emotions. The trick is learning to process them quickly so you can move on with your life.

What would you do with your time if you could compress the process of a 'Significant Emotional Event' (or 'SEE') from say, two months into two weeks, leaving you with six weeks to live and love life.

The key to emotional management success lies in:

- Disciplining your disappointment.
- Turning your frustration into fascination.
- Increasing your frustration threshold.

It's too often that you hear of self-sabotage through bad emotional management — for example Elvis Presley and Amy Winehouse.

Emotional Management Strategies

You have to be able to influence yourself before you can influence someone else.

You must be able to manage 'no's over 'yes's in school, college, university, work, business, relationships and life.

To do that, Jerry Clark suggests the following eight emotional management strategies by going on a thirty-day 'mental fast'.

Thirty-Day Mental Fast

Try this *thirty-day 'mental fast'* and detoxify your mind:

1. Read an uplifting and empowering book, such as:
   - Dr Napoleon Hill's *Think and Grow Rich.*
   - Andrew Carnegies' *How To Win Friends and Influence People.*
2. Switch your TV **OFF** and avoid the negative influences which come with it, such as the depressing news, etc. Remember, what goes in your mind comes out of all your self-expression.
3. Switch your radio **OFF** and listen to uplifting and empowering audio tracks instead.
4. Stop reading newspapers, especially tabloids.
5. Disassociate with negative people, and associate with positive, aspirational people.
6. Drink plenty of water. Jim Rohn said:

'Most people don't do well, because they don't feel well.

Most people don't feel well, because they're dehydrated.'

If you'd like to learn more about water, then go to the **'Be Like Water'** chapter in this book.

7. Exercise, and engage in some kind of beautiful motion, be it dance, martial arts or sports.
8. Reflect on goals and dreams, focussing on the good, being grateful for what you have, saturating your mind with positive thoughts. After all:

'*What the mind can conceive and believe, it can achieve,*' Dr Napoleon Hill.

Emotional Bank Account

When someone gives you a compliment, from now on, write it down in your own 'emotional bank account'. Accept it and embrace it with humbleness and humility.

So whenever you are feeling a little low, just look at all the riches you have in your 'emotional bank account' so you can put yourself back in a resourceful state when you received that 'emotional credit' just by making a little withdrawal from your 'emotional bank account'.

Physiology and Emotion

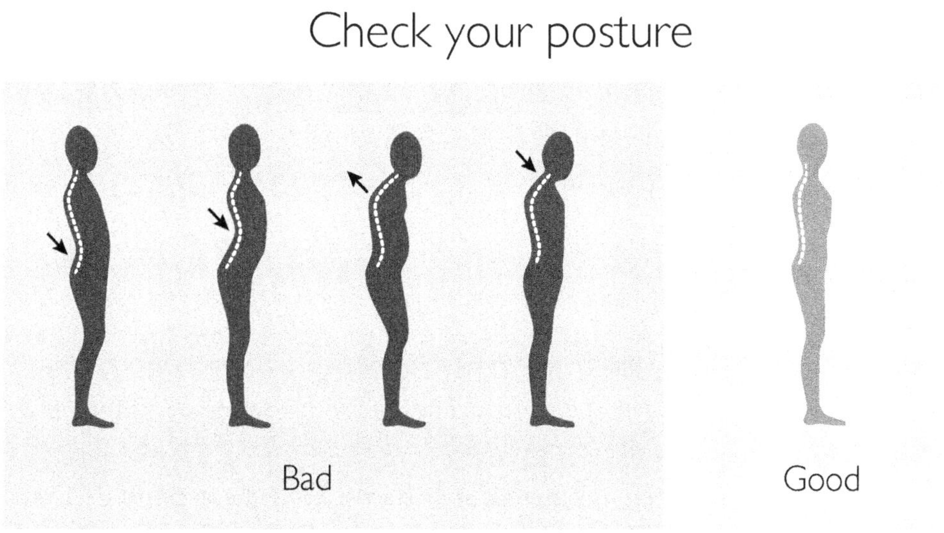

Check your posture

Bad

Good

Figure 20: Illustration of bad vs. good standing posture

There is scientific evidence that proves that your posture (your physiology) affects your mind and therefore your emotional state (our mood, thoughts and happiness).

Dr Deepak Chopra discovered that every cell in your body has a neuroreceptor. Each neuroreceptor responds to chemicals triggered and excreted by the brain's limbic system, consisting of structures such as the hippocampus, amygdala, hypothalamus, and mid-brain to name but a few.

Scientific evidence has also recently shown that these neuroreceptors get addicted to chemicals which persist over a prolonged period of time.

For example, if you have a 'hunched' physiology, you install a prolonged negative chemical state in every neuroreceptor in your body. As a result, your body gets addicted to feeling negative such as sad, depressed, anxious, etc., and this becomes your subconscious, programmed response.

If your physiology can change the way you feel, then that means that you can change your emotional state by simply changing your physiology, by standing up tall, projecting confidence.

A scientific study of saliva samples showed that expansive postures actually altered the participants' hormone levels, decreasing cortisol (C) and increasing testosterone (T). This neuroendocrine profile of High T and Low C has been consistently linked to such outcomes as disease resistance and leadership abilities.

It just goes to show that people don't *get* depressed, they *do* depressed.

To make this your new state going forward, develop a good posture by repeating it for the next fourteen to twenty-one days to embed the new habit, and voila you have revamped your total outlook on life within two to three weeks.

Dutch behavioural scientist, Erik Peper discovered that:

- When people nodded, it affected their opinions without them realising.
- When people hugged themselves, they were able to reduce their physical pain.
- When people stood up and stretched towards the sky, it put them in a more positive and resourceful state.

This is why physical motion such as martial arts, dance, sports and exercise has been directly linked to happiness.

Dr Deepak Chopra went on to famously quote:

'Every cell in your body is eavesdropping on your thoughts.'

State Change Drill

Do this drill on your own whilst standing, and notice how you feel when you do the following:

1. Slow slumped walk — this can drain us of energy and make us feel sad and depressed.
2. Skip or hop around the room — this can significantly increase energy levels.
3. Sit or stand up straight, and remember the first thing that comes to your mind. Positive memories should flood your mind.
4. Stand up tall with your chest out, looking up to the ceiling. Now try and become depressed. It's hard, isn't it?

Take ten minutes to experiment with these posture drills and be mindful of the feelings and thoughts that come to you in each posture.

Question

What do you think are the most common postural pain areas? Take five minutes to make a list.

Body language symbolizing power can actually affect our decision making subconsciously. Powerful postures not only give you the sense of being more powerful and in control, but are 45% more likely to make you take risks.

The following diagram illustrates the most common pain areas due to bad posture:

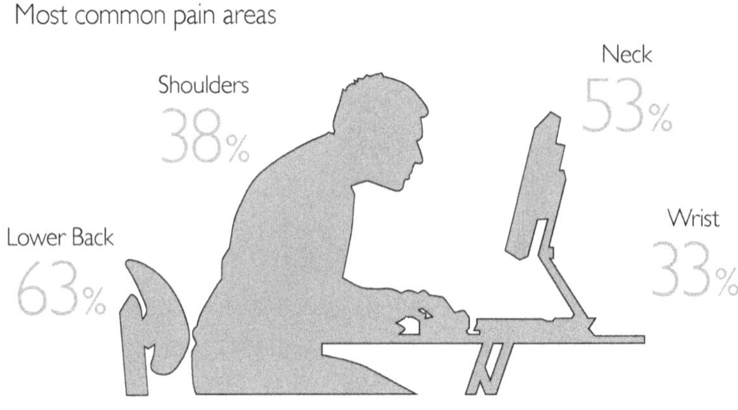

Figure 21: Illustration of most common pain areas.

Question
What do you think is the optimal sitting angle? Take a quick guess of the angle (in degrees), ninety degrees being sitting vertically upright.

The illustration below shows the optimal seating angle for your posture and emotional state:

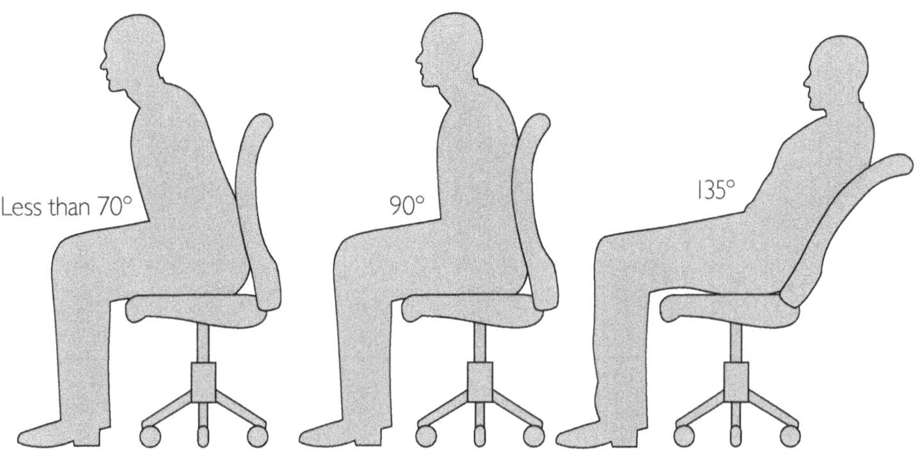

Figure 22: Ilustration of optimal seating position for your posture and emotional state is 135 degrees.

In short, the best posture is always the next posture, i.e. always keep moving. The human body was designed to fight or flight, not to freeze in one position for eight or more hours at a time at an office desk, staring at a computer screen.

What Do You Do When You Don't Have the Right Words?

Hug someone! Buddhists believe that hugging is good medicine. It transfers energy and gives the person hugged an emotional lift.

Buddhists say you need four hugs a day for survival, eight for maintenance and twelve for growth.

Scientists say that hugging is a form of communication, because it can say things you don't have words for.

And the nicest thing about a hug is that you can't give one without getting one.

Hug Therapy
So for the next drill you are going to do some hug therapy. Please ask someone if you can kindly give them a hug. Once the other person agrees, then put your arms around them with your left arm over their right shoulder, and your right arm under their left arm whilst tilting your head to your right, allowing your hearts to be aligned on top of one another's for the ultimate 'heart-to-heart' hug.

Develop a Strong Foundation

This section is based on the works of David Key (www.Auspicium.co.uk) and Tad James (www.NLPCoaching.com) as mentioned earlier.

In this section we are going to develop a strong foundation of tools and skills to 'express yourself' effectively, i.e. to build rapport to establish trust and confidence in the people you are communicating with.

Question
Firstly, what do you think is the highest positive intention of communication? Take five minutes to make a list.

The idea of positive communication is threefold:

1. To carry yourself with grace and confidence;
2. Communicate your message effectively by honouring the other person(s); and
3. To influence people in a congruent and ecological way, by creating a win-win situation.

Universal Language of Success Model

Successful communication comprises both internal and external communication, or as otherwise referred to as non-verbal and verbal communication.

There are three key components to the 'Universal Language of Success Model', which are:

1. Speak
    - Your ability to access a 'program' in your mind.
2. Communicate
    - The process of sending and receiving information.
    - Your values and beliefs.
    - Your map of the world.
    - Your interpretation and feedback.
3. Influence
    - Your ability to get someone to move using action towards your goal.

Old World Model vs. New World Model

As humans have evolved, so has human communication, and to communicate effectively towards your end desires, it is important that we upgrade our human communication programs from the 'Old World Model', to the 'New World Model', just like you upgrade your computer or smart phones software.

The 'Old World Model' was a passive one, where people 'anticipated, meditated and contemplated.'

The 'New World Model' is a dynamic and active one, where people 'activate, generate and innovate.'

In this section we are going to upgrade your programs to meet the demands of the 'New World Model'.

Perceptions vs. Facts

Perceptions are stronger than facts.

Question
Where do perceptions exist? Take a quick guess.

That's right, in the mind.

When influencing people, we are dealing with their perceptions. Perceptions are creations of the mind.

Sales and marketing companies try and get your interest (i.e. into your mind) and influence you to buy (i.e. take action, by you giving them your money in exchange for products and services).

Six Factors of the Mind

If you understand how the mind works, then you can utilise this knowledge in order to communicate effectively. There are six factors of the mind which you need to consider, which are as follows:

1. Minds Are Bombarded

   For example:

   - You are exposed to over 100k adverts per annum.
   - 300k new books are released per annum.
   - The internet overloads our minds with unnecessary information.

2. Minds Are Selective

   The mind works by distorting, deleting and generalising information.

   - Reticular Activating System (RAS) — for example, when you buy a new car, you see lots of similar cars everywhere. They were always there, but your RAS is more aware of them now by process of prioritisation and association of data.
   - Selective exposure — TV is an electronic income reducer, as are tabloids; they distract and misdirect your attention.
   - Selective attention — imagine that you are at a friend's party hosted at a bustling restaurant. Multiple conversations, the clinking of plates and forks and many other sounds compete for your attention. Out of all these noises, you find yourself able to tune out the irrelevant sounds and focus on the amusing story that your dinner partner shares.
   - Selective retention — people are sixteen times more negatively programmed than positively programmed. Therefore, they are more likely to recall negative experiences — hence they don't necessarily live a life of abundance.

3. Minds Are Simplistically Complex

   Your brain is amazing.

   - Scientists haven't figured out how it works yet.

- The brain consists of many complex components, such as nerves, neurotransmitters, ANS, PNS, etc.
- You have six senses: sight, hearing, touch, taste, smell and internal dialogue (which is the lesser known sense).
- To influence others, you must create an effective interpretation in other people verified through feedback using effective yet simple communication.
- For effective understanding, stick to the KISS formula — that is, 'Keep It Simple, Stupid'.
- If things are too complex, then the mind will simply reject it.

4. Minds Are Sensitive
   - Your unconscious mind stores everything.
   - Minds are sensitive to all stimuli — they have sensory acuity, so switch your senses on.

5. Minds Are Unsure
   - People do things based on what other people do. It's like a mental vote or primal pack mentality. It gives security and comfort to your decision.
   - People end up doing what other people do, and as a result end up getting the results most people get. That is why most people are broke.
   - This creates uncertainty, which is construed as risk.
   - There are five types of perceived risk otherwise known as the '5F's of Risk':

     i. Financial — loss of money.
     ii. Function — won't work.
     iii. Fear — afraid of being stupid for failing.
     iv. Feeling — especially guilt.
     v. Fundamental — your fundamental security is at risk.

6. Minds Are Stubborn
   - It's hard to change a mind when it's made up.
   - Minds require effort to change.
   - Minds remember what went in first rather than last.
   - There is a primacy and recency effect, which is why advertisers want to:

     i. Get into your mind first (primacy).
     ii. Keep repeating their message to keep it fresh (recency).

   - Buying decisions have got little to go with logical analysis; they are more likely to be determined by primacy and recency effect.
   - Advertisers drip-feed you products and services.
   - Who was the first person to walk on the moon? Who was the second? No one remembers the second.
   - Association — the first car was called a horseless carriage. People describe what something is not, for example sugar free, unleaded, fat free, etc. That is because the mind does not understand NOT.

Building Rapport Using Physiology

Since body language is the largest component of human communication, let's look at this first.

Rapport is built through three main physiological processes:

1. Matching.
2. Mirroring.
3. Crossover.

To build rapport using matching and mirroring, you can use:

1. Posture
    - Angle of spine when sitting (forward, back, rounded, to one side).
    - Head/shoulder relationship (upright, tilted, up, down).
    - Upper body position (upright, arched forward).
    - Lower body position (leg position, sitting/standing angles, etc.).

2. Gestures
    - Open or closed.

3. Facial expressions and blinking
    - Smile, frown, grimace, etc.
    - Rate (slow or fast).

4. Breathing
    - Rate (slow or fast).
    - Location (stomach, mid-chest, upper-chest).

So, when you have rapport, you know you have established trust and confidence. So how do you know you are in rapport with someone?

1. You may feel like you have 'clicked' with someone.
2. Colour shift — people become flushed, which indicates likeability.
3. They say something like, *'I feel like I've known you for ages'.*
4. You begin to lead them by having gained rapport. You can pace the other person by changing your body position and see if they follow you. If they do, you are 'leading' them; if not, return to matching and mirroring to 'pace' them.

Let's first explore posture and gestures through various exercises and drills as follows.

Combative Postures

Combative Posture Drill

Find a partner. Both of you will adopt a fighting posture.

Ask each other, how it feels as you both adopt the different postures described below. Now change your fighting postures as follows:

- Arched fighting position: leaning forward, shoulders rounded, arched back, eyes looking down.
- Neutral fighting position: natural plumb-line on shoulders and hips, eyes looking forwards.
- Upright fighting position: as above, with chest out, chin up, looking down slightly at opponent.

Take three minutes to explore the sensations you get as you both face each other in the various combative postures.

Now we are going to look at the daily life postures.

Daily Life Postures

Daily Life Posture Drill

Find a partner. One person adopts a standing posture (posturer) as described below, and the other person stands neutral (recipient).

Ask each other how this feels as the posturer adopts each of the different postures below, then swap it over. Now change your standing postures as follows:

- Arched standing position: leaning forward, shoulders rounded, arched back.
- Neutral standing position: natural plumb-line on shoulders, hips, knees and ankles, eyes looking forwards.
- Upright standing position: as above, with chest out, chin up, looking up slightly.
- Bear standing position: as above, with arms raised, standing up on your toes to make yourself as big and tall as possible, like a bear trying to ward off a supposed predator..

Take three minutes each way, and explore the sensation the posturer gives you when you stand neutral as he goes through the various postures.

Combative Gestures

Combative Gesture Drill

Find a partner. One person adopts a fighting posture (posturer) as described below, and the other person stands in a neutral fighting posture (recipient).

Ask each other, how this feels as you adopt the following combative gestures, then swap over.
Now change your fighting postures as follows:

- Low guard (i.e. open gesture): both hands in a low guard position.
- Neutral guard (i.e. neural gesture): both hands in a mid-guard position.
- High guard (i.e. closed gesture): both hands in a high guard position.

Take three minutes each way, and explore the sensations you get as you go through the various postures. Now we are going to look at the daily life gestures.

Daily Life Gestures

Daily Life Gesture Drill

Find a partner. One person displays one of the gestures in a neutral standing posture (gesturer) as described below, and the other person stands in a neutral posture (recipient).

Ask each other, how this feels as you work through each gesture, then swap over.
The equivalent neutral standing position gestures would be as follows:

- Open gesture: palms up with arms slightly raised.
- Neutral gesture: hands relaxed by sides.
- Closed gesture: both hands raised with fingers pointing upwards and palms facing forwards, like making a stop sign with both hands.

We can learn a lot from combative posturing, and apply this to building better rapport with people. Let's have a look at some key combative body language signals that we must avoid to ensure that we are not engaging in fighting talk, rather better rapport building.

Fighting Talk

Fighting Talk Drill

In pairs, one partner will be the defender who stands in a neutral posture, and the other the aggressor who will be in a more aggressive posture and perform the following:

1. Maintain fighting measure (or personal space):
   - The aggressor starts outside the fighting measure (a safe distance from which you cannot get hit easily), then steps inside it. How does the defender feel?
   - If an aggressor enters the fighting measure twice, then consider it an attack.
   - If an aggressor moves inside your fighting measure (or personal space), then that can be construed as an attack and gives you the legal right to pre-empt an attack 'with reasonable force' in your defence, if you truly felt like you were going to be attacked. The Police do not advertise this feature of the law for obvious reasons

2. Induce an adrenal reaction:

Be mindful that very experienced attackers can hide their adrenal response, but most people cannot control it. The expert eye will look out for:

- Erratic eye movement: looking out for not being caught by the police, public witnesses and possible rescuers.
- Adrenal reaction: pale face; eyes wide open from adrenaline-induced tunnel vision; stern facial expression; fidgeting in an attempt to hide the adrenal shake (like a cold 'shiver'); voice may quiver nervously.
- Splaying arms: used to make them appear bigger before an attack to intimidate the other person, like a bear.
- Beckoning finger: beckoning victims on with their finger.
- Nodding head: sporadically nodding their head.
- Neck pecking: aggressors may 'peck' their neck like a cockerel to protect their throat, which is a primary target.
- Eye bulge: eyes may appear wide and staring due to adrenaline-induced tunnel vision.
- Dropped eyebrows: eyebrows lower to protect eyes.
- 'Stancing up': people often turn sideways to take up an innate fighting stance and to hide their major organs from attack.
- Closedown distance: as aggression builds, the distance will close with more erratic movement.
- Concealed hands: it's not always the case, but concealed hands may hide a weapon

On a group basis, this is what most commonly happens.

Pincer Movement

Pincer Movement Drill

In small groups, one person will be the victim who stands in a neutral posture, one person will be the aggressor who will be in a more aggressive posture distracting the victim, while the rest of the group close into the victim from the back and sides.

They usually will not be seen in an adrenalised situation due to the adrenaline induced tunnel vision.

Take two minutes each, and take turns.

In order to therefore build strong rapport with people, it is really important to honour the other person's personal space, and manage their state with your non-verbal language through the effective use of gestures, which is what we are going to look at next.

Gesture Guessing Game

Gesture Guessing Game

In this drill, split into two groups. Each person in a group is to pick two or three items from the list below, and act out the gesture to their fellow group members. The group members have to guess what each gesture means.

The gestures are as follows:

Gesture	Meaning
Downward facing palm	Conveys dominance and control
Closed fist with pointing finger	Threatening and aggressive
Clenching hands	Negativity
Precision grip / pincing fingers	Demonstrates exactness
Thumb and forefinger not quite touching	Demonstrates uncertainty or hesitancy
Raised hand power fist	Demonstrates conviction and determination
Lowered steeple	A listening attitude
Raised steeple	Thoughtful authority
Hands on heart	Empathy and feeling
Stop sign with palm forwards, looking away	Unwillingness to speak

Table 6: List of gestures.

Gesture	Meaning
Index finger in front of lips	Instruction to be quiet
Hands cupped round mouth with open mouth	Surprise or shock
Hands on head with open mouth	Surprise or shock
Chopping hand to side	You mean business
Hands on colleagues shoulders	Empathy and care
One arm across body, and other hand under chin/on mouth, legs crossed	Holding back and seeking comfort
Hand(s) over heart, head tilted and open smile	Appreciation
One arm on lapel, the other hand in pocket, whilst standing upright	Conveys stature and authority • Vulnerable and pleading • Arrogance • Assertiveness
Downward tilted head and upcast eyes	Vulnerable and pleading
Hands clasped on tummy, with head titled upwards	Arrogance
Hands clasped on tummy, with head looking forward	Assertiveness
Furrowed brow and forward tilted head	Critical attitude
Hands behind head ('catapult')	Intimidation
Woman showing her neck (back, side or front)	Showing interest, vulnerable and appealing
Both hands on sides of head (clasp)	Acts as a shield
Both hands behind neck (cradle)	Comfort and security
Dropped head, glazed eyes and slack facial muscles	Boredom
2 people looking directly at one another, smiling, and close proximity	Attraction
Arms crossed, stern facial expression	Not prepared to be open
Chewing on lower lip whilst looking at person in pain	Pain connection
Tight muscles around eyes and mouth	Holding back negative emotion like sadness
Smile pulling eyes and mouth back	Genuine smile
Smile pulling mouth back only	Insincere smile
Looking downward on another person, with sneering lips, pulled up nose	Shows contempt
Tensely pulled back mouth, raised eyelids and exposed eye whites	Fearful
Arms raised with fingers facing up, open mouth with raised eyelids	Surprised
Holding gaze with relaxed eyes	Interested
Holding gaze with squinted eyes	Hostility

Gesture	Meaning
Arms besides sides, hips in front of shoulders	'Come to me' look
Visor eyes	Strong, dominant and in control
Pointing a pen to a presentation board	'Power lift' to draw attention
Sideways glance with a smile	Shows interest
Sideways glance without a smile	Disinterest
Eyebrow flash	Sign of recognition
Pout with furrowed brow	Tension
Pout with eyes looking up slightly	Sad
Prune lips	Measured thinking
Locked jaw with tight lips	Negative tension
Lop-sided smile	Contradiction and mystery
Full blown smile with head tilted down	Humbleness
Full blown smile with head tilted up	Pride
Arms raised, hands clenched, with big smile	Excitement
Arms cross	Protective measure
Arms crossed with thumbs facing up	Both apprehension and confidence usually in males
Fig leaf position – hands crossed over groin	Secure
Crossed arms stroking upper arms	Comforting
Double-handed hand shake	Bond and superiority
Touching colleague on elbows	Comforting and encouraging
Open palms facing up	Shows openness
Raised open arms and palms	Draws audience in
Open palm gestures towards colleagues in group discussion	Acknowledgment of a specific person
Downward facing palms	Dominance and control
Thumb gesturing towards another person	The other person is rude
Woman offering her handshake first	She's in charge
Soft handshake with soft body	Appealing
Palm facing down during handshake	Holds authority
Handshake with second hand clasping upper arm	Higher up the arm, the more intimacy and control
Tense lips	Emotions held back
Pull someone into your space with handshake	You're in charge – beware of personal space violation – extend arm to reinstate personal space
Hand to nose	Evaluation
Hand to chin	Disinterest
Hand on side of face	Boredom
Evenly place weight whilst standing upright	Firm foundation

Gesture	Meaning
Hands on hips with upright posture	Dominance and power
Parallel stance	Sign of uncertainty and submission
Stress stance, leaning on rear leg	You want to move
Scissor leg standing stance	Appealingly vulnerable
Leaning away from you, may point to door, feet pointing towards the door	Wants to leave
Sucking on an object like pencil or spectacles	Needs reassurance
Peering down on someone from over your spectacle frame	Make other person feel uncomfortable
Sitting in a corner position of a table with another person	Diffuses tension and promotes a positive attitude
Sitting side to side with someone	Cooperation
Leaning back in chair	Free thinking
Asymmetrical stances	Intriguing
Spread eagle seated position with legs apart, leaning forwards	Draw attention to manhood
Exposed wrists whilst stroking ear	Availability
Man with hands on hips with fingers pointing down to crotch	Drawing attention to his manhood
Sitting in a low soft chair	Lose authority
Hands waving above head	Flustered
Unbutton jacket	Open and receptive

Charades

Charades Game

For the next game, we are going to play charades to put your physiology skills to the test.
Split into two teams. The first team to play will nominate one person as an actor who will pick one of the movie, song or book titles shown below. You can also come up with your own.

They are not allowed to use any voice communication and make any letters using their body or limbs; they must use their physiology to communicate to the other team the title of the movie, song or book.

- *Enter the Dragon* (movie)
- *Pirates of the Caribbean* (movie)
- *Beat It* by Michael Jackson (song)
- *Staying Alive* by The Bee Gees (song)
- *Think and Grow Rich* by Dr Napoleon Hill (book)
- *Harry Potter and the Philosopher's Stone* by JK Rowling (book)

Take thirty-sixty minutes to play this fun game with your groups.

Now that we have explored postures and gestures and have a sound understanding of them, let's take a look at mirroring and matching now to develop our rapport-building tools and skills.

Mirroring

The idea of mirroring is to do the exact mirror opposite of what your partner or group is doing, to build rapport with them, by 'pacing' and ultimately 'leading' them.

Please note, building rapport is a means to 'honour' the other person, like in an elegant dance.

Combative Mirror

Combative Mirror Drill

Both partners adopt a fighting stance; one person drives (driver) and the other person mirrors (mirrorer). The objective is for the mirrorer to reflect every move of the driver, as the driver uses controlled and slow-to-medium paced footwork to simply move around the room. When you're finished, swap it over to the other side.

Take three minutes each way to get into the flow of mirroring.

Mirror Walk

Combative Mirror Drill

One person — the driver — thinks of something positive or negative and, holding that thought in their mind without saying what it is, walks around the room whilst embracing that thought. Their partner then follows their footsteps literally, mirroring their every move. The objective of this exercise is to understand what the driver is thinking, seeing, feeling and hearing just by mirroring their every movement. When finished, the driver should ask the mirrorer what they felt. Did they feel, see, hear, what the driver was thinking of, and try and guess what they were doing and where they were?

Take five minutes and then swap roles and repeat.

Matching

The idea of matching is to do exactly what your partner or group is doing, to build rapport with them, by 'pacing' and ultimately 'leading' them, again to honour the other person.

Matching Energy

Matching Energy Drill

Two partners have to greet each other with a handshake with the following energy levels (where one is least, and ten is most energy):

- Two versus ten.
- Six versus ten.
- Ten versus ten.

When you're finished, ask the other person how they felt, then swap it over.

Take three minutes each way, explore your own energy combinations and notice how they feel in contrast to one another.

Once you've done this, there is no excuse to ever not **change your energy levels and state.**

State Change

State Change Drill

You will need three people for this drill.

One person thinks of something, positive or negative, and holding that thought in their mind, they sit and embrace that thought.

The second person matches their posture, gestures, facial expressions and breathing, so they can feel what they feel, hear what they hear and see what they see, and they have to guess the first person's thought.

The third person observes and develops his/her sensory acuity to change in the physiological factors of human communication.

When finished, swap over.

Take three minutes each way.

Group Rapport

Group Rapport Drill

In this drill, split into two groups. Each group nominates one person to be 'it'. The 'it' person then has to momentarily step out of the room and close the door behind them.

The rest of the group then have to use their rapport building skills to get the 'it' person to say 'APPLE', but they are not allowed to use that word directly or indirectly (i.e. spell it) at all.

Take as long as it takes for you to convince the 'it' person to say 'APPLE', and notice how difficult/easy it is with/without rapport.

Broken Group Rapport

Broken Group Rapport Drill

In this drill, split into two groups. Each group nominates one person to be 'it'. The 'it' person has to momentarily step out of the room and close the door behind them.

The rest of the group first have to establish rapport at the beginning of the drill, then slowly break rapport.

The 'it' person is briefed to discuss a topic they are really passionate about and hold a conversation about it.

Take five minutes to go through the motions of this drill, and notice the physiology and state changes occurring throughout this process.

Rapport and Disagreement

Disagreement Drill

In this drill, both partners will pick something they disagree on, and using their rapport skills will try and explain their point of view to one another.

Take five minutes to discuss the item you disagree on, and notice how well or how badly you communicate with one another.

Typically, people find that they felt comfortable talking about something they disagreed on when they had rapport, and respected the model of the other person's world more when rapport existed.

If you can discuss something you have a disagreement with someone amicably, then you can maintain your state, remain in a resourceful state and achieve whatever end you desire with more calmness, clarity and certainty.

Crossover

Crossover is indirect matching, for example when one partner crosses his arms, then you cross your legs. You can practice doing this just as in mirroring and matching.

Building Rapport Using Tonality

The second largest human communication component is tonality. Therefore you can also build rapport using the qualities of your voice. This includes:

1. Tone/frequency/pitch.
2. Tempo/speed.
3. Timbre/quality.
4. Volume/Loudness.
5. Origin.

<u>Tonality Analysis</u>

<u>Tonality Analysis Drill</u>

Get into a group of five people, and each person will tell a short story for one minute. Write down the qualities of each individual's voice as you listen to them.

Take one minute each to talk and two minutes to write down their voice qualities.

Voice tonality consists of the following five components:

- Tone/frequency/pitch.
- Tempo/speed.
- Timbre/quality.
- Volume/loudness.
- Origin.

You can change these parameters to change the message of your communication, even if you say the same phrase.

<u>Auditory Cognition</u>

<u>Tonality</u>

Find a partner. Both partners should sit back-to-back. One person thinks of something positive or negative and holding that thought in their mind, counting from one to ten as they do so.

The other person has to guess whether it was a positive or negative thought by listening to the tonality of the numbers spoken.

Take three minutes each way, developing your auditory acuity to pick up on tonality cues.

Vocal

Vocal Drill

In this drill you are going to develop your tonal flexibility. Split up into two groups. Starting with one person and going round the group in a clockwise manner, each person is required to sing the nursery rhyme 'Jack and Jill' using the following moods (and therefore vocal tones):

- Cannot be bothered.
- Relaxed.
- Hysterical laughing state.
- Receiving an Oscar.

Take as long as it takes to go round the circle using all the different tonality types described above, and notice how the same nursery rhyme sounds with different tones.

Building Rapport Using the Right Words

Question

How do you know what words to use when communicating with someone for maximum effect?

Take five minutes to make a list.

You may have heard from an elder when younger the saying, *'Choose your words wisely.'* To do that, we can do the following:

1. Predicates

   These are words used predominantly using your primary 'Representational Systems'; we are going to look at this shortly.

2. Key Words and Phrases

   Words and phrases used particularly often.

3. Common Experiences and Associations

   These are 'Universal Experiences' common to us all, for example the weather, etc.

4. Values and Beliefs

   Values are what is important to you. For example, *'I love cars.'*

   Beliefs are what you hold to be true. For example, *'I'm sure most will agree that stealing is wrong.'*

5. Content Chunks

   If someone speaks in short sentences, then respond likewise.

   If someone speaks in long sentences, then respond likewise.

Representational Systems

For effective communication, we must also learn how to 'talk in the other person's language.'

You're probably wondering what that means. Well, we all have something called 'Representational Systems' that relate to our senses, which are:

Primary

1. Visual (sight).
2. Auditory (hearing).
3. Kinaesthetic (touch and feeling).
4. Auditory digital (inner dialogue).

<u>Secondary</u>

5. Gustatory (taste).
6. Olfactory (smell).

Representational System Preference

Representational System Preference Test

To find out what your primary Representation Systems are, please fill out the 'Representational System Preference Test' available on our website on www.MartialMindPower.com/Resources

When you have finished the test, tabulate your results in the 'Representational System — Preference Test Answers' sheet, which is also available on our website on www.MartialMindPower.com/Resources

Each 'Representational System' has typical behaviours, which can be used as indicators to tell how that person sees the world. These are shown on the 'Favoured Representational Systems Behaviour Indicators' sheet available on our website as well, on www.MartialMindPower.com/Resources

Predicates

The idea therefore is to assess what someone's favoured Representational Systems are using what's known as your sensory acuity. In order to talk in their language, use keywords called predicates and phrases that align with their Representational System.

Please refer to the following sheets for more information, which are available on our website on www.MartialMindPower.com/Resources

1. Representational System Sample Predicates.
2. Representational System Sample Phrases.

Sensory Acuity

Sensory Acuity refers to using your alertness and awareness to identify types of behavioural cues associated with internal thinking strategies, states and cognitive processes.

If you'd like to sharpen your alertness and awareness, then go to the **'Possess an Eagle Eye'** chapter.

Detecting someone's primary Representational Systems will mean that you can then communicate with them in their language as discussed in the previous section.

To discover someone's Representational System, the clue lies within the eyes. Scientists discovered that for 'normally organised' people, their eyes looked in a certain direction when accessing certain parts of their brains to remember, construct, feel or calculate things in their minds.

The following 'Eye Accessing Pattern Chart' shows you the eye pattern for normally organized people.

Please note, that some people may be 'reverse organised', in which case mirror the labels along the vertical axis.

When communicating with another (normally organised) person and their eyes look:

1. Up to the right, that person is recalling a visual memory (Vr - Visuual remembered).
2. Directly to the right, that person is recalling an auditory memory (Ar - Auditory remembered).
3. Down to the right, that person is having inner dialogue with themselves (Ad - Auditory digital).
4. Up to the left, that person is creating a visual image (Vc - Visual construct).
5. Directly to the left, that person is constructing an auditory sound (Ac - Auditory construct).
6. Down to the left, that person is feeling emotion (K - Kinaesthetic).

Eye Accessing Pattern Chart

Eye Accessing Pattern Diagram

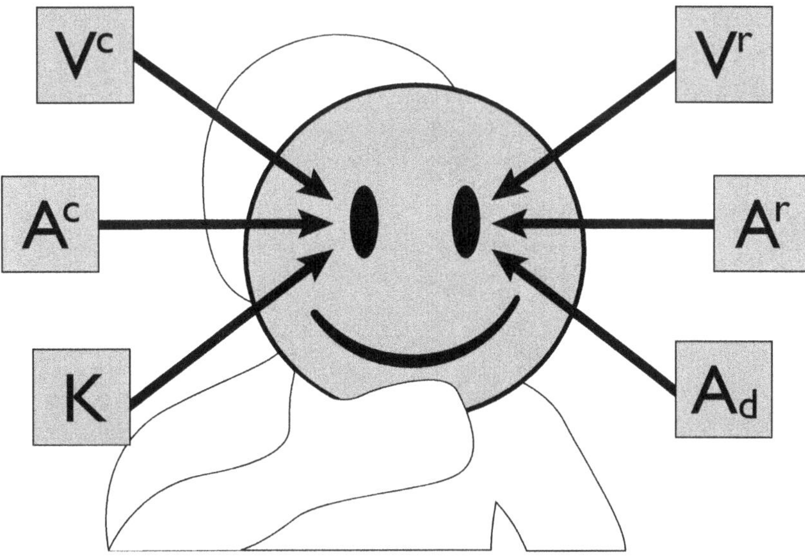

Figure 23: Illustration of eye accessing patterns for a 'normally organised' person.

Eye Pattern Elicitation

Eye Pattern Elicitation Drill

Find a partner. One partner will sit in a neutral posture, whilst the other will ask him/her questions as shown on the *'Eye Pattern Elicitation Questions'* sheet.

The objective is to see which way the eyes move when you ask specific questions — this may be quite sudden, so you will need to stay *'Switched ON'*.

When you swap the drill to the other person, then change the questions, as they will already be familiar with the questions already asked and have a mental representation for them, in which case you may not get an eye access response.

The 'Eye Pattern Elicitation Questionnaire' is available on our website on www.MartialMindPower.com/Resources

Calibrating Physiology

Sensory Acuity can also be used to calibrate someone's physiology. For example:

	Stressed or Anxious	Relaxed & Happy
Skin Colour	Pale	Flushed
Skin Tone	Asymmetrical Shiny	Symmetrical Not Shiny
Breathing	Fast Rate	Slow Rate
Lower Lip Size	No Lines	Lines
Eyes	Focused Not Dilated	Defocussed Dilated

Table 7: Physiological sensory acuity cues.

The BAGEL Model

This section can be beautifully summarised in Robert Diltz's BAGEL Model available on our website on www.MartialMindPower.com/Resources

Questions

This section is based on the works of Jerry Clark's audiobook called *The Magic of Influence.* Check out www.ClubRhino.com for more information.

Now that you understand Rapport and how to build it, the next stage is to get to:

- Know what you want.
- Direct questions with clarity and certainty to create your focus and expanse.
- Learn the art of influencing and its application in marketing and sales.

The problem is that people ask disempowering questions, and therefore get disempowering results. The question is, what has it cost you in the past to ask disempowering questions?

Empowering Questions

Empowering questions automatically assist you to get your goal.

For example, you ask someone to go to an exhibition and they reply, 'No I can't go.'

Question
How would you respond to the question above? Take five minutes to make a list.

Possibility Questions

Here are some possibility examples:

- *'OK, you can't go. What is the possibility of going?'*
- *'If you did go, where would you stay? Grosvenor or Dorchester?'*

What if they then say, *'I don't know'*, what would you say? Maybe something like:

- *'But if you did know, what would it be?'*

The answer WILL pop into their minds. That's a great example of how empowering questions lead to empowered answers and solutions.

Precision Questions

These are questions which narrow down responses. For example:

- Who's everybody?
- Who's all?
- Who specifically?

Most people think answers make the big difference between success and failure. I believe it's asking the right questions, as answers are simply premeditated by questions.

Whatever you focus on tends to manifest. Or as I like to say:

'Where your focus goes, energy flows -
and it expands.'

Question

Can you think of some more precision questions? Take five minutes to make a list.

BRIL-QI Question Elicitation Method

When eliciting questions, use the BRIL-QI method shown below:

- B — Breathe for calmness and clarity.
- R — Remove resistance.
- I — Interest their interest.
- L — Likes and dislikes elicitation.

- Q — Quality questions.
- I — Investigate and be inquisitive.

The idea of the BRIL-QI questioning method is to unlock people's potential.

One of the key functions of the human mind is to repress memories that contain unresolved negative emotions or pain, until such a time that it has the resources to deal with the underlying issue. On that basis, asking the right questions allows the person to liberate themselves from pain and move towards pleasure by resolving such repressed memories and negative emotions, and turn them into positives.

Good questions direct thoughts (called focus), which direct your feelings, which direct actions, which direct results, which direct your success.

What you focus on expands. Ask for what you want, not what you don't want.

In the King James version of the Bible, it states:

For every one that asketh receiveth;
and he that seeketh findeth;
and to him that knocketh it shall be opened.

'How is that possible?' I hear you ask. There's that word again: ask.

Brass Questions vs. Gold Questions

Brass is a cheap metal, which when cast into objects such as doorknobs, it tarnishes and discolours quite quickly. On the other hand, gold is expensive largely unreactive, highly fashionable, and when crafted into jewellery it is luxurious to wear. To live a life of abundance, *'create a gold mindset'.*

Here is an example of some 'brass' questions:

- Why am I always broke?
- Why do I always get bad luck?
- Why can't I lose weight?

Question
What are some examples of 'gold' questions? Take five minutes to make a list.

Cerebral Cleansing

Question
How can you cleanse your mind from negative thoughts and emotions? Take five minutes to make a list.

Here are seven things you can do to perform a 'cerebral cleanse' as follows:

1. Switch your TV OFF (the electronic income reducer) unless it's educational, inspiring and empowering. Avoid sitcoms and the news - if something important happens, you'll find out.
2. Switch your radio OFF.
3. Surround yourself with positive people.
4. Read an empowering, uplifting, inspiring book for fifteen minutes. Did you know that:

    - 58% high school graduates don't read a book ever again in their entire life?
    - 78% haven't visited a bookshop in the last five years?
    - 97% don't have a free library card?
    - The average child spends less than 1% of their time reading, and 54% of their time watching TV or playing video games?

5. Meditate and relax — reflect, seek wisdom, seek courage, give gratitude and thanks, ask peak performance questions. Wherever you direct your mind, you direct your results and create your own reality.
6. Listen to an empowering audiobook every day, and build up your library.
7. Cut out newspapers and tabloids — negativity and fear sells, so avoid the propaganda and think for yourself by seeing the bigger picture and staying switched ON!

Wake-Up Questions

Question
What self-empowering questions could you ask yourself first thing in the morning to get into a resourceful state?
Take five minutes to make a list.

Ask yourself empowering questions when you wake up in the morning, to help you focus your mind towards your end desires:

1. What am I positive about right now?
2. What am I excited about right now?
3. What am I purposefully pursuing right now?
4. Who or what do I give gratitude to what's happening in my life right now?
5. What am I persistent about being, doing and having in my life right now?

Wherever you move to, those things will be attracted to you. In order to GET, you must ASK.

Sleep-Time Questions

Question

What self-empowering questions could you ask yourself last thing before going to bed to get in to a resourceful state?
Take five minutes to make a list.

Ask yourself empowering questions before you rest at night to help you focus your mind towards your end desires, such as:

1. What did I do today that added value to another person's life?
2. What power philosophy did I practice and promote today, and how did that make me feel (check out *52 Power Philosophies* by Jerry Clark)?
3. What dream did I prepare through some small (or big) action today, and how did that make me feel?

Jerry Clark tells this wonderful story of a loyal employee, who happens to be a young man, who goes to speak to his boss one day. When he approaches his boss, he sees he is perusing the internet, looking at a picture of a grand home overlooking the ocean, with a swimming pool, tennis courts, a huge garage, etc. The boss turns around to his loyal employee and says, 'If you keep working hard, then this will be all… MINE!' Build your own dream or someone else's dream — it's your choice.

4. What payment did I receive today? Payment does not only have to be financial, it can also be mental, physical, spiritual, social, vocational and relational;
5. What prayer, thanks, and/or gratitude will I give before I rest my head to sleep tonight? Affirmation of asking for what you want is not religious, it's just being grateful to attract more of it.

How to Ask for What You Want

Question
How can you ask for the things you desire? Take five minutes to make a list.

Here are eight ways to ask for what you want:

1. **Ask with clarity** — be specific, have precision.
2. **Ask intelligently** — ask someone who has the ability to give you what you want.
3. **Use common courtesy** — I call it good spirituality, with a genuine sincerity.
4. You've heard the saying, **'Ask with salt'**; you can lead a horse to water, but you can't make it drink — *but*, if you salt its oats, it will drink when it gets there. Therefore, you can influence your own outcome. Provide incentive and use law of reciprocity through a psychic- or obligation-debt to set it up to come back to you
5. **Give** and it should be given unto you.
6. **Ask with posture** — permeate energy, believe you know what you want without ego or cockiness and without begging.
7. **Ask persistently** — never quit.

> '*No man is ever whipped until he quits — in his own mind*' — Napoleon Hill.

8. The harvest is in a different season to the planning...so **be patient** for the results. It takes time to sow the seeds, and for the fruit and flowers to blossom.

Two Barriers That Stop People Asking

Question
What two barriers do you think stop people asking for what they want? Take a quick guess.

In my experience, the two typical barriers that stop people from asking for what they want are **FEAR and EGO.**

Zig Ziegler calls FEAR 'False Evidence Appearing Real', because it's all in the mind, and not necessarily reality.

Have you heard the story about the bulldog chasing a boy on a bike? The bike's chain breaks one day as the dog is chasing the young lad, and the boy, scared for his life, picks up a brick. The dog suddenly stops, and the boy notices that it didn't have any teeth. Remember: most of the time **your fears have no teeth.**

Ego is a disease called statusitis, i.e. when you think you are above and beyond others, you feel like you don't need to ask. Unfortunately this is the ego trap.

Your ego can help at times, but more often than not it will hurt you. Let me tell you a story about four people that goes something like this…

This is the story of four people named Everybody, Anybody, Somebody, and Nobody.

There was an important job to be done and Everybody was sure that Somebody would do it.

Anybody could have done it, but Nobody did it.

Somebody got angry about that, because it was Everybody's job.

Everybody thought Anybody could do it, but Nobody realised that Everybody wouldn't do it.

In the end, Everybody blamed Somebody when Nobody did what Anybody could have done.

Healthy fear gets you out of the path of danger like a speeding bus, and alerts you to go to the doctors to check out a strange lump. Unhealthy fear is FEAR — false evidence that appears real but is mostly a fabrication of the reptilian brain and the EGO that wants to keep you imprisoned in your own mind, unwilling to be fully alive because it's too risky to venture out. Overcome this unhealthy fear, and you will wake up to an inner security that will put external threats into a new perspective.

There is a Chinese proverb that reads:

'He who asks a question is a fool for five minutes.
He who does not ask a question remains a fool forever.'

Furthermore, Sir Isaac Newton once noted:

'A body of motion continues to stay in motion until interrupted by an outside force.'

Moral of the story: don't let anyone interrupt your FLOW. If you'd like to learn more about how to find your flow, then go to the 'Be Like Water' chapter.

Influence

This section is based on the works of Jerry Clark's audiobook, ***The Magic of Influence.*** For more information, check out www.ClubRhino.com

Question

What does influence mean to you? Take two minutes to describe.

The Oxford Dictionary defines influence as:

'The capacity to have an effect on the character, development, or behaviour of someone or something, or the effect itself.'

The idea behind influencing people, their behaviours and, more importantly, moving their actions towards your desired results, is one which if not done with ecology will create distrust.

When influencing, we MUST think about the ecology — that is:

- Is it a win-win situation?
- This is a 'do-with' technology, not a 'do-to' technology.

Let's have a look at the art of influence and persuasion.

Principles of Human Nature

Question

Can you think of some of the principles of human nature? Take five minutes to make a list.

In order to influence a person, you must understand some underlying principles of their very human nature, which are as follows:

1. People are self-interested.
    - Get people to talk about themselves by asking good questions.
    - Questions should follow FORM — Family, Occupation, Recreation and Money.
    - Listen using their verbal and non-verbal messages.
    - Dale Carnegie stated:

'You can make more friends in two months by becoming interested in other people than you can in two years by trying to get other people interested in you.'

- Identify areas of dissatisfaction.
- Practice communicating.
- There are two magic questions:

    - Hoping to earn some additional income?
    - Do you have an extra X-Y hours a week?

- Survival mentality:

    - Some people think they have to 'get someone' to see something.
    - Others think, *What do they want from me?*

- A lot of people do not want to 'get someone'. This is a disempowering belief.
- Simply befriend the person genuinely, ask questions and identify areas of dissatisfaction.

2. People are self-important.
    - Smile.
    - Listen with undivided attention.
    - Stay open-minded.
    - Don't interrupt.
    - Feedback what was said.
    - Give sincere compliments.
    - Use their name frequently.
    - Use 'you' turns — i.e. turn questions back to them.
    - Give praise and recognition.

3. People are sceptical when you say something in your own favour.
    - Do not promote yourself — get others to do it.
    - Edification ('the moral or intellectual instruction or improvement of someone' — Oxford Dictionary) — edify, raise up, expand, show respect.
    - If you don't have something good to say, then don't say it all.
    - Build up people — e.g. Steven has a lot of powerful information to teach. He's a really busy guy so if you get some of his time you'll be blessed then Steven builds you up to give you power back. That is sponsoring. Whatever you say should be good and true about that person.
    - Three-way calling… the trust and respect factor — people you know don't respect you in a field they are clueless about.

4. Greed factor.
    - People have a desire for easy gain — something for nothing.
    - If the perceived value is greater than the perceived cost (money, time, responsibility, burden, likes), then people will proceed; if not, they will withdraw.
    - 'Opportunity meeting' — value meeting is always overplayed. For example, when you first meet a girl, you go to pick her up with a bunch of roses, show chivalry by opening the car door and treat her nicely. Two months later you're honking outside her house for her to come out. Similarly you start romancing material goods.
    - Free giveaways — stuff you don't need — easy gain.
    - Let them know what they're going to get — build the value and the product.

5. People like a sense of belonging.
    - See Maslow's *Hierarchy of Needs* on our website on: www.MartialMindPower.com/Resources

6. People are emotional by nature.
    - People recommend things all the time, for example, recommending a movie (without being paid to do so).
    - 80% of decisions are emotional, justified with 20% logic.
    - People buy states of mind.
    - They buy a product because of the state it makes them feel.
    - That's why people drink tea and coffee, because it makes them feel awake and alive.
    - Nothing is a bargain if there's no 'emotional want'.
    - People don't buy what they need, they buy what they want.
    - People are wanting stuff that makes them happy, and are always chasing something.
    - Learn how to speak at an emotional level with people, reasoned with logic.
    - Learn to talk benefits.
    - Check out *The Game of Influence and How to Play It* audiobook by Jerry Clark.

7. People want to 'avoid pain and gain pleasure'.
    - In the 1800s, Jeremy Benthony devised this concept as used by Tony Robbins.
    - People do more to avoid pain than gain pleasure; for example they would do more to avoid losing £100k than to gain another £100k.
    - 'What have you got to lose?' Give someone something to lose to stop people quitting or to gain traction.
    - Jerry Clark uses this powerful example…

      'I'm just calling to warn you and thank you.'

      'What are you warning me about?'

      'We've created enough business here I just wanted you to know if you wanted me to keep the £300 or if you wanted to keep it.'
    - Human nature principle (fear, greed, importance and pride).
    - People do things for two reasons: gain pleasure and avoid pain.
    - Sell consequences of doing and not doing something and create inner pressure.
    - As a leader, your job is to inspire, empower and lead by example.

8. People are creatures of habit.
    - People stay on a path because they will have to 'work' to get on another path.
    - Trial memberships create habit the people are reluctant to change.

What Is the Usefulness of Influence?

Influence is powerful to direct people's behaviours and actions towards your end desires. It is also knowing when it is being done to you.

Eleven Triggers of Influence

Question
What do you think are the eleven triggers of influence? Take five minutes to make a list.

There are eleven triggers of influence, which are as follows:

1. Emotional management.
2. Rapport.
3. Congruency.
4. Questions.
5. Anchors.
6. Pattern interrupts.
7. Flexibility.
8. Stories, metaphors, analogies and word pictures.
9. Framing.
10. Embedded suggestions.
11. Unconscious persuasion also known as indirect influence.

Repetition is the mother of all skill.

Martial Weapons of Influence

Question
Can you think of any martial weapons of influence? Take five minutes to make a list.

There are six key martial weapons of influence, which are as follows:

1. Reciprocity.
   - This is to create a win-win situation so someone will do something for you in return
   - Tell a secret.
   - Influence the person to confide in you.
   - Give the person something to get them to show up to a meeting with their commitment, so it induces a psychic debt — a report, presentation, etc. — something for them in return for showing up. Notice the little things people do to reciprocate.

2. Commitment and Consistency.
   - Use *'yes sets',* that is when people say *'yes'* in response to asking questions with small commitments leading up to the goals you achieved.
   - Conversational commitment and consistency — leverage their commitment.

3. Social Proof.
   - Social conformity. For example, people decide what to do based on other people's actions; it is the very principal upon which reviews are built. People say to themselves, *'If all these people are doing it, then they must know something I don't.'* A lot of people moving in a particular direction in a herd mentality.
   - Testimonials act as convincers for some people as proof something works.

4. Liking or Rapport.
   - The best way for someone to like you is to give them something they like; they will then feel obligated to give something back to you.

5. Authority and Contrast.
   - Communicate your credibility. It is best if someone else tells this person about you or sends a letter of introduction, to make it clear you're a genuine authority.
   - To look more attractive, put lesser attractive people around you.
   - People have a certain expectation of what an authority looks like, so dress accordingly. Dress the part, act the part. If you're not an authority, then don't be afraid to admit it if you're not there yet.

6. Scarcity.
   - Scarcity produces desire to want limited and rare products and/or services. Offer something unique that only your product/service can give.

Effect of Influence

Question
What kind of affect do you think influence has on people? Take a quick guess.

There are two effects of influence, and they are:

- **Positive experience:** When people have a positive experience, they will share it with another three people
- **Negative experience:** When people have a negative experience, they will share it with another nine people.

All the principles work across all cultures, but some principles work better than others.

Game of Influence

The secret to influencing is to connect with people by using the following formula: **EPIC-BV or to create EPIC Benefits and Values as follows:**

- E – Enchant and attract their attention.
- P – Profile their problem(s) by asking quality BRIL-QI questions.
- I – Invite them to look at your solution to resolve their problem(s).
- C – Connect them emotionally to be compelled to act now.

- B - Benefits recognition and sharing.
- V - Values recognition and sharing.

There are two driving forces behind basic human behaviour: **Pain vs. Pleasure.** For example, people sometimes have a limited amount of money but are willing to spend it on reducing pain and increasing pleasure.

People are always tuned into the **WIIFM radio station** — that is, **'What's In It For Me ?'**

They don't necessarily want money — usually they want something that the money can give them such as more family time, independence, etc.

Sell products and services on the pain vs. pleasure formula, otherwise known as *'The Art of Selling Without Selling'*, which we are going to talk about more shortly.

Marketing and Sales

Question

What does marketing and sales mean to you? Take five minutes to describe.

Marketing is any activity you do to acquire or keep an existing customer. It is not about convincing people to do this or that.

Selling is to transfer goods to or render services to another person in exchange for money or a price.

Sales personnel are the people who establish contact with the end-consumer to sell products and/or services, so they have a massive responsibility to do this in an ecological and congruent manner if they are to succeed.

A typical faux pas is when salespeople talk to potential customers. That is a big no-no!

Let's explore the art of selling without selling in an ecological and congruent manner.

Obstacles to People Spending Money

Question

Can you think of some obstacles to people spending money? Take five minutes to make a list.

Before you start selling, we should understand the obstacles that stop people from spending money in the first instance, so we can overcome them. The obstacles are:

- People don't buy what they *need*, they buy what they *want.*
- The product fails to meet goals before it's been fully utilised.
- Number one reason for failure — 'What will other people think?'

Do you believe and know people have desires? Can your product/service eliminate pain or give them pleasure? Will the customer be better or worse off after buying your product/service? Be sure to present it in a way so they can see the benefits and values. You owe it to your customer and their families to tell them.

Talk about the benefit of the service/product, not the features, because features focus on the product/service rather than the customer. Highlighting the benefits of your product/service answers the WIIFM ('What Is In It For Me?') question. So, lead with benefits then follow with some features. People make decisions based on emotions.

Build up the benefit vault for all your products.

The Art of Selling Without Selling

This section is based on the inspiring works of Sukhi Wahiwala. Check out www.SukhiWahiwala.com for more information.

Question
How do you sell something? Take fifteen minutes to describe.

It's Not About the Sell

Selling is not about selling at all.

Most people have been in situations where we have been on the receiving end of a hard sale, and all that does is create discomfort and unease, loss of momentary respect for sales people who are not respecting you as a human being and desperation to get out of the pressured sales situation.

Selling therefore is not a hard physical process, but a **mental and spiritual** one where most successful sales happen when people **change their mindset** around the sale that is happening and **you touch their hearts** with a product or service that is truly going to **benefit** them and create an **emotional connection** that they want.

This all happens when there is a **natural conversation** about the 'pitch' of your product(s) and/or service(s).

Talk the Talk, Walk the Walk

So how do you have a natural conversation about the 'pitch'?

We discussed this in detail earlier, and it is about creating rapport that leads to establishing trust and confidence in you and your offering(s). On top of that, it is about establishing congruency so that your customer's mind and body are in alignment and agreement, and this is established through the following three stages:

1. Thinking
    - Are you confident in what you do?
    - Do you believe in what you do?
    - Do you have congruency in your mind and body?
    - Do you know your worth?
    - Do you live your purpose or mission? That is, are you doing what you love, and loving what you do? Does what you do invigorate, inspire and empower you to do it more? Do you feel this is what you were put on this planet to do?

2. Believing
    - Know your product(s) and/or service(s) inside-out, back-to-front, upside-down.
    - Believe in your product(s) and/or service(s).
    - Be an expert consultant for your offering(s).

3. Talking
    - Are you adaptable to your customers' request(s)? To learn more about being adaptable, go to the **'Be Like Water'** chapter in this book.
    - Are you making referrals to other reputable product/service providers that can provide something you cannot? This is known as Santa Claus selling.
    - Are you saying 'yes' to the sales and money coming your way?

Finally, it is paramount that you establish an ecology — that is that the 'sale' is going to create a win-win situation, so everyone leaves with a sweet taste in their mouths.

Know Your Coffee Beans

When selling anything, ensure that 'you know your coffee beans', as the saying goes. That means make sure that you truly understand:

1. What you are selling currently.
2. How to package your offering(s).
3. How to communicate effectively with the end customer with tangible words that will serve their purpose.
4. Your target consumer so you can communicate in their language.
5. What results your customer will get from using your offering(s).
6. How your offering is going to benefit your customer.
7. How to be honest and ask yourself whether your offering something people want in the first place.
8. How to physically quantify what you deliver.

Tangibility Exercise
Pick five tangible words that describe your product or service. Take five minutes to make a list.

Your Product/Service Exercise
Outline your product/service.
What are the stages/levels/categories? What are the price points? What result does your product/service deliver?

List five key benefits of your product/service.

SPIN Selling

To help better understand what results the customer needs, Zerox created a list of selling questions using the simple SPIN formula, as follows:

- S ituation questions.
- P roblem questions.
- I mplication questions.
- N eeds payoff, analysis and benefits.

You can use this template as a means to better understand what results the customer is seeking in your product/service, and address them accordingly. If your product/service does not meet the customer's desired results, then see if you can offer any customisation around your offering, else do the right thing and refer them to someone who can better serve them. The customer will thank you for it and remember you as an ethical business and keep you in mind for future business when the results they seek change.

Sharing, Not Selling

In order to sell, share ideas and information that **adds value** to your customer's knowledge and experience of your offering, including its results and benefits to them, by:

1. Establishing rapport.
2. Asking yourself, how can I be of service to you? What can I do to help? What part of my offering can create positive change in that customer's life?
3. Match your customer's requirements with a solution (if you have the authority to do so).

Getting Customers

Question

Where will you get your customers from? Take five minutes to make a list.

Understanding where your customers are going to come from is important, so that you can create a plan with tactics and strategies to draw customers towards your offering(s). It is important therefore to understand:

1. Where are your potential customers?
   - Social media.
   - Events.
   - Magazines and newspapers.
   - Etc.
2. What events can you attend personally to interact with potential customers?
3. How do you follow up with the contacts you make?
4. Do you have a networking strategy?

Tribe Leader

Listed below are some critical facts about sales. Notice that these are all based on establishing yourself as an authority or leader figure on your offering(s), and having established some kind of emotional connection with your customers.

- Big sales come from repeat sales, not necessarily the first sales, so value your existing customers.
- People that have rejected your service are more likely to buy from you later compared to someone they haven't met, as they become familiar with strangers over time which is the premise on how strangers become friends.
- 80% of all sales come from referrals, which is why it is important to create sub-leaders (or ambassadors) for your offering(s), so they will do the selling for you.

As you can see, it is important to create a tribe, a following of people that share an interest in your offering(s), and will follow you and the knowledge and skills you share with them, to later convert that interest into sales.

Share, Share

The key to 'The Art of Selling Without Selling' is not to sell, but to share information as a tribe leader, to establish an emotional connection with you and your offering(s).

Question
What kind of things can you say or do to make a connection and share information with a potential customer?

Take five minutes to make a list.

Here are some ways in which to share information and establish an emotional connection:

1. Meet your customers wherever is most comfortable and convenient for them.
2. Share what you know selflessly.
3. Give a bit of yourself.
4. Create a mental shift and establish an emotional connection.
5. Make time to listen, then talk.
6. Listen from the heart.
7. Apply your knowledge and skill to their problem.
8. Add value at all times.
9. Always tell people the next step to make things happen.
10. Make an emotional connection with at least one person.

Question
What would you say to share information and establish an emotional connection with your potential customers?

Take fifteen minutes to draft a script.

The Perfect Pitch

The initial hook is usually what people refer to as the 'elevator pitch'; it's simply a quick statement you would use to describe what you do when you meet someone in an elevator, so it has to be short, sweet, snappy and straight to the point. That's the trick!

Here is a template for the perfect pitch:

'What inspired me was…(example).
Then in 1999 I nearly lost everything…(explanation).
But my life changed…(example).
I decided to…(explanation).
And today I am here to share my learnings.'

Let's break this down and analyse the components that make up the perfect pitch:

1. The single or double dip.
    - The dips refer to the two separate paragraphs, which take the listener into a hypnotic journey of your story with you.

2. *Match* people's requests to your skills and product benefits, rather than *selling* them your products or services.
3. Use your tangibility words.
4. Share your mission statement.

Here is my double-dip perfect pitch: *'What inspired me was Bruce Lee on the big-screen when I was a little child. The only way I'd sit still and eat my dinner as a young child of three or four years old was when my parents put on a Bruce Lee movie…and I just sat there, mesmerised.*

Later in life, in 2003, I nearly lost everything — I lost my job, my home and found out my wife was pregnant all at the same time. It was both the happiest and scariest day of my life.

But my life changed when I found one of Bruce Lee's Kung Fu schools in Manhattan to keep me strong and focussed, to help me keep going for my family.

I decided to become a third generation instructor in Bruce Lee's martial art and philosophy, a personal development and elite fitness coach, to help transform people's lives towards their own self-mastery. I call it Martial Mind Power! *And today I am here to share my learnings.'*

Question
Create your own (single- or) double-dip perfect pitch.

Take twenty to thirty minutes to draft your perfect pitch.

The Follow Up

So what happens when you've met someone (maybe in an elevator)?

Question
Write down some things you would do to follow up with a prospective customer.

Take five minutes to make a list.

In my experience, these actions are effective:

1. Exchange business cards or contact information.
2. Make a note of where you met the person (on their business card or on your smartphone, if you have one).
3. Establish contact with them within forty-eight hours. Request two or three possible dates to meet up, or to speak with them.
4. Arrange a free exploratory telephone session.
5. Arrange a physical meeting to show and share your offering(s).
6. Decide if the customer is the right match for your offering(s).

The Right Package and Price

Once you've established a customer is right for your offering(s), then the next step is to:

1. Create a package that is right for your customer.
2. Create a sales funnel, a staged sales process starting with a lower priced simpler offering to start with, graduating to more complex and pricier offerings further down the line if that suits their budget better.
3. Establish timings for delivery of each part of the sales funnel.
4. Establish prices for the sales funnel:
    - Establish a minimum price for your cheaper, simpler offering.
    - Establish a maximum price for your expensive, complex offering.
    - Ensure that you understand the market prices in your marketplace.
    - Understand why you are charging what you charge in confidence.
    - Ask yourself whether you feel congruent and ecological charging what you charge.

Sales Funnel Exercise
Select a product or service, outline your sales funnel, include timings and price and then take twenty to thirty minutes to create the sales funnel.

Customer Discipline

Question
What kind of discipline do you have with your customers (i.e. the things that you do for them, and the things that you do not do for them)?

Take ten minutes to make a list.

When speaking to customers, there is a rule of thumb that should be adhered to for the best results, as follows:

1. Stick to the plan.
2. Treat every customer equally.
3. Limit your accessibility.
4. Avoid *'chit-chats'.*
5. Above all, get results for your time.

Speaking Engagements

Question
Write down some things you would do when speaking to pitch a sale. Take five minutes to make a list.

When speaking to pitch a sale, these are some musts:

1. Know who will be in the room beforehand.
2. Speak to people who have the power to make decisions.
3. Give transformation there and then.
4. Solve a key problem.
5. Give the audience something unique and leave your mark.
6. Have no more than two or three clear and concise next steps.
7. Leave people with a 'branding hook' they will remember.

Eight Characteristics of Successful Marketeers

Question
What do you think are the eight characteristics of successful marketeers?

Take five minutes to make a list.

1. Patience

   Penetrate a customer's mind nine times, which creates total empathy to become purchase ready. Nine exposures prepares your customer's mind to be ready to buy. However, people usually quit in three exposures (three in one rule); therefore you have to expose your product to the customer twenty-seven times on average before they decide to buy.

2. Imagination

   Use your imagination. For example, put eleven stamps on a letter rather than one stamp to get their attention.

3. Sensitivity

   Be sensitive to what's on your prospective customer's mind right now.

4. Eagle strength

   Stand up to people that love you but try and put you off. Develop a thick skin.

5. Generosity

   Think, what can you give to your prospective customers as a gesture of goodwill to accessorise your sales?

6. Aggressiveness

   Use as many useful marketing tools as possible.

7. Seagulls

   Fly in circles, swoop down to eat and return to sky — i.e. remain in a constant state of learning.

8. Action

   Do something about it now!

In free enterprise it's a jungle out there, so be a guerrilla!

How Many Markets Do You Have?

Question

How many markets do you have? Take five minutes to make a list.

There are three main market segments, which are as follows:

1. Universe (anyone).
2. Prospects.
3. Existing customers. Guerrilla marketeers invest 60% of their time in this area, and it only costs one sixth to sell to existing customers.

Increase prospects, increase customers.

PLEASE NOTE, the most deadly enemy is apathy after the sale. So ensure you follow up after a sale and give the client some attention.

The most important long term goal is to establish a brand name.

How Many Businesses Are You In?

Question
How many different businesses do you think you are in when selling your offering(s)?

Take five minutes to make a list.

There are four businesses that you're in when you're in business, and they are:

1. The business you think you're in.
2. Marketing business.
3. People business.
4. Service business.

Question
What is the definition of the result of creativity and marketing combined?

Take five minutes to define these terms.

Profits! Creativity comes from the application of knowledge, and the skill of doing! Marketing your creation leads to directing people to act towards purchasing your offering effectively, which when done frequently ultimately leads to handsome sales and, in turn, profits.

As Bruce Lee quoted:

'Knowing is not enough;
we must apply.
Willing is not enough;
we must do.'

Therefore, the best time to launch a guerrilla marketing attack is TODAY!

Invest in What You Do with Emotional Content

Emotional Content relates to the depth of feeling a person puts into what they do, the emotional resonance of their action, if you will. For example, one can throw a poor punch half-heartedly/slowly or they can throw a punch with full intention and investment of oneself.

Half-hearted results lead to poor results or failure. Chris Kent quoted:

> *'When we invest in what we are doing with emotional content, it becomes the expression of the total self at that moment, and honest expression of the self. So ensure that your thoughts and actions are filled with sincerity and 'emotional content.'*

<u>Half-Hearted vs. Whole-Hearted Drill</u>

Find a partner. One partner holds two pads at head height, and the other partner tries to punch the pads:

1. Half-heartedly, i.e. slowly and lethargically. How does it feel?
2. Whole-heartedly, i.e. with intent, power and speed. How does it feel?

Take three minutes each way.

<u>Emotional Content Drill</u>

Find a partner. One partner holds two pads at waist height, and the other partner tries to punch the pads as hard as they can with a palm-up fist. This is not a strong punch, and lacks the emotional content of throwing a powerful strike. Can you feel it?

Take three minutes each way.

<u>VAK Storytelling</u>

In this drill, split into two groups. Each person thinks up a story of their own, and have to tell it in one minute chunks before moving onto the next person using the VAK (Visual, Auditory and Kinaesthetic) Representation Systems and add your emotional content into your storytelling expressions.

Make It Your Own

Chris Kent beautifully summarises this by saying:

'You take whatever it is that you do, integrate it with your personality, physical attributes, etc. and add your own personal modifications.'

For example, your driving style, talking style, walking style and so on.

<u>Question</u>
How do you identify your own style? Ask yourself the smart questions below, to identify your own style:

1. What is it?
2. Who are you?
3. What's your unique trademark?
4. What are you trying to say or do?
5. What is your vision?
6. How are you going to make it happen?
7. How will you make it your own?

Take fifteen minutes to answer these questions thoroughly

Bruce Lee famously quoted:

'Absorb what is useful,
discard what is useless and
add what is specifically your own.'

<u>Short Movie Exercise</u>
In this drill, you are going to work as a group and come up with a short martial arts movie sketch and act it out. You will use everything you've learnt to honestly express yourself, to give the most exciting and best performance you've ever given.

Take sixty minutes to create a short two-three minute play..

Rags to Riches

And then one day he noticed the sun. And he saw how the sun had power to do things he couldn't even dream of. He saw how the sun could turn all the fields from green to yellow, and from yellow to brown. He saw how the sun could dry up even the mightiest rivers and leave nothing but parched mud banks. He saw how the sun could starve the world of life.

And he knew unhappiness. *'I'm not happy. The sun has more power than I do. If only I were the sun, then I'd be happy.'*

And the angel appeared and said, *'You are the sun!'* And he became the sun. And he was happy. He felt his power and he felt his might. And he loved the way he could turn the fields from green to yellow to brown, dry up the rivers and change the whole world. And he was happy.

And he ruled the world from his zenith, exulting his power.

Until one day he noticed a cloud, a big black raincloud. And he saw how the cloud had the power to turn all fields from brown to green, refill the rivers with flowing water, and retrieve the life of the world.

And the depression filled him. *'I'm so unhappy. This cloud has more power than I. If only I was the cloud then I'd be happy forever.'*

And the angel appeared and said, *'You are the cloud.'* And he became the cloud, and he was happy. He felt his power and might. And he loved the way he could reverse the work of the sun and reinstate life where so little had been before. And he knew real happiness for the first time.

Until one day he saw, far below him, a rock. And he saw how the rock — black, strong, unyielding — was unchangeable. And he saw that no matter how much or how hard he rained, nothing he could do could challenge or destroy the rock. The rock was rugged and resistant.

And he knew the bitterness of unhappiness once again. And he said, *'I'm so unhappy. If only I were the rock then I'd be happy.'*

And the angel appeared and said, *'You are the rock.'* And he became the rock, and he felt his might and he felt his power, and he was happy. He exulted in his strength and sense of permanence. He loved his ability to withstand everything nature could throw at him. He laughed at the sun and he ridiculed the raincloud. Until one day, a quarryman arrived.

Conclusion

I started off by saying:

> *Expressing yourself is one thing. Honestly expressing yourself is another matter entirely. Honest self-expression demands that we express our own thoughts and feelings without conforming to styles, methods and systems expected by others. Without fear of not being understood, accepted or approved by others. Without compromising our values, beliefs or souls to satisfy others. All with honesty and integrity.*

To do this, we should feel confident that you can:

1. Communicate…
   - Without the fear of offending someone.
   - Without the fear of creating a conflict and confrontation.
   - With inspiration and empowerment!

2. Express yourself….
   - Without feeling that you're holding back.
   - Without trying to dilute your words and muddying your message.
   - Without avoiding saying what you mean.
   - With freedom of expression.

3. Honestly…
   - By not lying to oneself.
   - By not lying to others.
   - By being honest with yourself and talking from a place of wisdom.
   - In Thomas Jefferson's words, *'Honesty is the first chapter in the book of wisdom.'*

4. Trust and confidence…
   - Without distrust.
   - Without fear.
   - Without a lack of confidence.
   - With a sense of trust and confidence.
   - With a strong foundation of rapport.
   - Creating win-win situations.

5. Calmness, clarity and certainty…
   - Without confusion.
   - Without anxiety and panic.
   - With a sense of calmness, clarity and certainty.

In Bruce's book, *Artist of Life*, he quotes:

> *'Artistic skill must radiate from the soul.*
>
> *Artistic skill, therefore, does not mean artistic perfection. It remains rather a continuing medium or reflection of some step in psychic development, the perfection of which is not to be found in shape and form, but must radiate from the human soul.*
>
> *The artistic activity does not consist in art itself as such; it penetrates into a deeper world in which all art forms of things inwardly experienced flow together, and in which the harmony of soul and cosmos in the nothing has its outcome in reality.'*

How about you? Do you put on a show and act cool to impress? Do you do what you think other people expect you to do? Do you just honestly express yourself?

The only person that can answer that is YOU! It is not always easy to do.

In Bruce's TV interview on *The Pierre Berton Show* in 1967, Bruce explained, *'It is easy for me to put on a show and be cocky and flooded with a cocky feeling and then feel pretty cool and all that. Or I can make all kinds of phoney things and be blinded by it. But to express oneself honestly, not lying to oneself — that, my friend, is very hard to do.'*

After all, it's not about being like anyone else, it's about you BEING YOU!

Being 'in yourself' means knowing the real you so you can express your feelings, emotions and your essence honestly from the core of your being.

It is important to know your tools and skills, and cultivate them to be of service to the world in an undeniably honest, devoted, selfless and passionate way, so you love what you do, and do what you love.

By being in totality with yourself, giving 100% of yourself, 100% of your investment, with mind, body and spirit in complete sync, with absolute intent and emotional content in everything you do… you can truly have a unique and magical effect in your world and the people in it — be it at home, school, work and wherever else life takes you.

Let your actions, words, thoughts and ideas be real and come from your true authentic self, your honest expression of who YOU really are so you can liberate yourself, self-actualise and achieve your success goals.

In this stage, we looked at:

- Knowing yourself.
- Developing a strong foundation.
- Investing in what you do with emotional content.
- Making it your own.

And that brings us to the end of the Honestly Express Yourself stage of your self-mastery journey. Before you embark on your EXPRESS TO SUCCESS, please answer the following:

Question

1. Do you understand how to Express Yourself with Honestly and Integrity? (Yes or No)
2. Do you Know Yourself Better? (Yes or No)
3. Have you developed some tools and skills to communicate effectively with Poise and Confidence? (Yes or No)
4. Will you Act 'As-If' from now on? (Yes or No)

5. Do you understand how to **Invest Your Emotional Content** in whatever you are doing in the moment? (Yes or No)
6. Do you know how to make it your own and put your own **Signature or Trademark** on the things you say and do? (Yes or No)
7. Do you feel better equipped to **Win Friends, Influence People** and enrich relationships? (Yes or No)
8. Are you ready to **Express Your Way to Success**? (Yes or No)

My friend, I would like to deeply thank you for giving me the chance to take you through this **Master Your Life journey,** and remember:

'EXPRESS YOUR WAY TO SUCCESS!'

7

Be like water

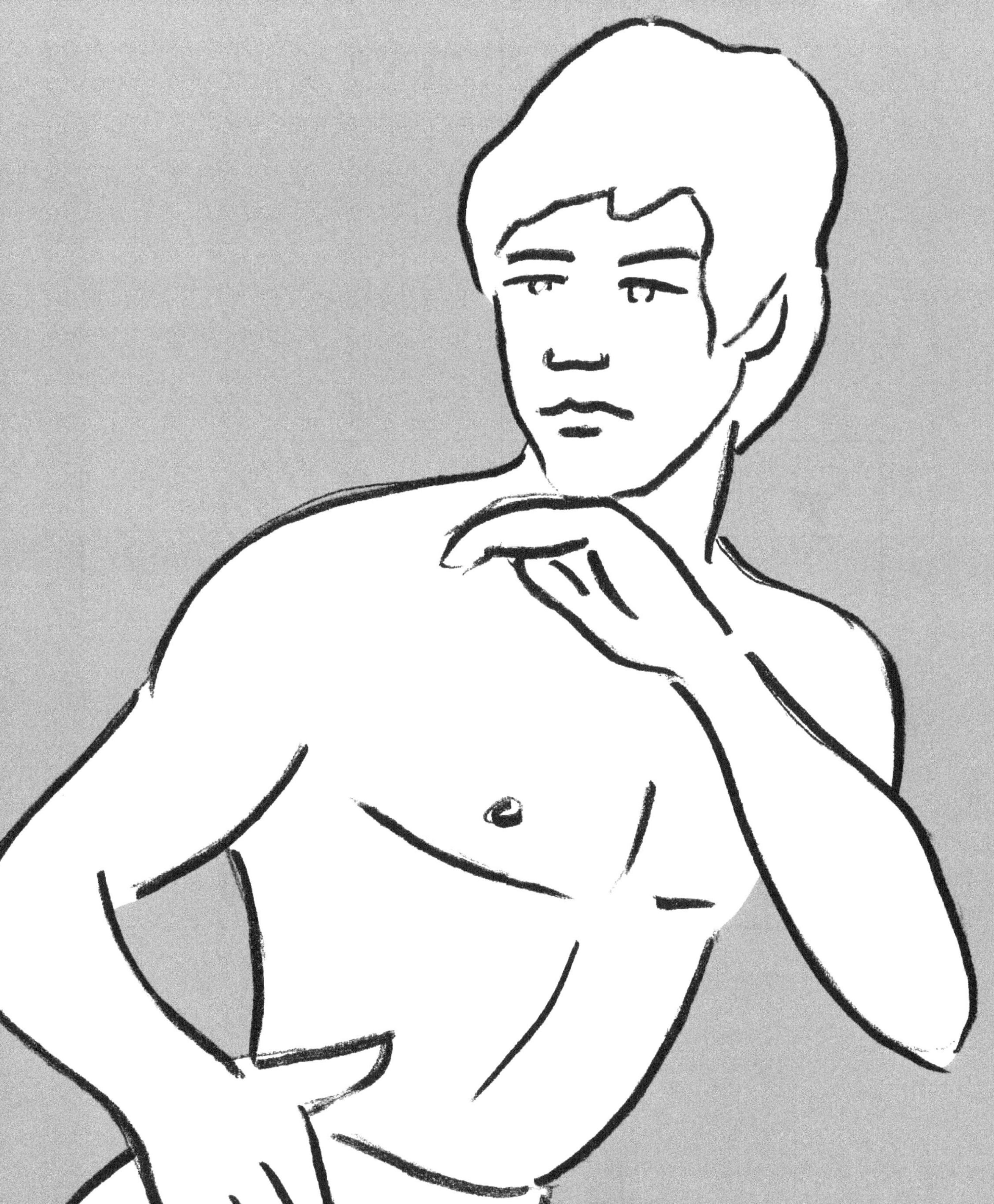

Be Like Water

STAGE 7 — PURPLE BELT

Master Your Flow

What's the Problem?

So, who are we trying to help in this Be Like Water stage of your self-mastery journey?

- People who are unhappy.
- People who do not have a vision.
- People who are not flexible and adaptable.
- People who are confused.
- People who are angry.

Objective

Outcomes and Results Question
What outcome(s) and result(s) do you expect to get when you Be Like Water?

Take ten minutes to list down all the positive changes you would like to see, hear and feel.

Water is one thing. But to BE like water is another matter entirely.

Being like water demands an in-depth understanding of what water is before you can be like it. Without understanding water's amazing facts. Without understanding water's properties. Without understanding water's behaviours. You cannot assimilate to water to Be Like Water.

Examples Question
Can you think of any examples when you have not been in the Flow? How did this cause you to feel? Take ten minutes to make a list.

Do you sometimes find yourself:

- Feeling unhappy and frustrated that things are not going your way?
- Lacking vision and drifting aimlessly?

- Being inflexible and unadaptable?
- Being stubborn and set in your own ways?
- Being too hard or too soft on yourself or others?
- Lacking patience, finding you cannot wait?
- Being easily put off when something stands in your way, and give up easily?
- Going in with all guns blazing when there's an issue?
- Feeling confused and angry?
- Feeling like you're stagnating in life?

If you have answered 'yes' to any of the above, then you're in for an amazing SPEEDBOAT THRILL RIDE.

Be Like Water is based on Bruce Lee's martial philosophy:

'Be formless shapeless, like water.
You put water into a cup, it becomes the cup.
Put it into a teapot it becomes the teapot.
Now water can flow, or creep, or drip, or crash.
Be water, my friend.'

And inspired by the works of Chris Kent's 'Be Like Water', in his famous book called *Personal Liberation* (www.PersonalLiberation.com) and the late Dr Masuro Emoto's works, which can be found in his book called *The Hidden Messages in Water* (www.masaru-emoto.net/english/water-crystal.html).

This stage of your self-mastery journey will help you to:

Belt	Pillars of Luck	Chapter	Success Goals
7. Purple	Pleasure	**'Be like water'** Master your flow	• Be adaptable and flexible to cope with any situation • Overcome obstacles that stand in your way • Create calm and clarity • Create a sense of vision and happiness • Achieve whatever ends you desire • Find your flow • Flow to success!

This stage is broken down into thirteen substages as follows:

1. Water facts.
2. Properties and Behaviours of Water.
3. Relate to Water.
4. Types of Fluidity.
5. Benefits of Fluidity.
6. The Water Principle.
7. Worksheet.

8. Dr Masuro Emoto.
9. What Are Water Crystals?
10. Water and Words.
11. Water and Thought.
12. Messages in Water.
13. Find Your Flow.

...so you can Be Like Water and FLOW TO SUCCESS!

Warm Up

Let's jump right in and start warming up by answering the following questions:

Question
Do you know what **Be Like Water** means? Take five minutes to write down your thoughts on this.

Question
Do you know any really **Amazing Facts About Water?** (Yes or No)

If 'no', then would you like to learn (Yes or No)

Question
Do you know any **Amazing Properties and Behaviours of Water?** (Yes or No)

If 'no', then would you like to learn? (Yes or No)

Question
Do you know how to **Be Like Water**? (Yes or No)

If 'no', then would you like to learn? (Yes or No)

Question
Do you know what **Fluidity** means? (Yes or No)

If 'no', then would you like to learn? (Yes or No)

Question
Do you know what **the Water Principle** is? (Yes or No)

If 'no', then would you like to learn? (Yes or No)

Question
Would you like to **Find Your Flow**? (Yes or No)

Question
Would you like to **Flow to Success**? (Yes or No)

If you do not know the answer to any of the questions above and are eager to learn, or answered 'yes' to the last question, then you're in the right place, so let's KEEP ON FLOWING.

The US Armada

An armada of the US Navy was engaged in naval exercises off the coast of Canada, when the following radio exchange was recorded:

US Navy: *'Please* **divert your course** *fifteen degrees to the north to avoid danger of collision.'*

Responder: *'Recommend that you* **divert your course** *fifteen degrees to the south to avoid danger of collision.'*

US Navy: *'We repeat.* **Divert** *north now to avoid collision.'*

Responder: *'Strongly recommend that* **you divert** *south soonest to avoid mishap.'*

US Navy: *'This is the Captain of a US Navy warship. I say again,* **divert your course** *with immediate effect.'*

Responder: *'Copy. We say* **divert** *south now.'*

US Navy: *'This is the USS Enterprise. We are an aircraft carrier of the US Navy.* **Divert your course** *now.'*

Responder: *'We are a Canadian lighthouse. YOUR CALL!'*

The Secret of Success

And so the little boy went to his father and said, *'Dad! Dad! What's the secret of success in life?'*

His father said, *'Son, that's a very difficult question. And I'm not the one to give you an answer. Why don't you ask your mother?'*

So the little boy went to his mother and said, *'Mum! Mum! What's the secret of success in life?'*

His mother said, *'Son, that's a very difficult question. And I'm not the one to give you an answer. Why don't you wait till the summer holidays and go see the Wise One who lives in the castle? The Wise One is sure to know.'*

And so, with barely concealed excitement and anticipation, the little boy waited through the winds of autumn, the frosts of winter, the unfurling of spring and the promise of early summer until the summer holidays arrived.

He packed his rucksack with all the things he might need and set off for the distant castle of the Wise One. He walked the lengths of deep valleys, climbed across high mountains, crossed fast rivers, swam broad lakes and trekked through dense forests until finally he reached the castle.

In the courtyard he was amazed to find it packed with people of every description. All were waiting to receive learning and knowledge from the Wise One. He was surprised that so many people from so many walks of life could be so interested in learning wisdom. There were actors, dancers and painters. There were lawyers, doctors and teachers. There were businesspeople, bankers and accountants. There were housewives and househusbands. There were bus drivers, plumbers and electricians. There were scientists, technologists and inventors. There were surgeons, dentists, opticians and nurses. There were even some politicians and academics.

The little boy waited patiently in turn. Finally he arrived before the Wise One. *'Please tell me, what is the secret of success in life?'*

'Son,' said the Wise One, *'that's a very difficult question. And while I think of an answer, take time to visit my castle and appreciate all its wonder and beauty. Remove your shoes, for it is the custom in this land, and feel the smooth coolness of the mosaic floors in my reception rooms. Take a look at the fine hanging tapestries in my bedrooms, noticing the richness of their colours and the detail of their description. Take time to listen to the harmonious music of my musicians, for the sounds they make will delight and enchant your ears and your soul. Be sure to visit my kitchens and taste the foods that my chefs produce, for the food they make — piquant or sweet, salt or sharp, sour or hot, spicy or subtle — whatever you eat will excite your senses as never before. And do not miss my gardens and orchards, for the sweet smells of the fruit in blossom and the tart aromas of the herbs will transport you to a land of long-forgotten memories.'*

As the little boy was about to leave, the Wise One stopped him, and took out from a concealed cloak pocket a small spoon and a bottle.

'Just one thing before you go... Take this spoon and be sure,' the Wise One said, putting two drops of oil from the bottle onto the spoon, *'that under no circumstances you spill these two precious drops. Be back in two hours and I will answer your question.'*

Introduction

In this Be Like Water stage, we must firstly ask ourselves the key question, 'What is water?'

To find the answer to this question, we are going to explore the 'depths' of what water is, to help us define it, so we can understand how we can possibly 'Be like water' through its closer examination, so that we can apply those key lessons to our daily life towards our personal liberation, self-actualisation, so we can achieve our success goals.

Are you ready to KEEP ON FLOWING?

Water Facts

Question
Name some facts about water. Take fifteen minutes to make a list.

Here are some interesting facts about water:

1. 70% of our planet is water.
2. Water is the only substance that exists as a solid, liquid and gas.
3. Water content in humans is as follows:
   - A fertile egg is 96% water.
   - A baby is 80% water.
   - An adult is 70% water.
   - An elderly person is 50% water or less.
4. Humans consume approximately two litres of water per day in food and drink.
5. Earth is the only planet with water known to man (at the moment).
6. Water is densest at four degrees Celsius.
7. In winter, the coldest water rises (unlike all other liquids), which is the main reason water life can survive in extreme cold temperatures.
8. Most substances expand when they get hot, but not water; when it reaches boiling point it micronises into steam.
9. Most substances contract when they get cold, but not water; when it turns to ice it expands by 9%.
10. When water turns to ice its density decreases, which is why ice floats in drinks. All other substances are denser in their solid state.
11. Water molecules are polar, i.e. they align themselves in certain ways.
12. Water creates vortices on opposite ends of the Earth — clockwise in the UK and anti-clockwise in Australia.
13. Water can travel upwards — for example water being soaked into a tissue, or travelling up a flower stem.
14. Bruce Lee is famously known as 'The Dragon'. Did you know that in Japan, dragons represent the God of Water.

We are going to use martial motion to explore water and its liquid and solid state properties, to get a closer feel for what water really is.

Liquid Ice Drill
Find a partner.
Stand natural and neutral.
Your opponent reaches out and places one hand on your shoulder and pushes gently; this should break your structure and balance.
This time, when your opponent touches you, imagine:

- That your body turns into solid ice, as you stiffen every muscle in your body.
- Your body becomes magnetised and your feet get stuck solid to the ground, pulling you towards the ground as you sink towards the ground below your feet by bending slightly at your knees.

Try it — do you notice any difference to your structure and balance?

Properties and Behaviours of Water

Question
Now that you've had a chance to discuss some water facts, list as many properties and behaviours of water as possible? For example, water can exist as a solid, liquid and a gas.

Take fifteen minutes to make a list.

Relate to Water

Question
For each property and behaviour of water you listed, relate and apply it to combat and/or daily life challenges?

Take fifteen minutes to relate.

Here is an extensive list of properties and behaviours of water, and their application in combat and/or daily life:

- Wholeness without form

  Water has no shape. Water moulds itself to whatever receptacle you put it in.

  The big idea is to be flexible, adaptive, co-operative to fit in whatever situation may arise.

<u>Wholeness Without Form Drill</u>
Find a partner.

Your opponent throws a lead punch, and you react to whatever comes. Here are some actions and some effective reactions for you to practice:

1. Defensive action — catch or parry your opponent's strike.
2. Aggressive defence — slip or heel-toe-sway past the strike.
3. Counter attack — simultaneous defence and attack, e.g. slip with strike or heel-toe-sway with lead strike.
4. Intercept — attack with intention or preparation, using your movement to strike and neutralise your opponent's attack as a defence.

- Embodiment of Yin and Yang

  Yin — water is soft. You cannot cut it or hit it. You cannot grab it — it slips away.

  The big idea is to understand when to be soft and yield to a situation, and on others you must be hard and be firm.

  Yang — when water seeps into cracks within stones and concrete and freezes, the ice can break stone and concrete, which causes millions of pounds of damage to UK's roads in the winter when it gets icy.

<u>Push-Pull Drill</u>
Find a partner. Partners stand in mirroring leads and extend lead hands, placing them palm-to-palm.

Drill 1: Both partners push — stalemate.

Drill 2: One partner pushes, the other partner pulls their hand back and slips of to one side — push-pull.

Notice the change in energies between drill 1 and 2.

- Patience

  Water can erode rock by gently washing it.

  The big idea is, no matter how impossible your dreams may seem, flow with them until you overcome the adversities you face in order to achieve your success goals through patience, perseverance and steady work. As they say, 'Slowly but surely.'

<u>Horse Stance Drill</u>
Stand in a squat position for one minute, then two minutes, then three minutes, until it doesn't bother you how long you sit in that position.

- No boundaries or obstacles

When water runs into an object, it immediately finds a way around it, over it, under it and through it.

The big idea is to understand that sometimes our actions and thoughts become blocked up by historical experiences. We must move on by finding a way around it, over it, under it and through it, just like water.

For example, Bruce Lee got turned down from the Hollywood TV show *Kung Fu.* He eventually went back to Hong Kong to make his blockbusters *Big Boss, Fists of Fury* and *Way of the Dragon*, only to be invited back to Hollywood on his terms to do his blockbuster movie *Enter the Dragon*, which catapulted him to superstardom.

Obstacle Course Drill
Get into a small group of four or five people.
One person stands on one end whilst the rest of the group spread out in a line, adopting various positions. The goal is to navigate from one side to the other by getting past the obstacles. For example:

1. Fighting stance — slip past them.
2. Legs open — slide through legs.
3. On floor — jump or roll over them.

Or simply move them out of the way.

- Clear when it is calm

A lake becomes muddied when disturbed and clear when it's calm. The big idea is to calm your thoughts and emotions like water and you will have clarity. Otherwise, if our thoughts and emotions are stirred, they become like muddied water, and we can end up making mistakes or missing opportunities because we cannot see them.

The Chinese philosopher Chuang Tzu said, *'If water derives lucidity from stillness, how much more the faculties of the mind'.*

Water Torture Drill — Calmness
Do this exercise on your own.

Get half a cup of water in a plastic cup. Perform a sidekick whilst holding the cup of water in your hand, without spilling any water.

Memory Drill — Calmness and Clarity
Get into a group of four or five people.
One person stands in the middle of a circle and has to remember the following shopping list of seven items:

1. Milk.
2. Bread.
3. Eggs.

4. Porridge.
5. Honey.
6. Almonds.
7. Water.

The person in the middle has to recite the shopping list within one minute. The rest of the group shout at the person in the middle, and even push him/her around gently for one minute.

- Generate great force

Force created by water can be used both positively (e.g. to generate power) and negatively (e.g. a force of destruction like a tsunami that devastated Japan).

The big idea is to direct and control our energies to whatever ends we desire rather than destructively.

Bamboo Principle Drill

Find a partner. They start in a high outer reference point — relaxed with zero energy.

Your opponent punches, aiming towards your chin. You yield to your opponent's energy by blocking whilst deflecting it to the side as you roll with the strike, and let your opponent's energy dissolve with minimal effort.

You can pull your opponent during their incoming attack once you have contact with the block in order to use the opponent's energy against themselves.

- Running water never becomes stale

The big idea is, as Bruce said, *'Do not stagnate, else you are just waiting, ready to die.'*

Running Water Drill

Find a partner.

One partner attacks the other with simple high-line attacks with 50% power and 50% speed, such as straight lead and rears, lead and rear hooks, lead and rear uppercuts. The objective is for the other person to use footwork to evade the incoming attacks with fluidity of motion. As you get better, you can start speeding up the motion.

Types of Fluidity

<u>Question</u>
There are two types of fluidity. Can you name them? Take a quick guess.

In conclusion, there are two types of fluidity in combat, which are:

1. Physical fluidity.
2. Mental fluidity.

I am going to elaborate on these as follows:

1. Physical Fluidity

   A good martial artist must demonstrate a state of physical fluidity in order to be able to transition from one technique to another swiftly and effectively without any hesitation.

2. Mental Fluidity

   Simultaneously, a good martial artist must maintain mental fluidity in order to adapt and respond to his opponents effectively. In doing so they can stay ahead and ultimately direct the fight.

Benefits of Fluidity

<u>Question</u>
What do you think are the benefits of being fluid? Take five minutes to make a list.

Maintaining fluidity of action and thought will allow you to reach your opponent by:

1. Penetrating through your opponent's defences.
2. Finding a way around an opponent's defences.
3. Avoiding an opponent's attack by yielding and/or dissolving it.

As Bruce Lee stated, a good martial artist must Be Like Water.

The Water Principle

Bruce also spoke about the water principle in both combat and daily life, referring to:

1. Fluidity in body movements.
2. Fluidity of the mind — never stagnating, always moving forward, growing and changing for the better.

Understanding the nature of water not only gave Lee the guiding principle for his martial art, but also a guiding principle for daily living.

In order to Be Like Water, we need to understand what water *is* before we can be like it.

Fluidity in Combat

- Water has no constant form.
- Likewise there are no constants in combat.
- Combative circumstances change from moment to moment.
- For an effective outcome, you must be adaptable, flexible and cooperative to the situation to be able to flow with the situation.

The famous poet Michael McGriff MD once said:

'Blessed are the flexible, for they shall not get bent out of shape.'

Fluidity in Life

Similarly, life is not constant; it changes all the time. Most people are reluctant to change because it puts people in a place of adversity, but change and adversity is the space in which a human grows with each challenge.

If you can flow with any situation, then change is welcomed, and you can experience positive personal development.

Fluidity in the Art of Self-Expression

Bruce Lee's philosophy of fluidity inspired Parkour or freerunning.

British Freerunner, 'Freeflow', says:

'The ultimate goal with freerunning is to be fluid, to attain flow — to adapt to any given situation, so you never stop at obstacles — you just keep flowing and find a way around them.'

Worksheet

We are now going to tackle the accompanying worksheet, which is available on our website **www.MartialMindPower.com/Resources**, to get you thinking about the application of the things we learnt about earlier.

As part of this worksheet, I'd like you to ask yourself several questions for each property and/or behaviour of water. As we explored earlier, there are many properties and behaviours of water to choose from which we can learn and grow. In your own time, feel free to expand on the list of these questions with your own to keep on growing.

Dr Masuro Emoto

In this part of the course, I am going to change the way you look at water, and in turn, expand the possibilities of BEing LIKE WATER.

Bruce Lee often stated that he didn't like the idea of 'thinking outside the box', as there was still confinement in the fact that a box still existed in the picture. Lee preferred to think of thinking as 'being at the centre of a circle without a circumference' — i.e. boundless. So, before we start, please may I ask you all to 'empty your teacups' so we can pour new tea in — open your mind! To learn more on how to open your mind, please go to the 'Empty Your Teacup' section.

Figure 25: *Dr Masuro Emoto, The Hidden Messages in Water*

I want to introduce you to a scholar called Dr Masuro Emoto, who performed an academic study on water based on the cultural sciences rather than natural sciences.

What he discovered has changed the way people look at water. What Dr Emoto found was that water consisted of crystals which exhibited motion, and that water crystal behaviour evidenced many outstanding theories and gave birth to many new hypotheses.

Figure 26: *A water crystal, The Hidden Messages in Water*

Firstly, when Dr Masuro Emoto returned to Japan from the USA, he bought back a vibration-measuring machine called an MRI machine. He used this to transfer vibrational energy on micro clustered water, a special type of water which he called HADO water.

Since, Dr Masuro Emoto has used this water to cure 15,000 people, which has been hard to accept by medical doctors.

So what is this super fandango water. Well it's based on a simple idea that:

1. No two snowflakes are the same;
2. Snowflakes are water; and
3. If snow has crystals, then so should water when it's frozen.

It took Dr Masuro Emoto and his team two months to capture water crystal photos.

After examining tap water from various cosmopolitan cities, Dr Masuro Emoto found that the water in London, Tokyo and Paris had no crystalline structure to it.

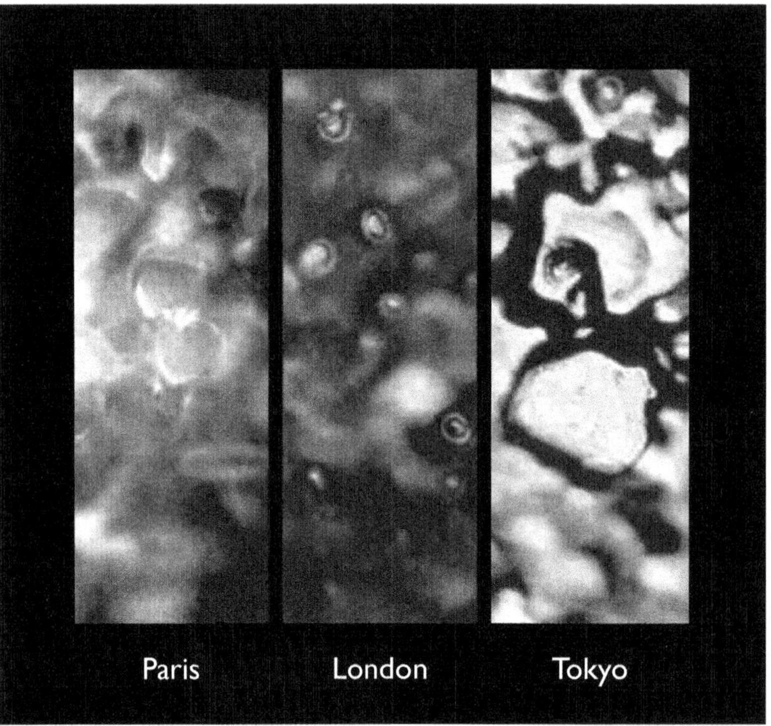

Figure 27: Water crystals from tap water in Paris, London and Tokyo, The Hidden Messages in Water

So how did Dr Masuro Emoto capture the water crystal photos? Well, he started by:

1. Activating the water samples by tapping the bottom of the water bottle.
2. He took fifty x one millilitre water samples and placed them in a petri dish.
3. The water sample was then frozen at minus twenty-five degrees celsius for three hours.
4. He then analysed the water at minus five degrees celsius under a microscope.
5. As the water warmed from minus twenty-five degrees celsius, water crystals started to form, creating a 3D shape like a pyramid.

What Are Water Crystals?

Figure 28: Albert Einstein and his famous formula for energy.

Physics has shown that everything in existence vibrates, and that vibration is another word for energy.

Dr Masuro Emoto believed that water crystals represent the life force of Mother Nature and that the absence of water crystals implies life force in that area has been compromised energetically.

Dr Masuro Emoto performed experiments using distilled water exposed to different types of music. To his amazement, he discovered that different music formed different crystals, expressed as the water 'followed' the music.

Figure 29: Water crystals formed from water exposed to different types of music, The Hidden Messages in Water

Dr Masuro Emoto believed that music was created to bring our vibration back into its intrinsic state. For example, after WWII, Japan went through a lot of turmoil, which spawned a lot of positive music during that specific time to restore vibrations distorted by history.

That is why Dr Masuro Emoto believed that music is a form of healing before it is an art.

Water and Words

Dr Masuro Emoto went on to discover that people whose energies were not in sync with the natural frequency of 7.83Hz (known as the Schuman Frequency) needed rebalancing. He used his findings from his water experiments, and created bespoke HADO water that his patients started to drink in order to heal themselves. Dr Masuro Emoto cured some 15,000 people.

But not everyone could be present in person, so they sent him pictures. Dr Masuro Emoto discovered that vibrational energy could be extracted from pictures too.

Then he decided to try people's names, and he learnt that he could use names too. Words in fact retained vibrational information so he exposed water to words and discovered that beautiful words, created beautiful crystals, and vice versa.

As they say, *'words breathe life'*, so be careful what you say, but say what you have to using intelligence and good spirituality.

The word angel	The word peace	The word spirit	The words you disgust me	The words you fool
Air on a G string by Bach	Imagine by John Lennon	Amazing Grace	Photo of dolphins	Photo of lotus

Figure 30: Water crystals from water exposed to different spoken words, The Hidden Messages in Water

Water and Thoughts

Dr Masuro Emoto went on to experiment even further.

He took two glasses of tap water. A group communicated by projecting positive thoughts in silence to the first glass of water, and said, *'Thank you, water, we love you.'* This created a beautiful crystal. Shortly after they insulted the second glass of water, saying, *'You fool.'* This created demonic looking water crystals.

Dr Masuro Emoto concluded that:

- Water is telling us it can act as a mirror.
- Water nurtures life on Earth.
- Water crystals carry a universal message.

Figure 31: Water crystal after prayer, The Hidden Messages in Water

Figure 32: Water crystal after feeling love and gratitude, The Hidden Messages in Water

Messages in Water

So what is the message?

I think we would all agree that it is important that the water around us produces beautiful crystals to indicate that the life force is energetic and vibrant, meaning healthy and happy.

It tells us what's important for the planet and its living creatures.

If we are all energy, and we can project our thoughts onto things as Dr Masuro Emoto has proved with his water crystallisation experiments, then that surely that is enough proof that our minds have the power to change things through conception and belief.

In Dr Masuro Emoto's own words:

> *'Absolutely, thought alone can change the body. Most people don't affect reality in a consistent, substantial way because they don't believe they can. They write an intention and they erase it because they think it's silly, and repeat the cycle. So, on a time average, it has a really small affect. Just boils down to the fact that they don't believe.'*

If you can accept with every ounce of your being that you can achieve your success goals, will it happen? Yes it will.

It's like positive thinking — but what this usually means is that you have a smear of positivity which conceals a whole mass of negative thinking. So thinking positively is not really thinking positively, it's just disguising the negative thinking that you have. You have to eradicate *all* negativity through to the core and build a positive foundation.

When we think of things, then we make reality more concrete than it is, and that's why we become stuck in the sameness of reality. We think that if reality is concrete, obviously we are insignificant. We cannot really change it.

But if reality is our possibility — possibility of consciousness itself — then we are immediately prompted to ask, 'how can we change it? How can we better it?'

Question
How can you Change the Way You Think from the OLD concrete reality-based way, to the NEW experiential consciousness way?
Take five minutes to make a list.

In essence, the answer is to FIND YOUR FLOW!

Find Your Flow

Question
How can you **Find Your Flow?** Take fifteen minutes to describe.

States of Flow

In conclusion, there are four psychological states, as follows:

Stage	Happiness	Vision	Cause & Effect	Resolution
1	No	No	Depression	Seek psychological help
2	Yes	No	Not growing or contributing	Create vision
3	No	Yes	Constantly stressed	Detatch happiness from goals. Do not tolerate stress/worry
4	Yes	Yes	Peak state; happy in the now; in flow	• Maintain peak state: • Maintain emotional control; • Stay happy in the now; and • Stay in flow (more important than productivity)

Table 8: Four psychological states of flow.

But a lot of people struggle to achieve FLOW.

Question
Why do you think you struggle to **Achieve Your FLOW?** Take five minutes to make a list.

In conclusion, people can sustain being 'happy in the now' internally for a short period of time before they start to doubt whether change is taking place externally. This usually results in a disappointed and frustrated reaction to the outside, which reinforces that you haven't changed, so why should the outside. That's the paradox.

It's like making jelly (or 'jello' for our American brothers and sisters). Let's say the set jelly is our 'desired goal', and the fridge is the 'universe' which is going to set the jelly (i.e. manifest our **'desired goal').**

If you place the hot liquid jelly mixture in the fridge and keep opening the door every five minutes, the jelly will not set.

In order for the jelly to set you have to trust the fridge to manifest the liquid and set it into the wobbly jelly which you so desire, and leave it to it for a few hours, and voila — you will get your end goal!

In other words, don't care what the outside looks like. Just decide what you're going to be, how you want to feel and what you want to experience.

Then BELIEVE.

And give the outside a chance to change time appropriately.

To understand flow, let's explore a couple of flow drills.

Flow Drill

Find a partner.

The first partner stands square and raises one arm to his side whilst making a strong fist.

The second partner pushes down on the first partner's arm at the wrist, and the arm should yield somewhat.

Now the first partner should imagine that a jet of water is flowing down from his mind, through his head, neck, shoulder, along his arm and out of his fingertips, aiming the water on a fixed point to his side like a laser beam.

The second partner now tries to push down on the first partner's arm at the wrist. Notice any difference?

Hubbad Flow Drill

Find a partner.

Both partners stand in a neutral fighting stance outside the fighting measure.

One person attacks the other on the chin with the straight lead, and the second person shallow slips and parries, carries, moves, traps and returns a straight lead.

The first person then repeats the process, and so on until you have flow in your counter movements.

And this brings us to the conclusion of the Be Like Water chapter.

The Secret of Success Unveiled

Exactly two hours later the little boy returned. The Wise One asked, *'And did you feel the cool texture of my floors, see the deep richness of my tapestries, inhale the powerful aromas from my gardens, taste the delicious fare prepared by my chefs and hear the sweet sounds of my musicians?'*

The little boy shook his head and said, *'No. No. I did none of these things. But look, I still have the two drops of oil on my spoon.'*

The Wise One paused for a moment. And then said, *'My son, never trust anyone whose house you do not know. Go back again. This time take all the time you need to appreciate all there is to be appreciated. This time use the powers of all your senses to notice the richness and glory that is around you. And then return once again, having noticed everything that is remarkable, with the spoon and the two drops of oil.'*

And so the little boy revisited the castle. When he returned four hours later, he was ecstatic. His whole body was lithe and fluid, his eyes shone, his gestures were broad and expansive.

Full of wonder and amazement, he spoke to the Wise One. *'Oh it's wonderful, all so wonderful. I saw the tapestries with their deep colours and fine details. I heard the rich and mellow strains of the musicians. I tried each and every one of the mouth-watering tastes in the kitchens. I smelled each of all the perfumes in the gardens and orchards; and I felt the cool smoothness of the mosaics on the soles of my feet. Everything here is completely wonderful.'*

'Yes, indeed it is,' said the Wise One. *'It is completely wonderful. But what has become, may I ask, of the drops of oil that were on your spoon?'*

And of course in his excitement the little boy had dropped the precious oil.

'The secret of success in life,' continued the Wise One, *'is really very simple. In order to absorb, understand and use the richness of the world that surrounds you, pay attention through every one of your five senses, for each is a priceless gift. Only then will you begin to notice how the whole world conspired to serve you in reaching whatever it is you want.*

And as you begin to discover how to move in the direction you desire, engaging with all the resources that surround you, you must equally learn to place your attention with care and flexibility. So, just as you notice how magnificent and wonderful the whole world is, you must equally never cease to pay attention to the drops of oil on your spoon.'

Conclusion

In this chapter we have explored the 'depths' of what water is, in order for us to *Be Like Water*, which has helped us to expand our understanding of it. We have discovered water has magical properties and behaviours that are still in their infancy of scientific understanding, but have led to some profound ways of thinking and some radical discoveries. We have a whole bunch of bonus materials showcasing some radical discoveries such as a car which runs on water and much more available on our website on **www.MartialMindPower.com/Resources**

Coming back to Bruce Lee... Bruce understood water, and discovered the importance of **going with the flow** as opposed to trying to resist external forces or force outcomes against such pressures, which allowed him to **adapt to any circumstance** until he overcame whatever adversity he was faced with.

Bruce also discovered that when emotionally stirred, that **calmness created clarity** to avoid making mistakes or avoid missing valuable once-in-a-lifetime opportunities.

Bruce Lee famously quoted this philosophy in what became known as 'The Lost Interview' on the Pierre Berton show in 1971. Bruce quoted:

'Be formless, shapeless, like water. You put water into a cup, it becomes the cup.
Put it into a teapot it becomes the teapot.
Now water can flow, or creep, or drip, or crash.
Be water, my friend.'

Do not stagnate; keep on growing, keep on achieving towards your personal liberation, self-actualisation and achieving your success goals.

To do this, start by directing your Martial Mind Power to whatever ends you desire. Remember, if your internal emotions and thoughts born in your mind can change the structure of water, it can change us and our external realities. After all, our bodies are approximately 70% water, and most importantly of all, our brains are 93% water. And since we only use 3% of our brain, our real selves lie in the subconscious undiscovered depths — in water.

So after all, there is a mountain of evidence that supports Dr Napoleon Hill's philosophy, *'What the mind can conceive and believe, it can achieve.'*

In this stage, we looked at:

- What is water? And amazing water facts.
- What are water's properties and behaviours?
- Related to water.
- Types of fluidity.
- Benefits of fluidity.
- The water principle, for fluidity in combat and life.
- Dr Masuro Emoto's water crystal experiments.
- How to find your flow and the states of flow.

And that brings us to the end of the **Be Like Water** stage of your self-mastery journey. Before you embark on **FLOWING TO SUCCESS**, please answer the following questions:

Questions

1. Do you understand how to **Be Adaptable** and cope with any situation better now? (Yes or No)
2. Do you understand how to **Overcome Obstacles** that stand in your way better now? (Yes or No)

3. Do you feel an improved sense of **Calmness and Clarity**? (Yes or No)
4. Do you understand how to create a sense of **Vision and Happiness**? (Yes or No)
5. Are you more **Confident** you can achieve whatever ends you desire? (Yes or No)
6. Do you understand how to **Find Your Flow**? (Yes or No)
7. Are you ready to **Flow to Success**? (Yes or No)

My friend, I would like to deeply thank you for giving me the chance to take you through this Master Your Life journey, and remember:

'BE LIKE WATER and

FLOW TO SUCCESS!'

8

Power side forward

Power Side Forwards

STAGE 8 — BROWN BELT

Master Your Visions

What's the Problem?

So, who are we trying to help in this **Power Side Forwards** stage of your self-mastery journey?

- People whose lives are imbalanced and need improvement.
- People who do not know their strengths and weaknesses.
- People who do not know if they're coming or going, and keep making the same mistakes.
- People who do not know what their purpose or mission is on this planet.
- People who are looking for their own success formula.

Objective

Outcome & Results Question
What outcome(s) and result(s) do you expect to get when you start to use your **Power Side Forwards**?

Take ten minutes to make a list of all the positive changes you would like to see, hear and feel.

Incredible change happens in your life when you decide to take control of what you do have power over, instead of craving control over what you don't.

Examples Question
Can you think of any examples when you have craved control over something you do not have any power over? How did it cause you to feel? What was the outcome?

Take ten minutes to make a list.

Do you sometimes find yourself:

- Feeling frustrated and angry?
- Feeling imbalanced in your life — working too hard, enjoying yourself too little?
- Not knowing your strengths (and weaknesses, for that matter)?

- Feeling like you do not know if you're coming or going?
- Repeating the same mistakes?
- Being unable not see your purpose, mission, or definite chief aim in this life on this planet?
- Wondering what you were put on earth to do?
- Trying to find a success formula, but failing?

If you have answered 'yes' to any of the above, then you're in for an POWERFUL EXPERIENCE.

Power Side Forwards is based on the following Bruce Lee philosophy:

'The leading straight punch is the backbone of all punching in Jeet Kune Do. It is used both as an offensive and defensive weapon to "stop" and "intercept" an opponent's complex attack at a moment's notice.

When you are standing right foot forward, your right punch and right leg become the main offensive weapons because of their advanced position. With your right foot forward, your right hand is much closer to your opponent than your left. The reverse is true for the left foot forward stance.

When fighting, keep your strongest side up front.'

I call this POWER SIDE FORWARDS.

It is also inspired by Sharon L. Lechter, Greg S. Reid with The Napoleon Hill Foundation book called *Three Feet From Gold.* Check out www.NapHill.org for more information.

Power Side Forwards will help you to:

Belt	Pillars of Luck	Chapter	Success Goals
8. Brown	Prosperity purpose passion	**'Power side forwards'** Master your visions	• Understand what power side forwards means • Accept and recognise areas of your life that need improvement to create harmony and balance in all areas of your life • Find your passion so you can love what you do, do what you love • Create a burning desire • Understand and calibrate your strengths and weaknesses • Identify how to use what you got to your maximum advantage by putting your strengths forward • Discover your definite major purpose in life • Create a vision • Identify creative opportunities • Power forwards to success!

This stage is broken down into six key substages as follows:

1. The Race Begins.
2. Power Side Forwards.
3. Yin and Yang.

4. Success Formula.
5. Definite Chief Aim.
6. And the Winner Is…

Now you can POWER FORWARDS TO SUCCESS!

Warm Up

Let's jump right in and start warming up by answering the following questions:

Question
Do you know what **Power Side Forwards** means? (Yes or No)

If 'no', then would you like to learn? (Yes or No)

Question
Do you know what the **Tao of Life** is? (Yes or No)

If 'no', then would you like to learn (Yes or No)

Question
Do you know all **eight key areas of your life**? (Yes or No)

If 'yes', then take five minutes to make a list.

The eight generic areas of your life include:

1. Physical.
2. Mental.
3. Spiritual.
4. Financial.
5. Social.
6. Career/vocation.
7. Family and friends.
8. Romance.

Question
Which areas of your life would you like to **Improve**? Take five minutes to make a list.

Question
List all your **Strengths** and weaknesses? Take five minutes to make two separate lists.

Question
Would you like to learn how to **Use What You've Got** to your maximum advantage? (Yes or No)

Question
What do you think **Success Formula** means? Take five minutes to describe.

Question
Would you like to **Discover Your Success Formula**? (Yes or No)

Question
Would you like to **Discover Your Major Purpose** in life? (Yes or No)

If you do not know the answer to any of the questions above and are eager to learn, or answered 'yes' to the last question, then you're in the right place, so let's POWER ON!

The Race Begins

You may have seen it on TV, or heard about it on the radio, or read about it in the newspaper, but recently the Annual World Logging Championship was held in British Columbia. The two finalists were Canadian and a Norwegian.

Their task was straightforward. Each had a sector of the forest. Whoever could fell the most timber between eight o'clock in the morning and four o'clock in the afternoon would be the winner.

At eight o'clock sharp, the whistle blew and the two lumberjacks set to with attitude. It seemed that they chopped stroke for stroke until, at eight-fifty, the Canadian heard the Norwegian stop. Sensing his chance, the Canadian redoubled his efforts.

At nine o'clock the Canadian heard the Norwegian start chopping again. Once more, it seemed as if they chopped stroke for stroke until, at nine-fifty, the Canadian heard the Norwegian stop. Again the Canadian continued, determined to make the most of his opponent's weaknesses.

At the stroke of ten o'clock, the Norwegian began cutting again — until ten-fifty, when he paused once more. With a growing sense of confidence, the Canadian sensed victory, and continued in his steady rhythm.

And so it went on throughout the whole day.

Power Side Forwards

In this section, I am going to lay down the big idea behind the meaning of Power Side Forwards from Bruce Lee's Kung Fu standpoint. Later in this chapter, we are going to take these ideas, and apply them to our lives.

The Big Idea

The big idea behind Bruce Lee's Power Side Forwards principle is to encourage Jeet Kune Do practitioners to develop devastating primary weapons such as the Straight Lead and Shin Knee Kick (i.e. stop-hits) for stealth, speed, accuracy and power, so that they can be used effectively in combat to incapacitate your opponent within fifteen seconds or less. This idea was developed over the classical martial arts which tend to have a longer development period to achieve the same result.

The 80:20 Rule

As a rule of thumb, Bruce Lee talked about fighting Power Side Forwards 80% of the time, as opposed to 20% on the weaker side. The Power Side is synonymous with the hand you write with, for example if you are right-handed then you would adopt a fighting stance ('*Bay Jong*' in Cantonese) with your right-leg forward (south-paw stance) or vice versa (orthodox stance).

Figure 33: Lak Loi is right-handed, hence his Power Side Forwards is with his right leg and right hand forwards.

Question

Get into a fighting stance with your Power Side Forwards.

Take five minutes to get used to the feeling of putting your Power Side Forwards.

Philosophy

Bruce Lee's philosophy behind Power Side Forwards implies that if you train your weaker side, then it may become stronger, but not necessarily as proficient as the Power Side due to your dominant side of the brain overpowering the weaker side. This neurological process is known as Hemispheric Dominance.

Therefore training the weaker side merely makes the weak side less weak, but it's still weaker nonetheless. To gain a competitive advantage in combat, it seems essential to Develop Your Power Side First.

Figure 34: Left-handed people have a dominant right-brain.

Statistics

Approximately 85% of the world's population is right-handed, which implies that the left side of their brain is the more dominant — usually referred to as left-brained (or right-brained for left-handed people). Therefore, this is the side of the brain which can be developed the quickest (and vice versa for left-handed people).

Things get a little trickier when we start to deal with ambidextrous people who are proficient on both their left- and right-sides because they have better neurological messaging between the two hemispheres. As a general rule of thumb, I would recommend that they try training on both sides, and develop the side which they feel most comfortable with as a starting point.

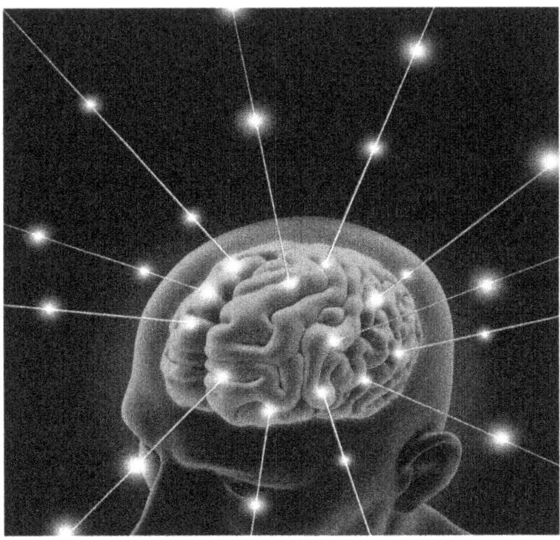

Figure 35: Ambidextrous people have active left and right brain hemispheres.

Train on Both Sides

This is a common question, and is best answered by example. Let's say it takes six months to develop a straight lead on your power side, which can be used effectively in combat, having trained twice per week for an hour during each session.

If we then go and split the training session into two halves focusing on developing straight leads on both your Power Side and weaker side, then we effectively half the time trained on each side every training session. On that basis, it will take at least twice as long, i.e. twelve months, to cultivate straight leads that are effective on both your Power Side and weaker side which can both be effectively used in combat. In the meantime, you do not have any effective weapons on either side.

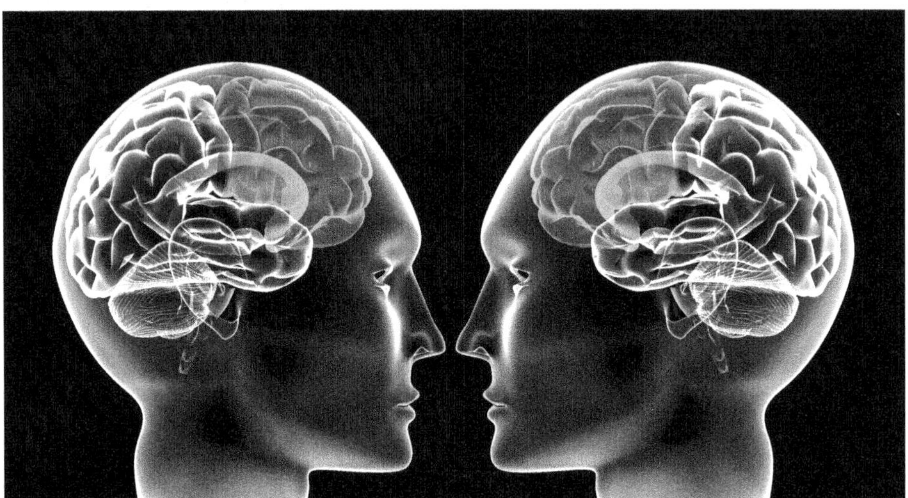

Figure 36: Ultimately train on both sides to develop your left and right brain hemispheres.

Train the Weaker Side

As a rule of thumb, I would recommend beginners to develop weapons on their Power Side so that they have some arsenal that they could use effectively in combat in a shorter space of time. Once you become proficient on your power side, then you should start developing weapons on your weaker side.

The Best Side

In the context of street-fighting, there are many environmental variables that dictate how you will fight. For example:

- What's the surface like?
- How much space have you got?
- How many people are you fighting?

These environmental variables will dictate how you will fight for effectiveness and could potentially change your structure to adapt for composure during combat. For example, have you ever tried to push step (or forward lunge) on an icy pavement? It is instinctive to want to lower your centre of gravity, centralise and spread your weight evenly across both feet and naturally place them more laterally, and adopt a wider but lower stance which is more stable. In this circumstance, your Power Side Forwards technique adapts and changes. What matters is that you just hit your foe in order to incapacitate them before they harm you, so there may be times when using the **Power Side Forwards** has to adapt and change.

Training Methods

In order to train martial arts techniques which you are trying to develop for effectiveness in combat application, start with your Power Side Forwards as we have been discussing. As an example let's say your Power Side is your right. On this basis you should train against your partner as follows:

- Right vs. right
- Right vs. left

Once you have become proficient training on your Power Side, then you should start developing your Weaker Side as follows:

- Left vs. left
- Left vs. right

Try not to just train right vs. right, as this is not realistic and will limit your combative experience and expression. You should train in this way to develop well-rounded vocabulary of responses for any given martial arts technique.

Summary

In summary, **Power Side Forwards** is a principle to help you develop your primary weapons, the straight lead and shin knee kicks (i.e. stop-hits). You may not always have your **Power Side Forwards**, but at least when you do you know how to use your weapons effectively in combat with stealth, speed, accuracy and power.

When you don't, then you must adapt and **JUST HIT**, using the longest weapon to the nearest target with economy of motion for a speedy attack.

I would like to summarise **Power Side Forwards** in Bruce Lee's own words:

'Using no way as way.'

This means, do not presuppose a way. Be in the moment. Be present. Be open to the best way to meet the moment in which you find yourself, rather than planning beforehand what way will be best.

The core teachings from the **Power Side Forwards** principle therefore are as follows:

1. To develop useful tools quickly and effectively.
2. To use your Power Side 80% and weaker side 20% of the time.
3. To develop your Power Side first so you have effective tools available for your utilisation (then to develop the weaker side tools).
4. To develop tactics and strategies to develop your tools effectively on the Power Side then the weaker side.
5. To practice using your tools on the Power Side and then the weaker side.

We will be revisiting these core teachings later in this chapter.

Yin and Yang

To understand the Tao of Life, let's take a look at Yin and Yang.

The idea of Yin and Yang comes from Chinese philosophy, which is an integral part of Taoism, Ch'an (Zen) Buddhism, and the I Ching. The philosophy behind Yin and Yang describes the natural order of the universe.

It is a common misconception in the western world that Yin and Yang represent a dualistic view of the world, such as:

- Black and white.
- Good and bad.
- Light and dark.
- Gentleness and firmness.
- Hot and cold.
- Life and death.
- Male and female.
- Active and passive.
- Strength and weakness.
- Cause and effect.
- Fire and water.
- Sun and moon.
- And so on.

However, Yin and Yang actually represents a monistic view, one which is complementary, interconnected, and interdependent. For example, 'darkness is the absence of light' and 'silence is the absence of sound.'

Yin and Yang therefore represent a dynamic relationship of an indivisible whole, in which the whole is greater than the sum of the assembled parts. For example, 'a shadow cannot exist without light' and 'an echo cannot exist without sound.'

Bruce Lee stated:

> *'So neither gentleness nor firmness holds any more than half of a broken whole, which, fitted together, forms the true Way of Gung Fu. Gentleness/firmness is one inseparable force of one unceasing interplay of movement. They are conceived of as essentiality one, or as two coexistent forces of one indivisible whole.'*

Now that you understand the true essence of Yin and Yang, you can start to manage it by perceiving Yin and Yang as equal and opposite energies of an indivisible whole.

For example, let's say you get into a heated argument. If the situation is managed poorly, then you may respond to aggression, i.e. Yin, with agitation, frustration and even anger which is also Yin, and the whole situation will become imbalanced and escalate due to compounding energies.

To re-balance the Yin and Yang, you could stay silent and be calming to introduce Yang energy to alter the state of the whole to lower the Yin energy, and restore balance and harmony to the situation.

This is what Lao Tzu depicts in *Tao Te King*:

'Tao engenders one,

One engenders two,

Two engenders three,
Three engenders all things.
All things carry the yin
while embrace the yang.
Neutralising energy brings them into harmony.'

In this case the Tao is one. The heated argument and silence are the two opposing Yin and Yang energies in the equation, which refer to two. And the way they interact to create a new outcome is three. The outcome, is therefore the result of the two energies neutralising, restoring balance within the Yin and Yang formula, therefore maintaining harmony and happiness.

In life, our ultimate goal is to apply this philosophy of Yin and Yang energy management, to create balance and maintain a constant state of harmony and happiness.

The Yin and Yang Symbol

Figure 37: *Yin and Yang Symbol, known as Taijiti.*

The Yin and Yang symbol shown above is also known as the Taijiti, which literally means 'Ultimate Potential'.

The circular symbol is comprised of two colours, where black represents Yin and white represents Yang.

The roundedness of the two 'fishlike' halves, seemingly 'flowing in motion' shows a continual interplay of the two halves of a complimentary, interconnected, interdependent parts of an indivisible whole.

In each half, there is a dot of the opposite energy, symbolising that Yin is rooted in the Yang, and that Yang is rooted in the Yin, inseparable, opposing, yet complimentary and interchangeable to create a new relational state.

The challenge for us in life is to balance the Yin and Yang in everything we do, to find harmony. As Lao Tsu describes:

'The Sage who is
Forthright but not hurting;
Sharp but not wounding,
Candid but not being crude;
Shining but not dazzling.'

The Law of Harmony / The Bamboo Principle

The application of the principles of Yin and Yang in Gung Fu are expressed as the 'Law of Harmony', also known as 'The Bamboo Principle'.

The Law of Harmony states that one should be in harmony with, not in rebellion against, the force of the opposition. This means that one should do nothing that is not natural or spontaneous: the important thing is not to strain in any way.

As Bruce Lee said:

> *'So neither gentleness nor firmness holds any more than one half of a broken whole which, welded together, forms the true way of martial art. The tendency to guard against is from getting too firm and stiff. Notice that the stiffest tree is most easily cracked, while the bamboo or willow survives by bending with the wind. This is why a gung fu man is soft yet not yielding, firm, yet not hard. The best example of gung fu is water. Water can penetrate the hardest granite because it is yielding. One cannot stab or strike at water and hurt it because **that which offers no resistance cannot be overcome.'***

To learn more about water, please attend the **'Be Like Water'** Martial Mind Power Experience.

From a combative standpoint, Bruce Lee went on to say:

> *'When the opponent expands, I contract.*
> *When he contracts, I expand.'*

The Tao of Life

The idea behind the Tao of Life, or the Way of Life, is to maintain harmony and happiness by balancing the Yin and Yang energies in all aspects of your life.

To do that, the Tao of Life methodology allows you to take an eagle eye perspective of your life by evaluating the balance of your life currently, in order to identify areas that need attention so that you can rebalance your life to create the future you want today. The *Tao of Life* diagram shown below provides a visual snapshot and tool for your current and ideal future life. The next section explains step-by-step how to use the Tao of Life to achieve your end desires.

Question

Take five minutes to list up to eight key areas of your life. As a guideline, I have provided eight generic areas of life below:

1. Physical.
2. Mental.
3. Spiritual.
4. Financial.
5. Social/hobbies.
6. Career/vocation.
7. Family and Friends.
8. Romance.

How to Use the Tao of Life

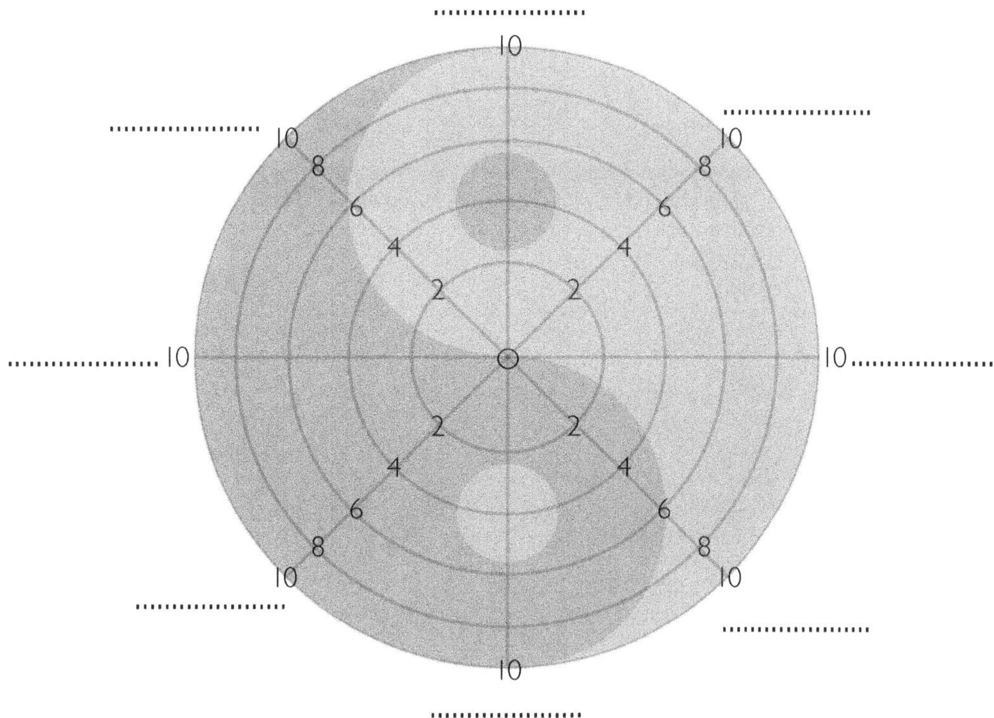

Figure 38: The Tao of Life

1. Print Tao of Life

   Start by printing or drawing the Tao of Life diagram as shown above.

2. Genius Storm Areas of Your Life

   Genius storm up to eight different dimensions which are important in your life. You can use one of the following methods:

   - Key areas of your life: physical, mental, spiritual, financial, social/hobbies, career/vocation, family and friends, and romance.
   - Roles you play in your life: brother/sister, husband/wife, father/mother, friend, colleague, team player, etc.
   - Important things in your life: financial freedom, freedom of speech, artistic expression, contribution, growth, love, environment, etc.

3. Write Down the Tao of Life

   On each spoke of the Tao of Life, write down each area you identified in the step above.

4. Analyse Each Dimension

   The big idea is that if you find the right balance of attention in each dimension you identified in your life, then you will also find fulfilment and gratification in them. In this step, analyse the amount of attention you're paying to each dimension, and mark a dot on the corresponding spoke on a scale from one (lowest) to ten (highest).

5. Join the Dots

   As they say in dot-to-dot, join the dots to see the bigger picture. Where the wheel kinks, you will be able to clearly see areas of your life where you need to give more attention to re-balance your life.

6. Visualise Your Ideal Life

   Now start to visualise your ideal life in all the dimensions you identified, and start thinking if the score you gave should stay the same, lower or higher. As before, draw the dots for your ideal life on the Tao of Life using a different colour so you can differentiate between the current and ideal future states.

7. Act Now!

   The big idea now is to identify the gaps between your current and ideal future life states, and figure out what you need to do to bridge the gap by either:

   - Increasing attention in a dimension of your life because there's currently not enough attention in it.
   - Decrease attention in a dimension of your life because there is currently too much time spent in it, which is sapping energy and enthusiasm from other areas of your life.

Once you have a clear idea of the gaps and how to bridge them, write down a list of simple actions that you need to take to achieve the ideal future state to restore the balance in your Tao of Life, using the following as a guideline:

- Increase attention: what extra things do you need to start doing now?
- Decrease attention: what things do you need to re-prioritise, delegate to someone else, or stop doing all together?

Finally, DO IT NOW!

As Bruce Lee said:

'Knowing is not enough,
one must apply.
Willing is not enough,
one must DO!*'*

Success Formula

We are now going to look at your Success Formula, whose equation looks like this:

$$S = ((P + T) \times A_1 + A_2) + F$$

In the following steps, we are going to unravel each variable in this equation one-by-one, to help you discover your personal Success Formula.

'S' stands for Success Formula. This is the process we are going to go through now to help you discover your personal Success Formula. Before we start, take a piece of paper and lay it out in a landscape orientation. Mark out five columns of equal width with a title row as shown below.

Table 9: The Success Formula planner.

'P' stands for Passion. At the top of the first column, put the title 'Passion'.

These are the things that you are passionate about. The things that make your heart sing. The things that fill you with joy and happiness. The things that make you feel like a child, delirious with excitement. The things that make you want to stay up late and wake up early.

For this step, list up to ten passions in order of priority, listing the most intense passions at the top of the list.

Passion
1.
2.
3.
4.
5.
6.
7.
8.
9.
10.

Table 10: The Success Formula — list of passions.

'T' stands for Talent. At the top of the second column, put the title 'Talent'.

These are the things that you excel in. The things that you are naturally good at doing. The things that you have invested time, effort, money and energy becoming an expert in. These are the things you have experience doing. These are things you find fun and easy to do. These are the things you have a natural flair for.

You Have It or You Don't. A king was watching a great magician perform his act. The crowd were enthralled and so was the king. At the end the audience roared with approval. And the king said, *'What a gift this man has. A God-given talent.'*

But a wise counsellor said to the king, *'My Lord, genius is made, not born. This magician's skill is the result of discipline and practice. These talents have been learned and honed over time with determination and discipline.'*

The king was troubled by this message. The counsellor's challenge had spoiled his pleasure in the magician's art. *'Limited and spiteful swine. How dare you criticise true genius. As I said, you either have it or you don't. And you most certainly don't.'*

The king turned to his bodyguard and said, *'Throw this man into the deepest dungeon. And,'* he added, for the counsellor's benefit, *'so you won't be lonely you can have two of your kind to keep you company. You shall have two piglets as cellmates.'*

From the very first day of his imprisonment, the wise counsellor practised running up the steps of his cell to the prison door carrying in each hand a piglet. As the days turned into weeks, and the weeks into months, the piglets steadily grew into sturdy wild boars. And with every day of practice the wise counsellor increased his power and strength.

One day the king remembered the wise counsellor and was curious to see how imprisonment had humbled him. He had the wise counsellor summoned.

When the prisoner appeared, a man of powerful physique, carrying a wild boar in each arm, the king exclaimed, *'What a gift this man has. A God-given talent.'*

The wise counsellor replied, *'My Lord, genius is made, not born. My skill is the result of discipline and practice. These talents have been learned and honed over time with determination and discipline.'*

Your next task is to list up to ten talents, in order of priority, listing your best talents at the top of the list.

Talent
1.
2.
3.
4.
5.
6.
7.
8.
9.
10.

Table 11: *The Success Formula — list of talents.*

'A1' stands for Association. At the top of the third column, put the title 'Association'.

These are successful people and organisations that are already in the space you aspire to be in. These are the people that are already established. These are the people that have already achieved the goals you seek. These are people you can elicit expert council from. These are the organisations that can endorse and certify you. These are the people and organisations that can support you in your goals.

These are the people that can help point you in the right direction. These are the people that can edify you. These are the people you want to associate with.

Your next task is to list up to ten associates, in order of priority, listing the most important associates at the top of the list.

Association
1.
2.
3.
4.
5.
6.
7.
8.
9.
10.

Table 12: The Success Formula — list of associations.

Now that you have identified the people and organisations you want to be associated with, just put a little '+' sign next to the associate name if they are currently not in your life, to indicate you need to add them.

On the flip side, make a note of all the people that are in your life, but did not make your associate list. This may be an indicator that you may need to leave some people behind as you POWER FORWARDS towards your SUCCESS!

Transmutate Your Learnings. To identify your personal Success Formula and major purpose in life, simply and easily let the following happen now:

1. Lay out your Success Formula in front of you, so you can **see your success in the first three columns.**
2. Imagine you are a majestic golden eagle **sitting comfortably on top** of the paper in front of you.
3. You **decide to take off now,** flying high above the lists whilst maintaining a crystal clear eagle-eye view of your Success Formula.
4. You start to **see the bigger picture from above.**
5. As you continue to look at the Success Formula, you will start to **transmutate the relationships between your passions, talents and associations.**
6. As you soar high above, you will **start to see your major purpose in life.**
7. When you **get the insights and learnings from your Success Formula,** review the Success Formula variables to ensure that they accurately reflect your new findings. For example, you may realise that you need to acquire some additional talent for which you will need to take adjust your talent variable list, and add an **Action** (the next step) to obtain that talent by writing it in to the actions variable list.

'A2' stands for Action. At the top of the fourth column, put the title 'Action'.

These are simply the definitive steps you need to take to achieve the success goals you just identified.

Your next task is to list up to ten actions, in order of priority, listing the most important action at the top of the list. To be more precise, you could also note a deadline for when you want to have successfully completed that action.

Action
1.
2.
3.
4.
5.
6.
7.
8.
9.
10.

Table 13: The Success Formula — list of actions.

'F' stands for Faith. At the top of the fifth column, put the title 'Faith'.

The Staircase. Remember the time when you walked into a new building and had to climb the stairs to get to the floor you had to meet someone on? Being unfamiliar with the building and what lay at the top of the staircase, you decided to **take one step at a time** until you finally **climbed to the top**.

Bruce Lee also quoted Dr Napoleon Hill:

'If you ***think*** *you are beaten, you are,*
If you ***think*** *you dare not, you don't*
If you like to win, but you ***think*** *you can't*
It is almost certain you won't.

If you ***think*** *you'll lose, you're lost*
For out of the world we find,
Success begins with a fellow's will —
It's all in the ***state of mind****.*

If you ***think*** *you're outclassed, you are,*
You've got to ***think*** *high to rise,*
You've got to be ***sure of yourself*** *before*
You can ever win a prize.

Life's battles don't always go
To the stronger or faster man,
But sooner or later the man who wins
Is the man ***who thinks he can****.'*

Faith therefore is your unwavering belief in yourself, that you can **achieve your success goals.** Faith binds all the other variables of the Success Formula together, to allow you to **focus your energy towards your definite success goals,** allowing you to apply energy so you can **manifest your success goals.** As they say:

'Where your focus goes, energy flows -
and it will expand.'

In the final task, list up to ten things that you can do to **keep the faith** and maintain absolute self-belief towards achieving your success goals, listing the strongest beliefs that need enforcing at the top of the list.

Faith
1.
2.
3.
4.
5.
6.
7.
8.
9.
10.

Table 14: *The Success Formula — list of faith or beliefs.*

In summary, **the Success Formula** reads:

Success Formula = ((Passion + Talent) x Association + Action) + Faith

Sharon Lechter, one of the creators of the Success Formula in *Three Feet from Gold* states...

'All experts and successful people have tremendous faith.
That if they found their passion, applied their talent and took action with the right association,
eventually good things would come to pass.'

You already **have the passion, talent and ability** to create great success in your life. **Surround yourself with the right people** and **take massive action,** with a heap of **faith,** with a directed focus and energy you will expand your bliss.

Your personal Success Formula and major purpose in life lies within the lists of variables you have just created.

Definite Chief Aim

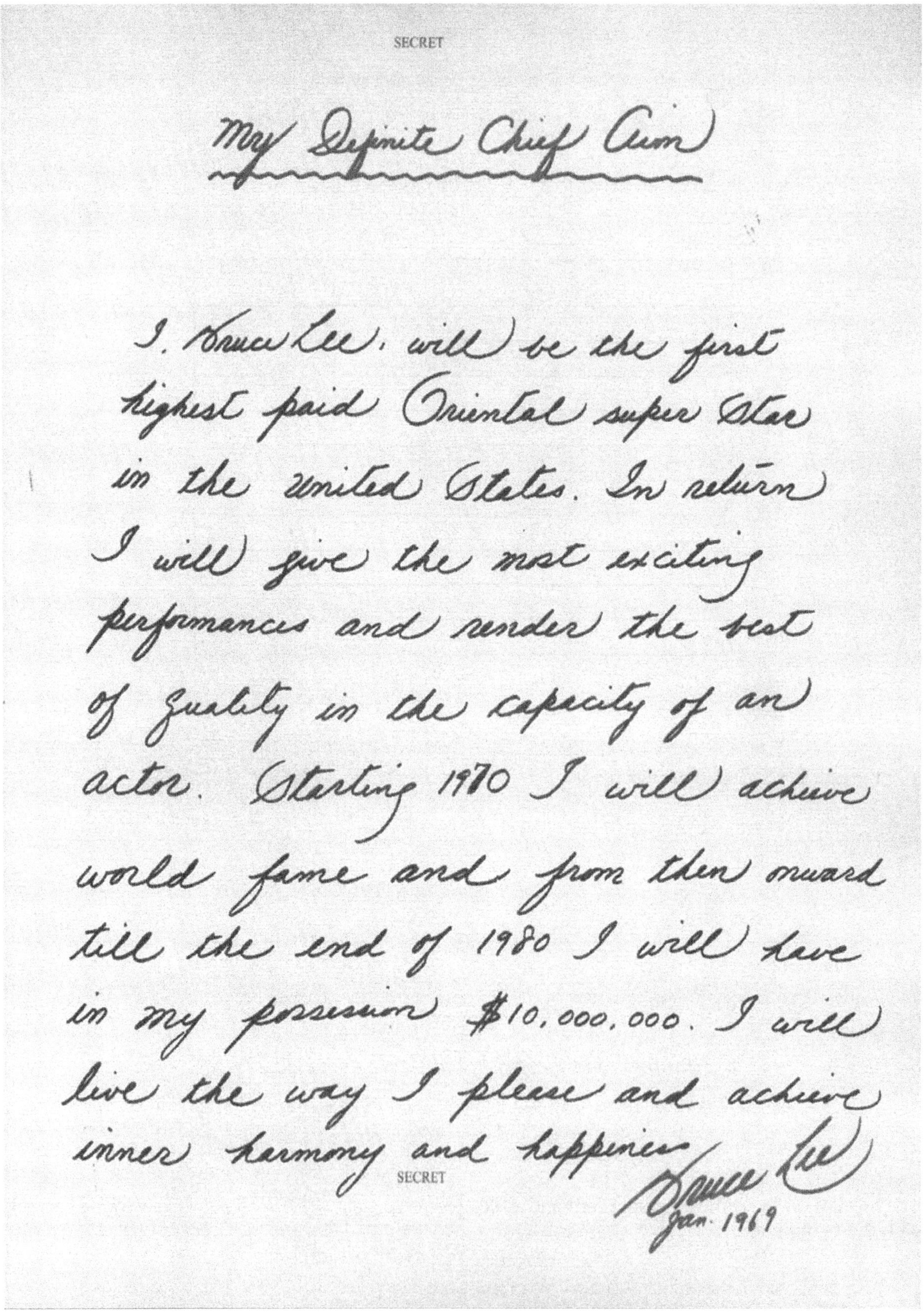

SECRET

My Definite Chief Aim

I, Bruce Lee, will be the first highest paid Oriental super Star in the United States. In return I will give the most exciting performances and render the best of quality in the capacity of an actor. Starting 1970 I will achieve world fame and from then onward till the end of 1980 I will have in my possession $10,000,000. I will live the way I please and achieve inner harmony and happiness

Bruce Lee
Jan. 1969

SECRET

Figure 39: Bruce Lee's Definite Chief Aim.
Bruce Lee Foundation

Bruce Lee studied profound philosophers, both past and present. One such philosopher was Dr Napoleon Hill (26th Oct 1883 — 8th Nov 1970), who wrote the bestseller book *Think and Grow Rich.*

He presented the idea of a 'Definite Major Purpose' or 'Definite Chief Aim' as a challenge to his readers in order to make them ask themselves, *'In what do I truly believe?'* According to Hill, ninety-eight percent of people had few or no firm beliefs, and this alone put true success firmly out of their reach.

Bruce wrote the following 'Definite Chief Aim' — at which time Bruce would have been twenty-eight years of age and a minor TV star in the United States, having featured in a number of shows which included, most notably, the ill-fated Green Hornet series. With his second child recently born and no financial security to speak of, the clearly determined founder of Jeet Kune Do decided to put his 'Definite Chief Aim' down on paper:

> *'I, Bruce Lee, will be the first highest paid Oriental superstar in the United States. In return I will give the most exciting performances and render the best of quality in the capacity of an actor. Starting 1970 I will achieve world fame and from then onward till the end of 1980 I will have in my possession $10,000,000. I will live the way I please and achieve inner harmony and happiness. '*

The rest is history.

My Verdict

I would like to breakdown Bruce Lee's Definite Chief Aim and analyse it piece-by-piece as follows:

'I, Bruce Lee, will be the first highest paid Oriental superstar in the United States.'

Enter the Dragon grossed over $25 million in the US alone, and Bruce Lee was the first major oriental actor to make it onto the big screen in the USA. On that basis it's probably safe to assume that Bruce Lee was the first highest paid Oriental superstar in the United States.

'In return I will give the most exciting performances and render the best of quality in the capacity of an actor.'

Bruce Lee's exciting performances are revered today as the pinnacle of martial artistry, often copied but never equalled, as Bruce's legend and martial art Jeet Kune Do continues to inspire millions worldwide, including Tyson, Quentin Tarantino, The Wu Tang Clan, and many more.

'Starting 1970 I will achieve world fame…'

Bruce Lee died on 20th July 1973 at the young age of thirty-two, two weeks before the release of his blockbuster movie *Enter the Dragon.* After Bruce's death, *Enter the Dragon* catapulted him into superstardom, not only in the USA, but worldwide.

'…and from then onward till the end of 1980 I will have in my possession $10,000,000.'

As mentioned above, *Enter the Dragon* grossed $25 million in the US alone. Today the Bruce Lee Estate continues to make $7 million per year (according to www.Suggest.com, August 2014).

'I will live the way I please and achieve inner harmony and happiness.'

As for inner peace and harmony, before his untimely passing Bruce had mentioned to his wife Linda that he felt unhappy and trapped by the fame. I personally feel that Bruce's fame bought him physical, mental and spiritual unrest on Earth and, chillingly, I feel that his passing dealt him the 'inner harmony and happiness' that he longed for, but in another realm.

As they say, *'Be careful what you wish for!'* On the same token, *'If you don't ask, you don't get.'* In the next section, we are going to look at exploring your truest potential by taking your power sides as identified in the Tao of Life and your Success Formula, and put it in your own Definite Chief Aim so you can move forwards towards your own success.

To find out more about Dr Napoleon Hill read his most famous book called *Think and Grow Rich*, and visit www.NapHill.org

Create Your Own Definite Chief Aim

To define your own Definite Chief Aim, follow the seven practical steps to your success below:

1. Set a **definite amount of money** you desire in your mind. Bruce Lee stated that he would have $10,000,000 in his possession. 'To be rich and wealthy' or 'to achieve financial freedom' are not sufficient, so be precise with the exact amount of money you so desire.
2. Determine **what definite service(s) and/or product(s)** you are going to give in return for the money or payment you receive. Bruce Lee stated that he would 'give the most exciting performances and render the best of quality in the capacity of an actor'.
3. Establish a **definite date by when you intend to acquire the money.**
4. **Develop a definite plan** to achieve your desire, and **act now.**
5. **Write down your Definite Chief Aim** like your personal mission statement, as follows:
    - Exact amount of money you desire.
    - Describe what service(s) and/or product(s) you are going to give in return for the money or payment.
    - Define when you intend to acquire the money.
    - Describe your plan clearly.
6. **Read your Definite Chief Aim** twice a day, first thing in the morning when you wake up, and last thing before going to sleep.
7. **Create a 'burning desire' to achieve your Definite Chief Aim** and **'act as if' you already have it** (without spending it before you've actually taken possession of it, of course).

Andrew Carnegie, the steel magnate who yielded a fortune of over $100 million dollars, and Thomas A. Edison, famous for inventing the light-bulb amongst 1,093 US patents, both abided by these principles to help them achieve their own successes and accumulate a fortune.

To do this, you must open your mind to the possibility of consciousness to allow yourself to become a practical dreamer. To learn how to do that, then attend the 'Empty Your Teacup' Martial Mind Power workshop.

Remember, the same amount of effort is required to dream a big life full of abundance and prosperity, as it is to accept poverty and misery. A great poet called Jessie B. Rittenhouse once wrote these powerful words of universal truth:

I bargained with Life for a penny,
And Life would pay no more,
However I begged at evening
When I counted my scanty store.

For Life is just an employer;
He gives you what you ask,
But once you have set the wages,
Why, you must bear the task.

I worked for a menial's hire,
Only to learn, dismayed,
That any wage I had asked of Life,
Life would have willingly paid.

If you would like further information on setting goals, then please read on to refine your Definite Chief Aim.

Goal Setting

Before we start, I'd like you to perform a quick sanity check, to ensure that your goal is in fact a goal and not a state. These are easily confused and if you are not sure what the difference is, then you can think of a 'state' as being something that is ambiguously expressed such as:

- Something you can have right now, such as, 'I want to be happy'. If you attended the **'Honestly Express Yourself'** Martial Mind Power Experience, we looked at several techniques and methods that you can use to change your state to a more resourceful one immediately.
- Something that is infinite, such as, 'I want to be wealthy'. The question is, 'How much wealth do you desire exactly?'… £1,000? £10,000? £100,000? £1,000,000? … £1,000,000,000?
- Something that is expressed for yourself and others, such as, 'I want world peace'. The truth of the matter is, you cannot change others, rather you can only change yourself, and by being peaceful you start the process of creating a more peaceful world and leading by example.
- A state that can be accessed, such as, 'I want peace and harmony', which can be elicited at any time, and accessed using anchors such as a meditation audio (audible anchor) or relaxing on the beach (spatial anchor).
- Something that does not require any steps to achieve, such as, 'I am grateful for being alive'. If you're reading this, then you're very much alive and there is nothing else to do.

On the other hand, a 'goal' or a 'well-formed outcome' is something that is specifically expressed like your own Definite Chief Aim. As an example, let's have another look at Bruce Lee's Definite Chief Aim:

> *'I, Bruce Lee, will be the first highest paid Oriental superstar in the United States. In return I will give the most exciting performances and render the best of quality in the capacity of an actor. Starting 1970 I will achieve world fame and from then onward till the end of 1980 I will have in my possession $10,000,000. I will live the way I please and achieve inner harmony and happiness.'*

A goal or a well-formed outcome is something that is specifically expressed. I'll use Bruce Lee's Definite Chief Aim as an example to illustrate this as follows:

- Something that takes time to accomplish, for example Bruce wrote his Definite Chief Aim in 1969, and he stated '*Starting 1970 I will achieve world fame and from then onward till the end of 1980 I will have in my possession $10,000,000*'.
- Something that is measurable, for example Bruce stated he wanted to be in possession of $10,000,000 by 1980, a measurable target by 1980.
- Something that is expressed for oneself only. Bruce Lee's Definite Chief Aim is written in the first context only, i.e. for himself only.
- Something that has clearly defined goals, or what I call 'well-formed outcomes', such as: '*first highest paid Oriental superstar in the United States*'; '*I will give the most exciting performances and render the best of quality in the capacity of an actor*'; '*Starting 1970 I will achieve world fame*'; '*till the end of 1980 I will have in my possession $10,000,000*'.
- Something you have to take definitive steps towards if you are to achieve your goal or Definite Chief Aim. Bruce clearly quoted what he was going to do in return… '*I will give the most exciting performances and render the best of quality in the capacity of an actor*'.

I can confidently say that Bruce Lee did achieve his Definite Chief Aim.

Question
Now take your Definite Chief Aim or other success goal and check it against the table shown below. If your success goal is in fact a state, then pick another success goal or go through the **'Power Side Forwards'** chapter again to determine your Definite Chief Aim now to clearly understand your well-formed outcomes.

State	Goal or Well-Formed Outcome
Ambiguously expressed (e.g. I want to be happy)	Specifically expressed (e.g. Your Definite Chief Aim)
Something you can have right now (immediate gratification)	Takes time to achieve
Infinite	Measurable
Expressed for self &/or others	Expressed for oneself only
Elicits states and anchors	Writes down goals and well-formed outcomes
No steps required	Need to take steps to reach goal

Table 15: States versus goals.

Well Formed Outcomes

Question
In this step, I would like you to reflect on what it is that you want and don't want, and fill out the table below appropriately.

Take fifteen minutes to fill this form out thoroughly.

Once you've filled out this Well-Formed Outcomes worksheet, the big idea is:

- If you have any entries in the 'Don't Want and Have' box, then ask yourself, 'If I don't want that thing, then how can I get rid of it? What do I want instead of what's in this box?' and put your positive insight into the 'Want and Don't Have' box.
- Prioritise all your entries in the 'Want and Don't Have' box.
- Ideally, you should have NO entries in the right-most boxes, i.e. the 'Don't Want and Have' and the 'Don't Want and Don't Have' boxes should be empty. For the simple reason, if you 'Don't Want' them, then forget about them.

Want & Have	Don't Want & Have
Want & Don't Have	Don't Want & Don't Have

Table 16: Wants and don't wants.

Change the Tune

Question
Focus on a problem, and reflect on it by running the following set of questions against it.

Question
Answer these questions: What did you have for breakfast yesterday? What is the weather like outside? What colour was your bedroom when you were little?

Question
Now focus on something you want, and reflect on it by running the following set of questions against it.

Problem Questions	Your Answers
What is my problem?	
How long have you had it?	
Where does the fault lie?	
Who is to blame?	
What is my worst experience with this?	
Why haven't I solved it yet?	

Table 17: Problems and answers.

Want Questions	Your Answers
What do I want?	
How will I know when I've got it?	
What resources do I already have that can help me achieve this outcome?	
What is something similar that I have succeeded in doing?	
What is the next step?	

Table 18: Want questions and answers.

Question
Finally, compare and contrast the internal representations in [Wants and Don't Haves] to those in [Want Questions and Answers].

Too many people focus on what they do not want, and wonder why they keep getting that and not that which they do want. Simply change the tune.

The big idea behind this exercise is for you to DECIDE WHAT EXPERIENCES YOU WANT. I like to say:

'E-motion is energy in motion.
E-Motion puts your thoughts into action.
Actions create experience.
Experiences create life.
Choose the experiences you want, and
LIVE THE LIFE YOU WANT.'

Create Captivating Goals

Dr Napoleon Hill believed that ninety-eight percent of people did not know what they wanted in life. It is a bit like asking someone:

Question:	*'What would you like?'*
Answer:	*'Financial freedom.'*
Question:	*'What does financial freedom mean to you?'*
Answer:	*'Lots of money.'*
Question:	*'How much money is "lots"?'*
Answer:	*'I'm not sure.'*
Question:	*'£1,000, £10,000, £100,000, £1,000,000, £10,000,000…? Tell me.'*
Answer:	*'£1,000,000'*
Question:	*'Is that before tax or after tax?'*
Answer:	*'After tax, of course.'*
Question:	*'So, with an approximate thirty percent tax, you would need £1,300,000.'*
Answer:	*'I* Get It Now.*'*

See what I mean? It's a bit like being on a boat without a rudder, drifting aimlessly in the sea. All seems OK whilst the seas are tranquil, but what happens when you hit a storm?

As Dr Napoleon Hill stated, *'The difference between a dream and a goal is a deadline.'* To make this so, is a matter of taking 100 percent responsibility and control of your life to make it happen - that is the art of self-mastery.

Self-mastery is:

- The ability to make the most out of your physical, mental and spiritual resources.
- The realisation of your major purpose in life, and then using your passions and talents coupled with action and association with a huge dollop of faith towards your end desires.
- The ability to take responsibility and control of your life without being blown off course by feelings, urges and circumstances, having 'stickability' with a burning desire.

However, a lot of people mistake tasks for outcomes. A series of tasks are the actions you perform to get closer to the outcome you want to achieve.

All outcomes require the investment of time, effort, money and, most importantly, an output. If you have calmness, clarity and certainty, as explored in the 'Think and Become' Martial Mind Power Experience, you will be able to focus on the things you want, rather than those that you don't. As mentioned before:

'Where your focus goes, energy flows -
and it expands.'

People intrinsically focus on negatives, and often live in past experiences, feeling sorry for themselves as victim of cause-and-effect. It's a bit like driving forward whilst looking in your rear-view mirror. It is an accident waiting to happen. As C. Bard stated:

'Though no one can go back and make a brand new start,
Anyone can start from now and make a brand new ending.'

This is why negatively stated goals are not as effective as positively stated ones. For example, 'giving up smoking' is not as impactful as 'I want to be a healthy non-smoker', which is a goal stated with positive results attached to it. Similarly, 'losing weight' does not have half as much impact as 'I want to be a size X because that'll confirm that I am fitter and healthier'.

Therefore, the big idea is not to 'take away', but to state a goal in a **Positive 'Gaining Goal'** Statement with calmness, clarity and certainty. The most effective way to do this is to model someone who has already achieved your outcome, so you can understand their mindset. This is what is called 'the difference that makes the difference' — i.e. the tweaks in your mindset that create demonstrable and observable success in high-achievers, to truly understand the 'essence of what works'. This is the strategy Bruce Lee used to explore the essence of what made certain martial art techniques so effective, so Bruce could refine his own process of becoming a fine-tuned street-fighter and the best martial artist ever!

When you define your outcome 'as if' you have already achieved it, you will be able to describe and define it in the way in which it looks, sounds, feels, tastes and smells. An outcome is what you really want emotionally, *not* what you do not want. Your outcome must be ecological (see the 'Ecology of Success Goal' section), and stated in the positive.

SMART Goals

The idea of setting SMART goals is to turn a dream into a goal by giving it parameters that will help you steer your actions and their output towards the desired Well-Formed Outcome by a given deadline. This allows you to control and monitor your progress en route to your destination, so you can Enjoy The Journey!

Question
To do this, clearly define each of the SMART variables for your goal, to form your strategy to achieve it.

	Description	Questions
S	Specific Simple	• Is your goal well defined in a clear and concise manner? Do you know the whats, whens, whys, wheres, and hows? • Is your goal specific to an area of improvement, innovation, etc? • Can you explain your goal to someone simply? • Can you define key specific & simple steps to achieve your goal?
M	Measurable Meaningful Motivational	• Is your goal meaningful? • Does your goal align with your major purpose in life? • Do you believe the goal is achievable? • Do you know when you expect to achieve your goal? • How are you going to measure & quantify your progress towards reaching your goal? • How would you know when you have achieved this goal? • What would you see, hear, feel, taste and smell when you achieve your goal? • How would you celebrate when you achieve your goal? • How do you plan on staying motivated towards achieving your goal?
A	Act 'As-If' All Areas of Your Life Achievable Assignable Actionable Aspirational	• Do you believe you can achieve this goal? • Are you acting 'as-if' you have already achieved the goal? • Will the goal enrich all areas of your life? • Have you got all stakeholders agreed to help support you in reaching your goal? • Do all your stakeholders understand what you are trying to achieve?

	Description	Questions
A	Continued from above...	• Do all your stakeholders know what they need to do? • Do you have a plan of distinct actions that need to be fulfilled towards achieving your goal? • Have you broken your actions down into manageable chunks that are simple and easy to follow? • Who can you aspire to and model who has already achieved a similar goal? • Have you modelled your aspirational role model?
R	Realistic Responsible/Ecological	• Do you think that your goal realistic? Remember, shoot for the moon, and even if you miss you'll land amongst the stars • Do you believe you can achieve your goal with your available resources? • Do you have or can source the knowledge and expertise required to achieve your goal? • Are you prepared to take full responsibility for delivering your goal? • Is your goal ecological? (See section on Ecology of Goals)
T	Timely Towards Trackable	• Do you feel that you have enough time to achieve your goal? • Are all your tasks and actions moving you closer towards achieving your goal? • Are you able to track your progress towards your goal?

Table 19: SMART goal setting.

Ecology of Your Success Goals

The big idea behind creating ecological goals, is to maintain a level of harmony and happiness between all the key components of your life.

For example, John lives in London. John got married to his wife Jane when he was twenty-five, and they both celebrated their marriage by visiting Hawaii for their honeymoon. Both John and Jane fell in love with Hawaii, and John has dreamt of relocating there ever since.

John, now in his fifties, reflecting back on his life wondering why he has not fulfilled his twenty-five-year-long dream of relocating to Hawaii yet.

When John was asked to look at the ecology of his goal against his eight key components in his life, he had the following insights.

Area of Life	Ecology
1. Physical	Moving to Hawaii would be a healthier choice, because the weather is better than in the UK, and John would be able to exercise more in the great sunny outdoors
2. Mental	Moving to Hawaii would be more relaxing, being surrounded by nature compared to living in a busy cosmopolitan city like London
3. Spiritual	Moving to Hawaii would allow John to spend more time on his own, to find himself through stillness in motion by spending time on his own and in nature whilst exercising outdoors
4. Financial	Moving to Hawaii would allow John to continue his on-line business with no impact
5. Social / Hobbies	John is an outdoorsy person, and Hawaii would allow John to spend more time outside pursuing his outdoor activities
6. Career / Vocation	Moving to Hawaii would allow John to continue his on-line business
7. Family & Friends	John has two children at college, both whom do not want to move anywhere because all their friends live locally, and this would create a major problem in Johns' life
8. Romance	Jane does not want to move anywhere without the children, and since they do not want to move, this is creates a major concern for John

<u>Table 20</u>: *Ecology in life.*

Having analysed John's ecology, it is clear that both his family and romance components of his life would have severe negative impact if he was to move to Hawaii, and hence subconsciously John has been sabotaging this dream for the past twenty-five years.

However, if John had had some insight into this sooner, he could have come up with a solution to buy a time-share or holiday home in Hawaii, which would afford him and his family the opportunity to spend time in Hawaii during the children's holidays without compromising the ecology in his life.

Hence it is important that your goals are ecological, else you could sabotage your own goals unconsciously without truly understanding why.

<u>Question</u>

So for this exercise, I would like you to:

1. List up to eight key areas of your life in the left-hand column of the table below.
2. Describe the ecology of achieving your goal against each area of life, expressed as a positive, negative or neutral impact, as in the example above.

Take fifteen minutes to write this down.

Area of Life	Ecology
Physical	
Mental	
Spiritual	
Financial	
Social/Hobbies	
Career/Vocation	
Family & Friends	
Romance	

Table 21: Ecology in your life.

Questions to Create Achievable Outcomes

This section lists a series of questions which will help you create achievable outcomes, by highlighting potential obstacles that you need to conquer.

Questions

State the question and the answer in the positive — 'What specifically do I want?'

Specify the present situation compared to the outcome — 'Where am I now in relation to the outcome?'

Specify the outcome in sensory detail — 'What will I see, hear, feel, taste and smell when I've achieved this goal?'

Specify evidence procedure — 'How will I know when I've achieved my goal? What will I see, hear, feel, taste and smell when I've achieved this goal?

Is it congruently desirable? What will this outcome get for me or allow me to do that I otherwise would not have?

Is it self-initiated and self-maintained? Is this outcome only for me?

What resources are needed? What do I have now, and what do I need, in order to get my outcome? Have I ever had or done this before? Do I know anyone who has? Can I act 'as-if' I've already achieved it?

Is it ecological? What is the impact on others around you? For what purpose do I want this? What will I gain if I have it? What will I lose if I have it?

Take thirty minutes to go through exercise this thoroughly.

Cartesian Coordinates

Question
In this exercise, please answer these questions honestly. Take ten minutes to answer thoroughly.

What will happen when I get it?	What won't happen when I get it?
What will happen if I don't get it?	What won't happen if I don't get it?

Table 22: Cartesian coordinates

And the Winner Is...

Remember the Norwegian and the Canadian logging competition?

Every hour at ten minutes to the hour, the Norwegian would stop and the Canadian would continue. When the whistle blew to finish the contest at four o'clock in the afternoon, the Canadian was supremely confident that the prize was his.

You can imagine how surprised he was to discover that he had lost.

'How did you do that?' he asked the Norwegian. *'Every hour at ten to the hour I heard you stop. How the hell were you able to cut more timber than me? It's just not possible.'*

'It's really very simple,' said the Norwegian bluntly. *'Every hour, at ten minutes to the hour, I stopped. While you continued to cut, I was sharpening my axe.'*

Conclusion

In this section, we firstly looked at what Bruce Lee meant by **Power Side Forwards** from a combative aspect.

The Power Side Forwards principles identified are:

1. To develop useful tools quickly and effectively.
2. To use your Power Side eighty percent and weaker side twenty percent of the time.To develop your Power Side first so you have effective tools available for your utilisation (then to develop the weaker side tools).
3. To develop tactics and strategies to develop your tools effectively on the Power Side then the weaker side.
4. To practice using your tools on the Power Side and then the weaker side.

We then took these core principles and applied them across the following:

1. **Tao of Life:** To create harmony and balance in all areas of your life.
2. **Success Formula:** Once you have a solid foundation in all areas of your life, the next stage is to help you identify your strengths and use what you've got in a purposeful way to create your own personal Success Formula and identify your Major Purpose in life.
3. **Definite Chief Aim:** Finally, once you have the vision, the idea is to create a mantra by which to live by for your own personal success which you can practice on a daily basis with a burning desire for ultimate self-actualisation and transcendence.

Each of these applications clearly addressed the Power Side Forwards and can be summarised in the following table:

	Develop Tools Quickly & Effectively	Use Power Side 80% Weak Side 20%	Develop Power Side 1st Then Weaker Side	Develop Tactics & Strategies to Develop Tools	Practice Using Tools
Tao of Life	Take current life and build on it to create your ideal future life	Identify strong areas of your life Identify weaker areas of your life	Identified gaps and bridge them	Identified actions to bridge gaps	Action steps identified
Success Formula	Take existing passions & talents and build on them	Use existing passions and talents	Identify talent gaps and bridge them	Identify associations and actions Identify actions to bridge talent gap	Action steps identified

	Develop Tools Quickly & Effectively	Use Power Side 80% Weak Side 20%	Develop Power Side 1st Then Weaker Side	Develop Tactics & Strategies to Develop Tools	Practice Using Tools
Definite Chief Aim	Using your success formula	Using your success formula	Using your success formula	Define exact amount of money desired Describe what you'll give in return for money Define by when Describe plan clearly	Repetitively action Definite Chief Aim with a burning desire everyday

Table 23: Power Side Forwards summary.

And that brings us to the end of the **Power Side Forwards** stage of your self-mastery journey. Before we embark on POWERING FORWARDS, please answer the following questions:

Question

1. Do you understand what **Tools You Can Develop Quickly** and effectively towards achieving your own personal success goals in life? (Yes or No)
2. Do you understand what **Your Power Side** is (i.e. passions, talents, association, actions and faith), so you can use it eighty percent of the time as opposed to your weaker side twenty percent? (Yes or No)
3. Do you understand what to **Develop on Your Power Side** first so you have effective tools available for your utilisation (then to develop the weaker side tools)? (Yes or No)
4. Do you have some **Tactics and Strategies** to develop your tools effectively on the Power Side (than the weaker side)? (Yes or No)
5. Do you now have some definitive **Actions to Practice** using the tools you identified in the Power Side Forwards process? (Yes or No)
6. Are you ready to **Power Forwards** to your success? (Yes or No)

My friend, I would like to deeply thank you for giving me the chance to take you through this *Power Side Forwards* journey, and remember:

'WHEN FIGHTING, KEEP YOUR STRONGEST SIDE UP-FRONT and POWER FORWARDS TO SUCCESS!'

9 Stay ahead

Stay Ahead

STAGE 9 — BLACK BELT

Master Your Success

What's the Problem?

So, who are we trying to help in this **Stay Ahead** stage of your self-mastery journey?

- People who have just discovered their vision, mission or definite major purpose in life, but are not sure how to achieve it.
- People who have not got into the groove of getting closer to their goals.
- People who don't understand The Rhythm of Life.
- People who do not know how to orchestrate their goals to fruition.
- People who do not know how to deal with and cope with obstacles that may present themselves on their journey of life.

Objective

Outcome & Results Question
What outcome(s) and result(s) do you expect to get when you start to **Stay Ahead**?

Take ten minutes to list down all the positive changes you would like to see, hear and feel.

Getting ahead is one thing; *staying* ahead once you get ahead is another matter entirely.

To stay ahead demands that we understand our purpose inside out, and we are prepared for what life throws at us. Without giving up. Without being the victim to external forces. Without losing faith and self-belief. All with a passion, drive and hunger, that allows you to stay ahead of yourself!

Examples Question
Can you think of any examples when you have fallen behind? How did it cause you to feel? What was the outcome of the situation?

Take ten minutes to make a list.

Do you sometimes find yourself:

- Having a vision, a mission, or a Definite Chief Aim, but still being unsure how to get there?
- Having not got into the groove of getting closer to your goals?
- Failing to understand the Rhythm of Life?
- Feeling like the outside is controlling your destiny, and your life is out of control?
- Being unable cope when some obstacles get in the way?
- Losing the will and lacking motivation to keep going, and giving up too easily?
- Not knowing how to manage your journey to your end desires?

If you have answered 'yes' to any of the above, then you're in for an AMAZING DANCE.

Stay Ahead is based on Bruce Lee's martial philosophy:

'A good fight should be like a small play...but played seriously.
When the opponent expands, I contract. When he contracts, I expand.
And when there is an opportunity, I do not hit, it hits all by itself.
Any technique, however worthy and desirable,
becomes a disease when the mind is obsessed with it.'

I like to think of it as rhythm, a dance, and I say:

'Orchestrate Your Success and
Dance to Your Own Rhythm.'

I call it STAY AHEAD!

This stage of your self-mastery journey will help you to:

Belt	Pillars of Luck	Chapter	Success Goals
9. Black	Planning Practice	**'Stay ahead'** Master your success	• Develop an understanding of rhythm and broken rhythm • Develop an understanding of The Rhythm Of Life • Find your own rhythm • Orchestrate your success strategy to overcome obstacles and challenges • Dance to your own rhythm • Stay ahead of your success!

This stage is broken down into five key substages as follows:

1. Being on Top.
2. Rhythm and Broken Rhythm.
3. The Rhythm of Life.
4. Dance to Your Own Rhythm.
5. Staying Ahead.

Are you ready to ORCHESTRATE YOUR SUCCESS, DANCE TO YOUR OWN RHYTHM, and STAY AHEAD OF YOUR SUCCESS?

Warm Up

Let's jump right in and start warming up by answering the following questions:

Question
What do you think **Stay Ahead** means? Take five minutes to define.

Question
What does **Rhythm** mean to you? Take five minutes to define.

Question
What does **Broken Rhythm** mean to you? Take five minutes to define.

Question
What does **The Rhythm of Life** mean to you? Take five minutes to define.

<u>Question</u>
Would you like to **Orchestrate Your Success**? (Yes or No).

<u>Question</u>
Would you like to learn how to **Dance to Your Own Rhythm**? (Yes or No)

If you answered 'yes' to the last two questions, then you're in the right place, so let's **GO AHEAD.**

Being on Top

A merchant, a staunch pillar of society, wanted to protect his daughter from shame. When he realised she had become a ripe and succulent apple, he took her aside one day and said, '*My daughter, wicked and slippery are the ways of men in this world, and you must exercise the greatest of care if you are not to bring disgrace on yourself and your family.*'

Now that he had his daughter's attention, he continued. *'Men are after only one thing; they are exceedingly devious and will stop at nothing to fulfil their lustful desires. I want only to keep you from harm and disgrace. So listen carefully to what I am going to tell you, so you will know how to protect yourself when the time comes.*

At first a man will admire and praise your beauty and charms. Then he will flatter you, and invite you to spend time with him. The next thing is that he will walk you by his house, as if by chance, and remember he has something important inside that he needs to fetch. And of course he will invite you to come in while he looks for it.

While you are waiting he will offer you a seat and, as if out of politeness, something to drink in order to refresh yourself. He will sit down next to you, and you listen to music together. When the moment is right, he will make his move. He will force himself on top of you, and in this way you will be violated. You and your family will be shamed and our reputation ruined.'

The daughter was much impressed by this forceful and passionate speech of her father. She took serious notice of it and resolved never to bring shame upon herself or her family.

Rhythm and Broken Rhythm

What Is Rhythm?

The word **rhythm** comes from the Greek word '*rhythmos*', meaning *'any regular recurring motion, symmetry'* (Liddell and Scott, 1996). Rhythm therefore describes a *'movement marked by the regulated succession of strong and weak elements, or of opposite or different conditions'* (Anon, 1971).

Regular recurring patterns in time can be applied to a wide variety of cyclical natural phenomena having a periodicity or frequency over a period of time, from microseconds to millions of years.

In the performance arts rhythm is the timing of events on a human scale: of musical sounds and silences, of the steps of a dance, the meteor of spoken language and poetry.

In the martial arts embodying a visual presentation, we are looking at rhythm as a *'timed movement through space'* (Jirousek, 1995), and this is united through a common language of pattern using rhythm and geometry.

In the book called *Thinking and Destiny* by Harold W. Percival, he defined rhythm as *'the character and meaning of thought expressed through the measure or movement in sound or form, or by written signs or words'* (Percival, 1946).

Why Is Rhythm Important?

Howard Goodall presented a theory in his series called *How Music Works*, stating that:

> *'Human beings have an inherent rhythm in the way in which they walk and their heart beats.'*

Other research suggests that there is indeed a human rhythm, but it does not necessarily relate to the heartbeat directly, but rather the speed of emotional affect which indirectly influences the heartbeat.

Yet other research suggests that beat-based rhythmic human processing is anchored in our ancient evolutionary roots (Patel, 2014).

Therefore, it seems human beings are inherently rhythmic beings, and therefore it is important for us to understand rhythm to maximise our true potential.

How Can We Understand Rhythm?

Liddell and Scott, Anon and Jirousek all described rhythm as:

- A timed movement through space.
- Something that can be sensed audibly, visually and kinaesthetically.

This means that we can understand rhythm through:

- Music.
- Physical motion.

If rhythm can be found in music and motion, then it can be found in all aspects of life. Today, we are going to look at rhythm in music, express it using martial motion, and apply it to better understand the rhythm of our lives towards our own personal success goals.

Understanding Rhythm Through Music

We are going to:

1. Study some music terminology, to develop a foundation for how rhythm is described and looks like in musical terms and written notation.
2. Listen to the music (available on our website on www.MartialMindPower.com/Resources) so we know what the described rhythm in step (1) sounds like.
3. We are going to express the musical rhythm through martial motion to get a better insight into what rhythm feels like.

Figure 40: Illustration of the beat in contrast to division and multiple levels.

In music and its theory:

- The **pulse** consists of a number of recurring beats within a defined period of time, usually within a minute. A typical example would be 120 BPM pulse.
- The **beat** is the basic unit of time in music, and is usually characterised by the sounds and silences making up music to which people dance to.
- In martial arts, a strike — let's take a punch, for example — has two beats.
- The first beat is the time taken to fully extend your fist out, which is known as 'completion'.
- The second beat is the time taken to retract and recover your weapon back to its starting position.

In martial arts, a pulse would be described as a number of recurring strikes within a defined period of time, usually within a second. The Guinness Book of World Records has recorded 805 punches being thrown in sixty seconds; that is an average of thirteen point five punches a second by Robert Ardito in Sydney, Australia, on 18th March 2009.

Beat and Pulse Demo
Check out a demonstration of a beat and pulse on our website at:
www.MartialMindPower.com/Resources

In the demonstration, a metronome and music is used to help you understand the timing of a beat and pulse.

Take five minutes to practice throwing strikes using different beat and pulse timings, to better understand this concept.

Rhythm in music is characterised by a repeating sequence of stressed and unstressed beats, called strong and weak. These are divided into bars, which indicates the organisation of music by a time signature and tempo.

Figure 41: Simple examples of a 3/4 time signature, i.e. 3 quarter-notes (crotchets) in a 4-measure bar.

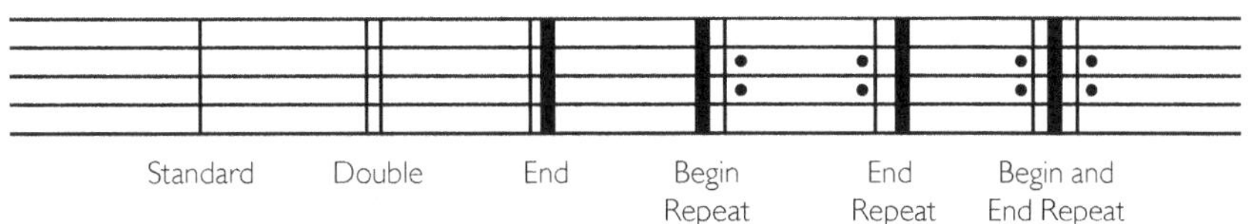

Figure 42: Types of bar lines.

In martial arts, a strong beat would be described as a strike which is heavy and powerful, whereas a weak beat would be lighter and faster.

Strong and Weak Beat Demo
Check out a demonstration of a strong and weak beat on our website at: www.MartialMindPower.com/Resources

Take five minutes to practice throwing heavy and weaker strikes such as a punch on a punch bag to better understand this concept.

Time Signature

A time signature denotes how many beats (pulses) there are in each bar and which note value is to be given one beat. This is usually illustrated on the musical score which is the music sheet which musicians read and play from; the time signature appears at the beginning of the piece. It appears as a time symbol or stacked numbers such as 𝄴 (which is called common time known as 4/4) or 𝄵(which is cut-common time such as 3/4, or a doubling of the time called proportia dupla) immediately following the clef.

The key signature refers to the clef symbol. An illustration of the simple treble g-clef and bass f-clef are shown below respectively. The clefs indicate which pitch the notes are to be played in. In laymen's terms, on a piano the treble clef represents where the right hand would play (higher pitch), and the bass clef represents where the left hand would play (low pitch).

Figure 43: Treble G clef.

Figure 44: Bass F clef.

In martial arts, this would denote the speed taken to perform a certain combination. In single-speed (or common time) this would take X seconds. In double-speed (cut time), this would take X/2 seconds, for example.

Treble and Bass Demo
Checkout a demonstration of a:

1. Single (𝄴 common-) time using 4/4, for example 1, 2, 3, 4 or a jab, cross, jab, cross.
2. Double time using 3/4, for example 1, 2, 3 or a jab, cross, jab, where the treble = jab (high pitch or lighter strike); and bass = cross (i.e. lower pitch or heavier strike).
3. This demonstration is available on our website at: www.MartialMindPower.com/Resources
4. Take five minutes to practice throwing single and double time strikes such as a lead and rear punches combinations on a punch bag, to better understand this concept.

- Simple 2/4, 3/4, 4/4
- Compound 9/8, 12/8
- Complex 5/4, 7/8
- Mixed 5/8, 3/8, 6/8, 3/4
- Additive 3+2+3/8
- Fractional 2.5/4
- Irrational Meters 3/10, 5/24

Figure 45: Example of time signatures.

Simple Time Signature

We are going to look at the simple time signature which are 3/4 and 4/4 to develop our understanding of rhythm.

- The upper number indicates how many **beats there are in a bar** grouped together, for example in a 3/4 time signature, 3 means three beats in a bar.
- The lower number indicates the note that represents one beat or the **beat unit**, for example in a 3/4 time signature, 4 means a quarter beat or a crotchet.

To summarise then:

- 3/4 means three quarter-note (crotchets) beats per bar.

- 4/4 means four quarter-note (crotchets) beats per bar.
- A more complex time signature would mean 3/8 means three eighth-note (quavers) beats per bar.

We are going to look at the different types of notes like crotchets and quavers shortly.

Single (Common) and Double (Cut) Time Demo
Check out the following demonstrations on our website at: www.MartialMindPower.com/Resources

1. Single (𝄴 common-) time using 4/4, for example 1, 2, 3, 4 or a jab, cross, jab, cross.
2. Simple time using 3/4, for example 1, 2, 3 or a jab, cross, jab.

Take five minutes to practice throwing single and double time strikes such as a lead and rear punch combinations on a punch bag, to better understand this concept.

Tempo

Tempo, meaning *'time'* in Italian, is described as the **Beats Per Minute (BPM).** This is usually denoted in musical notation as a description with a metronome mark, i.e. usually using a crotchet with a number next to it, written at the top of the piece of music.

Figure 46: Mozart's Sonata K. 331 with a Andanta Grazioso 120, i.e. a tempo of 120 BPM, meaning 'Walking Pace Graceful'.

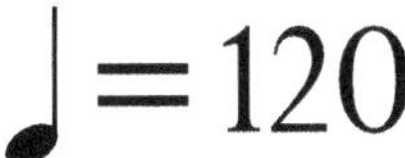

Figure 47: Metronome mark indicating a 120 crotchet BPM or tempo.

This implies that a particular note value, for example a quarter note (i.e. a crotchet), is specified as the beat, and the delay between successive beats is specified as a fraction of a minute. The greater the BPM, the shorter the delay between successive beats; therefore, the music needs to be played faster.

As an example, a piece of music played at sixty BPM implies one beat per second, while a tempo of 120 BPM implies doubling of the speed of play, signifying one beat per 0.5 seconds. A metronome is a tool which can be used to baseline tempo and BPM to time music to.

Thus, 'rhythms of recurrence' arise from the interaction of two levels of motion, the faster providing the pulse and the slower organising the beats into repetitive groups (Yeston 1976, 50-52).

These attributes of music are described by:

- The beat.
- The bar.

When asked what is the **measure or metric,** Lester (1986) replied, *'Once a metric hierarchy has been established, we, as listeners, will maintain that organisation as long as minimal evidence is present'.*

60 BPM and 120 BPM Demo
Checkout a demonstration of Beats Per Minute (BPM) on our website at: www.MartialMindPower.com/Resources

In the demonstration, a metronome and music is used to help you understand tempo using different strikes and combinations.

Take five minutes to practice throwing strikes using different Beats Per Minute (BPM), to better understand this concept.

Time Stretching

When tempo (or pitch) changes, this is called time-stretching, and is the first explicit component of music which changes the rhythm, which I call broken rhythm in martial arts.

Time Stretching Demo
Check out a demonstration of time stretching on our website on www.MartialMindPower.com/Resources

In the demonstration, a metronome and music is used to help you understand time stretching between 60 BPM to 120 BPM to 60 BPM using different strikes and combinations.

Take five minutes to practice throwing strikes using time stretching, to better understand this concept.

Tempo Markings

Tempo markings describe the rate and change in tempo, and are usually described in Italian.

Tempos are described by:

- Adding *-issimo* to the end of a tempo marker — meaning **amplified** or made **louder**.

- Adding an *-ino or -etto* to the end of a tempo marker — meaning diminished or made softer.

Basic Tempo Markers

Here are the basic tempo markers from slowest to the fastest:

- *Larghissimo* – very, very slow (24 BPM and under).
- *Grave* — very slow (25 to 45 BPM).
- *Lento* — slowly (45 to 50 BPM).
- *Largo* — broadly (50 to 55 BPM).
- *Larghetto* — rather broadly (55 to 60 BPM).
- *Adagio* — slow and stately (literally, 'at ease' — 60 to 72 BPM).
- *Adagietto* — slower than andante (72 to 80 BPM).
- *Andantino* — slightly slower than andante (although in some cases it can be taken to mean slightly faster than andante) (80 to 84 BPM).
- *Andante* — at a walking pace (84 to 90 BPM).
- *Andante moderato* — between andante and moderato (thus the name andante moderato) (90 to 96 BPM).
- *Marcia moderato* — moderately, in the manner of a march (83 to 85 BPM).
- *Moderato* — moderately (96 to 108 BPM).
- *Allegro Moderato* — moderately fast (108 to 112 BPM).
- *Allegretto* — close to but not quite allegro (112 to 120 BPM).
- *Allegro* — fast, quickly, and bright (120 to 144 BPM) (molto allegro is slightly faster than allegro, but always in its range).
- *Vivace* — lively and fast (132 to 144 BPM).
- *Vivacissimo* — very fast and lively (144 to 160 BPM).
- *Allegrissimo (or* Allegro Vivace*)* — very fast (145 to 167 BPM).
- *Presto* — extremely fast (168 to 200 BPM).
- *Prestissimo* — even faster than Presto (200 BPM and over).

Terms for tempo change:

- *Ritardando* or *rallentando* — gradually slowing down.
- *Accelerando* or *stringendo* — gradually accelerating.

Additional terms:

- *A piacere* — the performer may use his or her own discretion with regard to tempo and rhythm; literally *'at pleasure'.*
- *A tempo* — at the same speed from the beginning.
- *L'istesso tempo* or *Lo stesso tempo* — at the same speed.
- *Tempo comodo* — at a comfortable (normal) speed.
- *Tempo di...* — the speed of a ... (such as *Tempo di valse* [speed of a waltz, ≈60 bpm], *Tempo di marcia* [speed of a march, ≈120 bpm]).

- *Tempo giusto* — at a consistent speed, at the 'right' speed, in strict tempo.
- *Tempo semplice* — simple, regular speed, plainly.

Common style qualifiers:

- *Alla* — in the manner or style of.
- *Alla breve* — in short style, i.e., duple time, with the half-note (minim) rather than the quarter note (crotchet) as the beat; cut time; 2/2 instead of 4/4; often marked as a ¢ (see the 'Time Signature' section above).
- *Alla marcia* — in the manner of a march (e.g., Beethoven, op. 101).
- *All' ongarese* — in Hungarian style.
- *Alla (danza) tedesca* — in the style of the Landler c.1800, and similar dances in rather quick triple meter (see Beethoven, op. 79, op. 130).
- *Alla turca* — in the Turkish Style, that is, in imitation of Turkish military music (Janizary music), which became popular in Europe in the late 18th century (e.g., Mozart, K. 331, K. 384).
- *Alla zingarese* — in the style of gypsy music.
- *Assai* — very much, as in *allegro assai*, quite fast.
- *Ben* — well, as in *ben marcato* (well-marked or accented).
- Con — with.
- *Con bravura* — with skill.
- *Con brio* — with vigor and spirit.
- *Con dolcezza* — with softness; delicately.
- *Con fuoco* — with fire.
- *Con moto* — with motion.
- *Deciso* — decidedly, decisively.
- *Fugato* — in fugal style, usually part of a non-fugal composition; such passages often occur in the development sections of symphonies, sonatas and quartets.
- *In modo* — in the manner of, in the style of: *in modo napolitano* (in Neopolitan style), *in modo di marcia funebre* (in the manner of a funeral march).
- *Meno* — less, as in *meno mosso* (less quickly).
- *Appena* — almost none, as in *appena forte* (almost not at all loud).
- *Misterioso* — mysterious.
- *Molto* — much, very, as in *molto allegro* (very quick) or *molto adagio* (very slow).
- *Non troppo* — not too much, e.g. *allegro non troppo* (or *allegro ma non troppo*) means 'fast, but not too much'.
- *Non tanto* — not so much.
- *Più* — more, as in *più allegro* (more quickly); used as a relative indication when the tempo changes.
- *Piuttosto* — rather, as in *piuttosto allegro* (rather quick).
- *Poco* — slightly, little, as in *Poco adagio.*
- *Poco a poco* — little by little.
- *Polacca* — generic name for Polish dances, usually the polonaise, as in *tempo di Polacca*; note, however, that the *'Polacca'* in Bach's Brandenburg Concerto No. 1 shows little resemblance to the polonaise.
- *Primo* — principal or early, as in *tempo primo*, the same tempo as at the beginning;

- *Quasi* — almost, nearly, as if (such as *Più allegro quasi presto, 'faster, as if presto'*).
- *Senza* — without, as in *senza interruzione* (without interruption or pause), *senza tempo* or *senza misura* (without strict measure).
- *Sostenuto* — sustained, prolonged.
- *Subito* — suddenly.

Mood Tempo Markings

Some markings that primarily highlight a mood (or character) also have a tempo connotation:

- *Affettuoso* — with feeling/emotion.
- *Agitato* — agitated, with implied quickness.
- *Appassionato* — to play passionately.
- *Animato* — animatedly, lively.
- *Brillante* — sparkling, glittering, as in *allegro brillante, rondo brillante*, or *variations brillantes*; became fashionable in titles for virtuoso pieces.
- *Bravura* — broadly.
- *Cantabile* — in singing style (lyrical and flowing).
- *Calando* — dying away, slowing, diminishing.
- *Dolce* — sweetly.
- *Dolcissimo* — very sweetly and delicately.
- *Energico* — energetic, strong, forceful.
- *Eroico* — heroically.
- *Espressivo* — expressively.
- *Furioso* — to play in an angry or furious manner.
- *Giocoso* — merrily, funny.
- *Gioioso* — joyfully.
- *Grandioso* — magnificently, grandly.
- *Grazioso* — gracefully.
- *Incalzando* — encouraging, building.
- *Lacrimoso* — tearfully, sadly.
- *Lamentoso* — lamenting, mournfully.
- *Leggiero* — to play lightly, or with light touch.
- *Leggiadro* — lightly and gracefully.
- *Maestoso* — majestic or stately (which generally indicates a solemn, slow march-like movement).
- *Malinconico* — melancholic.
- *Marcato* — marching tempo, marked with emphasis.
- *Marziale* — in a march style, usually in simple, strongly marked rhythm and regular phrases.
- *Mesto* — sad, mournful.
- *Misterioso* — mystical, in a shady manner.
- *Morendo* — dying.
- *Nobilmente* — nobly (in a noble way).

- *Patetico* — with great emotion.
- *Pesante* — heavily.
- *Saltando* — jumpy, fast and short.
- *Smorzando* — dying away, decreasing to nothing in both speed and dynamic.
- *Sostenuto* — sustained, with a slowing of tempo.
- *Spiccato* — slow sautillé, with a bouncy manner.
- *Tenerezza* — tenderness.
- *Tranquillamente* — adverb of tranquillo, 'calmly'.
- *Trionfante* — triumphantly.
- *Vivace* — lively and fast, over 140 BPM (which generally indicates a fast movement).

Tempo Change

Composers may use expressive marks to adjust the tempo:

- *Accelerando* — speeding up (abbreviation: *accel.*).
- *Allargando* — growing broader; decreasing in tempo, usually near the end of a piece.
- *Calando* — going slower (and usually also softer).
- *Doppio movimento/doppio più mosso* — double speed.
- *Doppio più lento* — half speed.
- *Lentando* — gradual slowing and softer.
- *Meno mosso* — less movement/slower.
- *Mosso* — movement, more lively/quicker, much like *più mosso*, but not as extreme.
- *Più mosso* — more movement/faster.
- *Precipitando* — hurrying, going faster/forward.
- *Rallentando* — gradual slowing down (abbreviation: *rall.*).
- *Ritardando* — slowing down gradually; also see rallentando and ritenuto (abbreviations: rit., ritard.).
- *Ritenuto* — slightly slower, temporarily holding back. (Note that the abbreviation for ritenuto can also be *rit.* Thus a more specific abbreviation is *riten.* Also sometimes *ritenuto* does not reflect a tempo change but a character change instead).
- *Rubato* — free adjustment of tempo for expressive purposes (literally *'theft'*, so more strictly, take time from one beat to slow another).
- *Stretto* — in faster tempo, often near the conclusion of a section. (Note that in fugal compositions, the term *stretto* refers to the imitation of the subject in close succession, before the subject is completed, and as such, suitable for the close of the fugue. Used in this context, the term is not necessarily related to tempo).
- *Stringendo* — pressing on faster (literally *'tightening'*).

Notes and Rests

Musical notes represent the sounds played, and the rests describe intermittent silences between notes that make up a musical composition.

Musicians have been composing music using scores (or music sheets) since the thirteenth century, and they describe the pitch, rhythm, tempo and composition fundamentals.

Notes and rests on a score are relative, and played in proportionate duration to each other. For example, a quarter note (crotchet) is a quarter of the length of a whole note.

Note	British Name / American Name	Rest
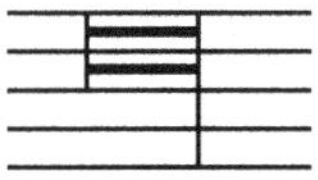	Large (Latin: Maxima) / Octuple whole note (octuple note)	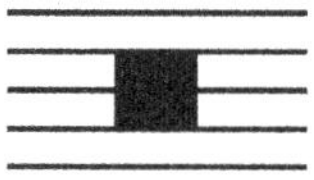
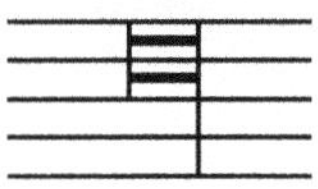	Long / Quadruple whole note (quadruple note)	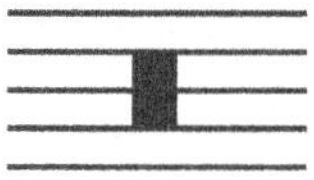
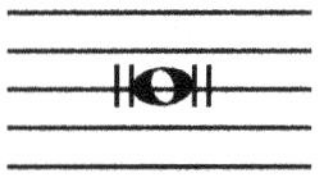	Breve / Double whole note (double note)	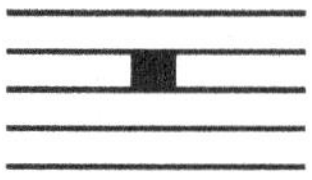
	Semibreve / Whole note	
	Minim / Half note	
	Crotchet/ Quarter note	
	Quaver / Eighth note	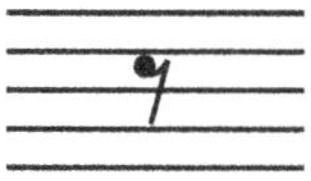

Note	British Name / American Name	Rest
	Semiquaver / Sixteenth note	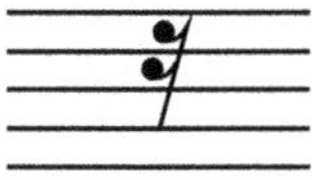
	Demisemiquaver / Thirty-second note	
	Hemidemisemiquaver / Sixty-fourth note	
	Semihemidemisemiquaver / Hundred and twenty eighth	
	Demisemihemidemisemiquaver / Two hundred and fifty-sixth note	
	Beamed notes Connecting eight notes (quavers)	N/A
	Dotted note One-half note extension	
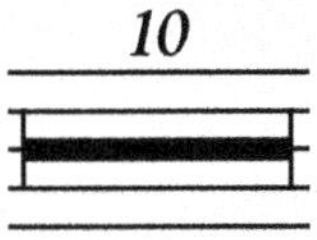 10	Multi-measure rest No of measures in a rest	N/A

Table 24: *Illustrates tempos of different notes (on left-hand side) and their respective rests (on right-hand side).*

In martial arts, tempo and notes would simply dictate the speed at which the strikes and footwork is executed. For example:

1. A semi-breve (whole note) would be equivalent to a strike on completion, i.e. 1-beat.
2. A minim (half note) would be a strike performed at twice the speed, i.e. on the half-beat.
3. A crotchet (quarter note) would be a strike performed at quadruple the speed, i.e. on the quarter-beat.
4. And so on.

I think you get the idea, THAT'S RIGHT!

Tempo and Notes Demo

Check out a demonstration of using different tempo and notes on our website at: www.MartialMindPower.com/Resources

In the demonstration, a metronome and music is used to help you understand tempo and notes using different strikes and footwork.

Take five minutes to practice throwing strikes and using footwork using the tempo and notes shown below, to better understand this concept.

1. Semi-breve (whole note) as one normal strike (A)

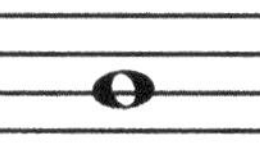

2. Minim (half note) as a strike x2 speed (B)

3. Crotchet (quarter note) as a strike x4 speed (C)

Notes and Rest Demo

Check out a demonstration of using different notes and rests on our website at: www.MartialMindPower.com/Resources

In the demonstration, a metronome and music is used to help you understand notes and rests using different strikes and footwork.

Take five minutes to practice throwing strikes and using footwork using the notes and rests shown below, to better understand this concept.

1. (Semi-breve, rest, semi-breve, double-rest)

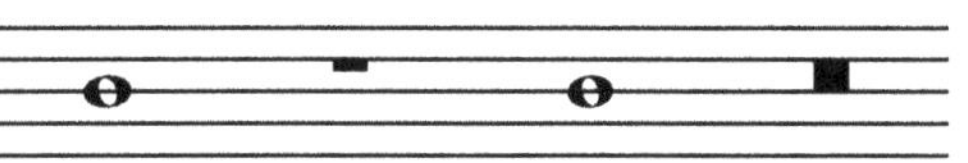

2. (Minim, minim, half-rest, minim)

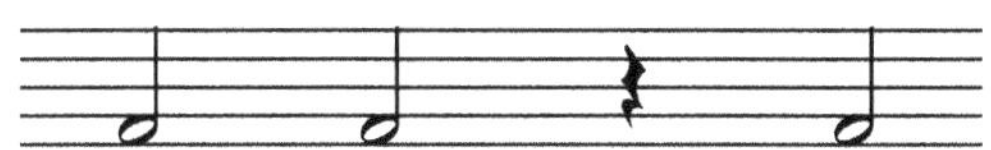

3. (Crotchet, quadruple-rest, semi-breve, crotchet, crotchet, crotchet)

Breaks

Breaks introduce pauses between notes as follows:

Note	Name / Description	Martial Application
	Breath mark Slight pause for non-wind instruments	Take a breath or break between strikes
	Caesura Pause until conductuor indicates to resume playing	Pause until opponent initiates an attack

Table 25: Breaks.

In martial arts, a break would simply be to momentarily pause or stop and literally take a break between strikes or footwork. This is described on the right-hand column in the table above.

Stopping is as important as continuing playing in music, else it would all sound like one big noise which merges into one long drone. Likewise, continuous movement without controlled pauses and breaks loses it grace and dexterity, and serves to drain the participant of energy.

Common Accidentals

Common accidentals adjust the pitch of the notes as follows:

Note	Name / Description	Martial Application
	Flat Lowers pitch of a note by a semitone	Strike held on target
	Sharp Raise pitch of a note by a semitone	Strike retracted from target quickly
	Natural Cancels previous accidental	Normal strike
	Double flat Lowers pitch by two semitones	Strike pushed through target
	Double sharp Raises pitch by two semitones	Strike snapped on target

Table 26: Common accidentals.

In martial arts, common accidentals/pitch would be equivalent to using:

1. High pitch: a high-line weapon, such as your hands for punching, hooking, upper-cutting, etc. or, shallow and rapid footwork covering short distances.
2. Low pitch: a low-line weapon, such as a straight kick, round kick, side kick, etc. or, deep footwork covering longer distance.

This is described on the right-hand column in the table above.

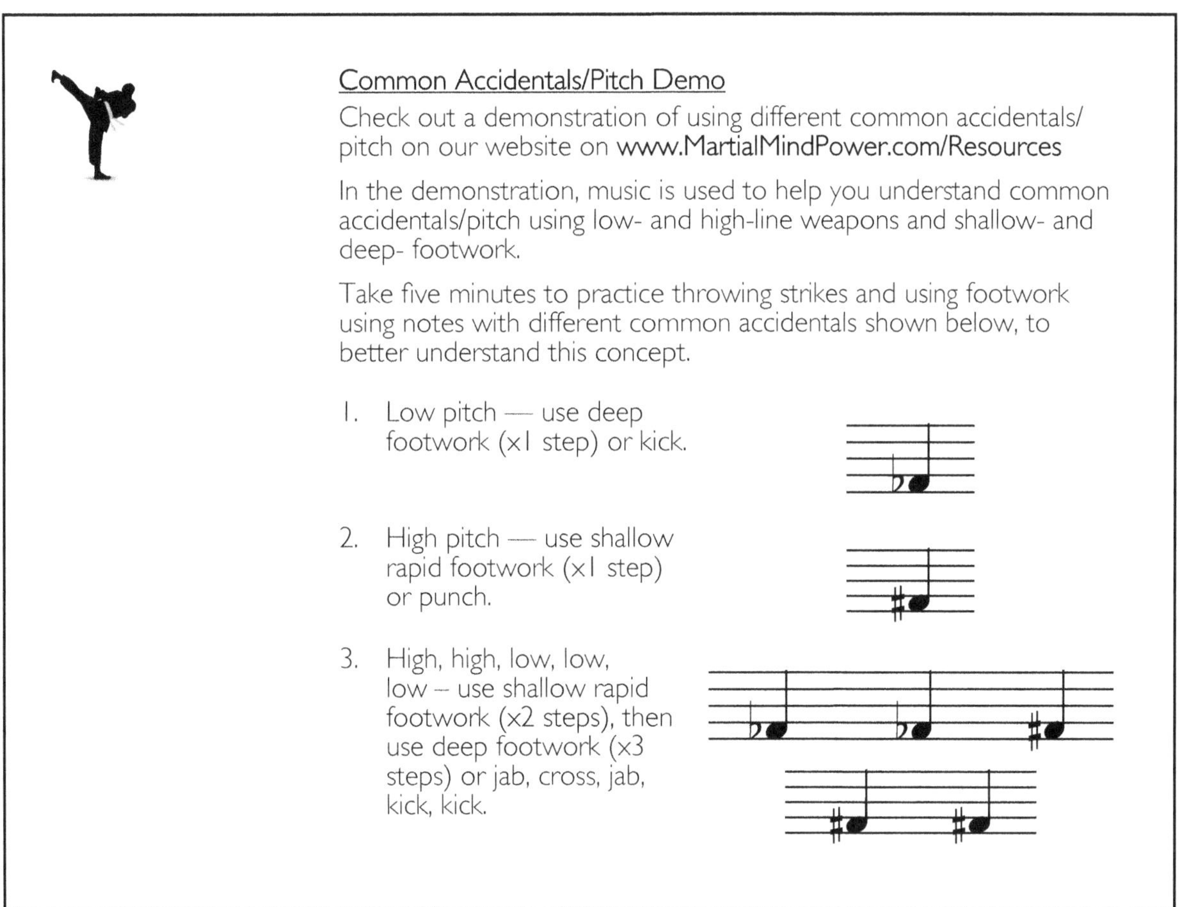

Common Accidentals/Pitch Demo

Check out a demonstration of using different common accidentals/ pitch on our website on www.MartialMindPower.com/Resources

In the demonstration, music is used to help you understand common accidentals/pitch using low- and high-line weapons and shallow- and deep- footwork.

Take five minutes to practice throwing strikes and using footwork using notes with different common accidentals shown below, to better understand this concept.

1. Low pitch — use deep footwork (x1 step) or kick.
2. High pitch — use shallow rapid footwork (x1 step) or punch.
3. High, high, low, low, low – use shallow rapid footwork (x2 steps), then use deep footwork (x3 steps) or jab, cross, jab, kick, kick.

Note Relationships

These symbols describe relationships between two or more notes being sounded as follows:

Note	Name / Description	Martial Application
	Tie Two or more notes played as one note with time durations compounded	Strike through opponents target

Note	Name / Description	Martial Application
	Slur Two or more notes played simultaneously	Simultaneous attack and defence e.g. Pak Da
	Phrase Mark or Ligature (Legato) Connects several notes over a phrase, not necessarily slurred	Succession of strikes
	Glissando or Portamento A continuous glide between the start and finish note indicated	Smooth succession of strikes
	Tuplet A number of notes played within a given number of notes, e.g. 5 notes played within 3 note duration	A number of strikes within timing disproportionate to their normal value
	Chord Several notes played simultaneously. Two-note chords are called dyads; three-note chords are called triads	Multiple strikes performed simultaneously
	Arpeggiated Chords A broken chord, where the notes are played in succession, usually ascending	Multiple strikes performed in succession

Table 27: Note relationships.

In martial arts, note relationships would be equivalent to a combination of strikes or footwork, and the harmonious relationship between the distinct strikes (i.e. notes) played within a unit of time (bar). This is described on the right-hand column in the table above.

Note Relationships Demo

Check out a demonstration of note relationships on our website at: www.MartialMindPower.com/Resources

In the demonstration, to help you understand note relationships, different strikes and footwork are used in combination as shown in the note relationships below.

Take five minutes to practice throwing strikes and using footwork in combination to better understand this concept.

1. Low-pitch note combined with a high-pitch note played simultaneously can be shown as...
   - Kick followed by a punch in one beat.
   - Or footwork with a deep step coupled with a shallow rapid double-step in one beat.

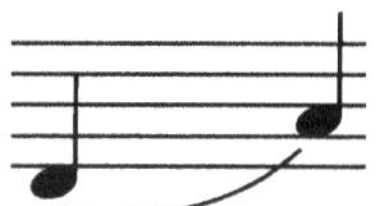

2. Low-pitch note graduated to a high-pitch note over time...
   - Low kick, medium kick, high kick, mid-line punch, high-line punch combination; or
   - Footwork with deep-step, medium-deep-step, normal-step, shallow-step, shallow-rapid step combination.

Dynamics

Dynamics indicate relative volume or intensity of a musical line as follows:

Note	Name / Description	Martial Application
ppp	Pianississimo Extremely soft	Strike extremely softly
pp	Pianissimo Very soft	Strike very softly
p	Piano Soft	Strike soft
mp	Mezzo Piano Half as soft as piano	Strike half-soft
mf	Mezzo Forte Half as loud as forte	Strike half-hard
f	Forte Loud	Strike hard
ff	Fortissimo Very loud	Strike very hard
fff	Fortississimo Extremely loud	Strike extremely hard

Note	Name / Description	Martial Application
sfz	Sforzando Forced, abrupt or fierce	Strike with abrupt fierce force
<	Cresecendo Gradual increase in volume	Gradually increasing intensity of strikes
>	Diminuendo A gradual decrease in volume	Gradually decreasing intensity of strikes
fp	Forte-Piano Loud then immediately soft	Strike hard then soft

Table 28: *Dynamics.*

In martial arts, this is equivalent to:

1. Piannissimo — striking extremely softly.
2. Sforzand — striking extremely hard and heavy.

This is described on the right-hand column in the table above.

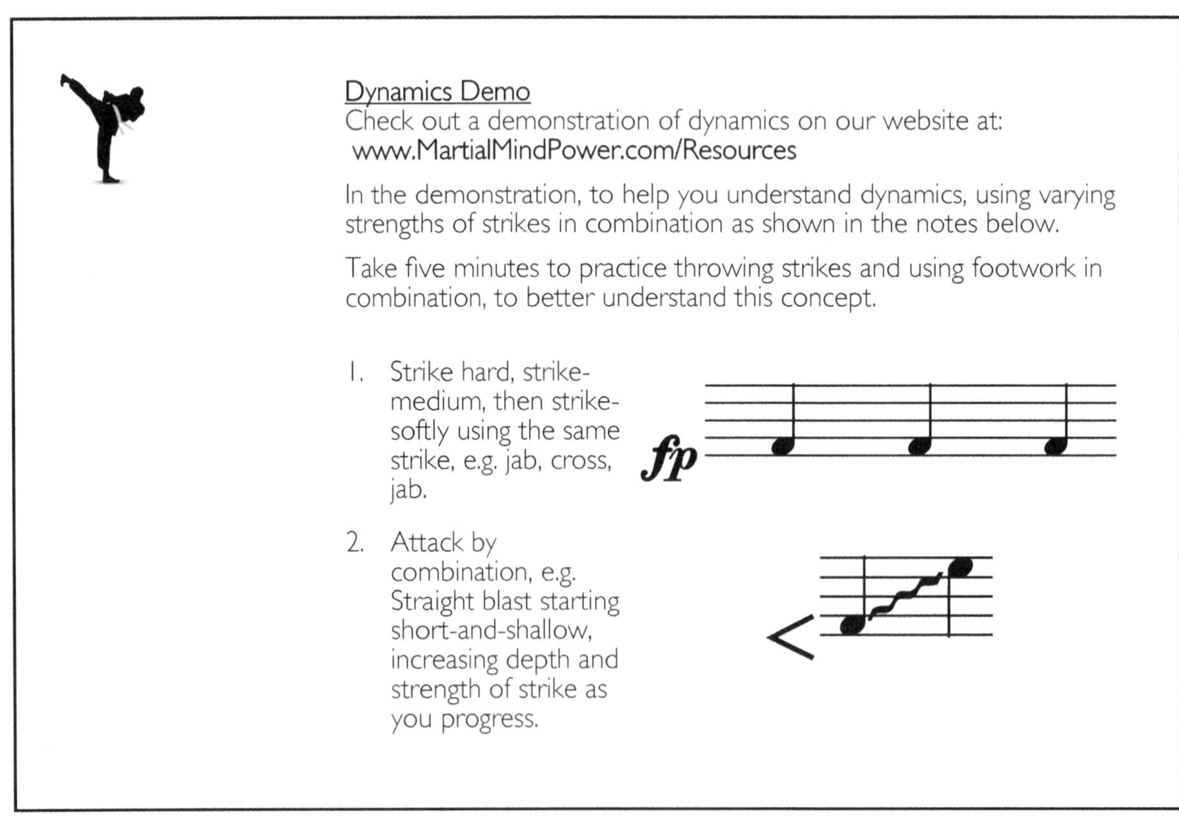

Dynamics Demo
Check out a demonstration of dynamics on our website at:
www.MartialMindPower.com/Resources

In the demonstration, to help you understand dynamics, using varying strengths of strikes in combination as shown in the notes below.

Take five minutes to practice throwing strikes and using footwork in combination, to better understand this concept.

1. Strike hard, strike-medium, then strike-softly using the same strike, e.g. jab, cross, jab.
2. Attack by combination, e.g. Straight blast starting short-and-shallow, increasing depth and strength of strike as you progress.

Articulation Marks

Also known as accents, these indicate how individual notes are to be played, and can be used in conjunction with phrase markers.

Note	Name / Description	Martial Application
	Staccato Play note shorter than notated, like a hop	Hop
	Staccatissimo or Spiccato After a staccato, this indicates a longer silence after the note	Pause after a hop
	Accent Play note harder/louder than other notes	Strike harder than usual
	Tenuto Play note to full value or slightly longer	Strike through target
	Marcato Play note harder / louder than accented note	Strike hardest
	Left-Hand Pizzicato or Stopped Note A note played with silencing	Strike from a closed guard
	Snap Pizzicato A note played on a string instrument, where the string is stretched away from the instruments frame making it snap against the frame	Snap strike
	Natural Harmonic or Open Note String instrument - note played in natural harmonic; Valved brass instrument - Note to be played open Organ - pedal note played with the heel Percussion - Open hi-hat or instrument allowed to ring	Strike from an open guard

Note	Name / Description	Martial Application
	Fermata or Pause A rest prolonged longer than the note value	Pause after a strike
	Up Bow or Sull'arco Bowed instrument - play note when drawing bow up. Plucked instrument - played with a pick on an upstroke	Upwards strike
	Down Bow or Giu'arco Bowed instrument - play note when drawing bow down Plucked instrument - played with a pick on a downstroke	Downward strike

Table 29: Articulation marks.

The martial arts application varies depending on the note, and this is described on the right-hand column in the table above.

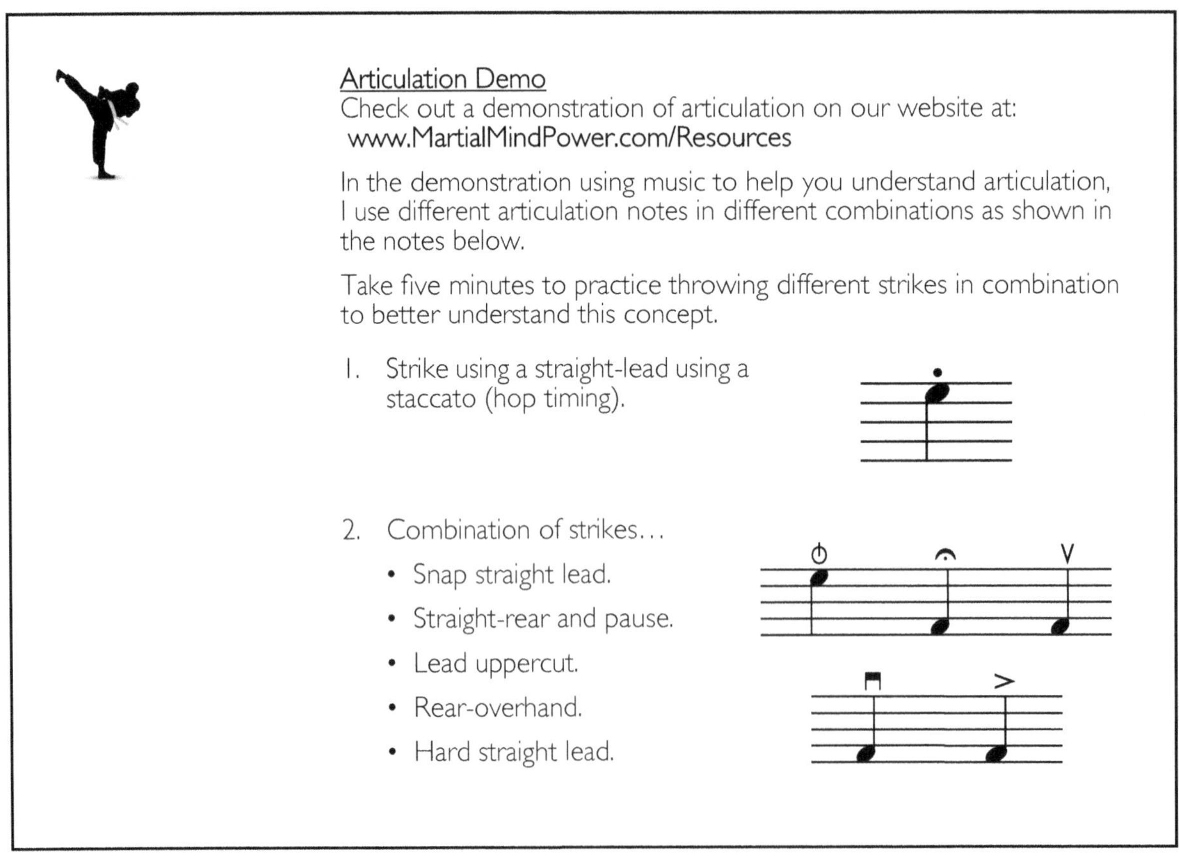

Articulation Demo
Check out a demonstration of articulation on our website at:
www.MartialMindPower.com/Resources

In the demonstration using music to help you understand articulation, I use different articulation notes in different combinations as shown in the notes below.

Take five minutes to practice throwing different strikes in combination to better understand this concept.

1. Strike using a straight-lead using a staccato (hop timing).
2. Combination of strikes…
   - Snap straight lead.
   - Straight-rear and pause.
   - Lead uppercut.
   - Rear-overhand.
   - Hard straight lead.

Ornaments

Ornaments adjust the pitch pattern of individual notes.

Note	Name / Description	Martial Application
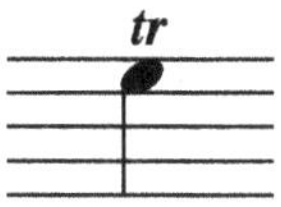 tr	Trill or Shake A rapid alternation between two specified notes	Blasting strikes with alternative ballistic aggressive attack to "shake" the opponent up
	Inverted Mordent Play the primary note, then the next note up, then return back to the primary note with rapidity	Attack by combination from lower-line to higher-line then back to lower-line to "shake" the opponent up (Low-High-Low or LHL)
	Inverted Mordent Play the primary note, then the next note up, then return back to the primary note with rapidity	Attack by combination from higher-line to lower-line then back to higher-line to "shake" the opponent up (High-Low-High or HLH)
 	Turn Placed on top of note - play next note up, play primary note, then next note down, and return to primary note Placed on right of note - play primary note, followed by above pattern Line through - play next note down, play primary note, play next note up, and return to primary note	Attack by combination from: High, Mid, Low, Mid-lines (L-M-L-M) Low, Mid, High, Mid-lines (L-M-H-M)
	Appoggiatura The first half of the primary notes duration has the pitch of the grace note	A Progressive Indirect Attack (PIA)
	Acciaccatura A note brushed on its way to the primary note, which is played to its full value	A Progressive Indirect Attack (PIA)

Table 30: Ornaments.

The martial arts application varies depending on the note, and this is described on the right-hand column in the table above.

Ornaments/Pitch Pattern Demo
Check out a demonstration of ornaments/pitch pattern on our website at: www.MartialMindPower.com/Resources

In the demonstration using music to help you understand ornaments/pitch pattern, I use different combinations as shown in the notes below.

Take five minutes to practice throwing different strikes in combination as shown below to better understand this concept.

1. Straight hook blast — using rapid alternating lead and rear hook strikes.

2. Low-high-low — straight-kick, straight-lead, then straight-kick.

3. A Progressive Indirect Attack (PIA).
    - Opponent leads with a hook.
    - You strike (or gunt) to the inside of the arm.
    - You then riposte with inverted straight-lead to chin.

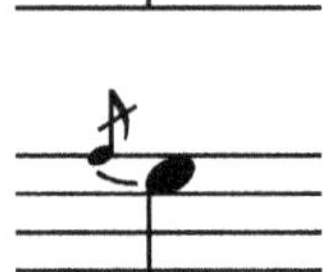

Repetition and Codas

These describe notes which are repeated as follows:

Note	Name / Description	Martial Application
	Tremolo A note which is repeated rapidly. If the tremolo is between two notes, then both notes are rapidly alternated	Rapidly repeating strikes e.g. straight blast
	Repeat Signs All notes within the passage are repeated more than once	Repeat a whole sequence of strikes
	Simile Marks Repeat preceding groups of beats	Repeat set of strike beats
1. 2.	Volta Brackets Repeat a passage with a different ending, marked with the no.	Repeat a whole sequence of strikes with different finishing strikes
D.C.	Da Capo or "from Top" Play music from the beginning	Repeat strikes from the beginning
D.S.	Da Segno or "from the Sign" Repeat playing music from nearest segno	Repeat strikes from a specified marker
	Segno Mark used to indicate a placeholder from which to repeat play	Repeat strikes from a specified marker
	Coda Indicates a jump forward to the ending passage, marked with the same sign	Jump forward and repeat strikes from a specified marker

Table 31: Repetition and codas.

The martial arts application varies depending on the note, and this is described on the right-hand column in the table above.

Repetition and Codas Demo
Check out a demonstration of repetition and codas on our website at: www.MartialMindPower.com/Resources

In the demonstration using music to help you understand repetition and codas, I use combinations as shown in the notes below.

Take five minutes to practice throwing different strikes in combination as shown below to better understand this concept.

Broken Rhythm

Rhythm is always changing. If you understand how it can change, then you can manage it, or be the one directing it.

When these variable components of music change, we change the rhythm and therefore the organisation of the sound of the music in time, orchestrated with perfect harmony.

When expressed in martial arts, any motion which exhibits a prolonged repetitive rhythm makes you vulnerable, as it affords your opponent more opportunities to take advantage of you to overpower you in combat, by exploiting windows of opportunity within your rhythm.

Therefore it is important to keep changing your rhythm in martial motion… I call this *'broken rhythm'.* If you can manage rhythm and broken rhythm in a fight, you will keep your opponent guessing so you can direct the fight and Stay Ahead.

This Stay Ahead stage of your self-mastery journey is inspired by Bruce Lee's a philosophy quoted by Bruce Lee during a conversation with his Shaolin master in *Enter the Dragon.* Check out a clip of this conversation on our website at: www.MartialMindPower.com/Resources, which goes as follows:

> The master asks Bruce, *'What is the highest technique you hope to achieve?'*
>
> Bruce replied, *'To have no technique.'*
>
> *'What are your thoughts when facing an opponent?'* the master continues.
>
> *'There is no opponent.'*
>
> *'Why is that?'*
>
> *'Because the word "I" does not exist,'* Bruce explains. *'A good fight should be like a small play, but played seriously. A good martial artist does not become tense, but ready. Not thinking, yet… not dreaming. Ready for whatever may come. When the opponent expands, I contract; when he contracts, I expand. And when there is an opportunity, I do not hit, it hits all by itself!'*

Bruce goes on to write more on this philosophy, saying:

'Any technique, however worthy and desirable,
becomes a disease when the mind is obsessed with it.'

In this chapter we have looked at music and broken it down by studying how music is composed. This has given us insight into the composition of rhythm and changing rhythms (broken rhythm), which in turn has given us valuable insight into how we can manage rhythm and broken rhythm in combat.

The following key musical variables can be applied directly to combat to help you direct the fight and Stay Ahead:

- The beat and pulse.
- Time signature.
- Tempo.
- Time stretching.
- Tempo markings (such as BPM, tempo change, terms, styles, and moods).
- Notes and rests.
- Breaks.
- Accidentals.
- Relationships.
- Dynamics.
- Articulation.
- Ornaments and,
- Repetition and codas.

<u>Broken Rhythm Drill</u>
Find a partner.

Make up a musical piece using a variety of musical variables from the list shown above, using a minimum of three musical variables.

Take thirty minutes to practice your musical piece and demonstrate it using martial movement such as footwork and strikes

<u>Dance</u>

Another effective way to understand rhythm and broken rhythm is through music and dance. In this section, I am going to take you through a dance lesson which employs a variety of the musical mechanics we have studied within this chapter to better understand these principles. This is available on our website at: www.MartialMindPower.com/Resources

Check it out so you can absorb these ideas discussed in this chapter using music and dance. Enjoy!

The Rhythm of Life

Miguel Angel Ruiz quoted:

'Life is like dancing.
If we have a big floor, many people will dance.
Some will get angry when the rhythm changes.
But life is changing all the time.'

Figure 48: *Yin and Yang symbol, known as Taijiti.*

In the section titled 'Yin and Yang', in the 'Power Side Forwards' chapter we looked at:

- Dualistic (dyad or duplet) relationships, where we separate and segregate equals and opposites, hence we do not recognise any *'in-between'* such as black and white, good and bad, light and dark, life and death, male and female and so on.
- Monistic (singlet) relationships of Yin and Yang. One which is complementary, interconnected and interdependent. For example, 'darkness is the absence of light' and 'silence is the absence of sound'.

Yin and Yang therefore represent a dynamic relationship of an indivisible whole, in which the whole is greater than the sum of the assembled parts. For example, 'a shadow cannot exist without light' and 'an echo cannot exist without sound'.

In essence, the monistic relationships of a higher realm are invariably dyads (duplets) bound by a third element making them triads (triplets). For example:

- Black, white and just colour.
- Good, bad and just a thought.

- Light, dark and time-space.
- Gentleness, firmness and nothing.
- Hot, cold and just feeling.
- Life, death and the journey.
- Male, female and being human.
- Active, passive and just being.
- Strength, weakness and character.
- Cause, effect and taking responsibility.
- Fire, water, and elements.
- Sun, moon and the all-encompassing universe.
- Energy, matter and anti-matter.
- Physical, non-physical and the meta-physical.
- Past, present and the future.
- Light, darkness and time-space.
- Sound, silence and time-space.
- Yin, Yang and the Taijiti — the all-encompassing circle of life.

This is what Lao Tzu depicts in his Tao Te King:

'Tao engenders One;
One engenders Two;
Two engenders Three;
Three engenders all things.
All things carry the yin
while embrace the yang.
Neutralising energy brings them into harmony.'

Hence, music, motion and life are also a triad — one which I call the 'Rhythm of Life'. Everything is subject to music and motion, which creates life. Life is a wave, a vibration, a pulsation at the very heart of All That Is.

Gabrielle Roth, known as the Mother of Modern Dance, writes about the idea of there being five Rhythms of Life as follows (found at http://www.5rhythms.com/gabrielle-roths-5rhythms/what-are-the-5rhythms):

'The Five Rhythms — Flowing, Staccato, Chaos, Lyrical, Stillness™ — are states of Being. They are a map to everywhere we want to go, on all planes of consciousness — inner and outer, forward and back, physical, emotional and intellectual.

They are markers on the way back to a real self, a vulnerable, wild, passionate, instinctive self.

In Flowing, we physically practice the art of being fluid in our bodies. Flowing is the pipeline to our inner truth, the impulse to follow the flow of one's own energy, to be true to oneself—listening and attending to our needs, receptive to our inner and outer worlds. When we open up to the flow of our physical beings, all other pathways open. It is one of the most beautiful and fascinating ways of dancing — to be in, to be around and to watch.

Men and women that embody the Rhythm of Flowing are supple, flexible, surrendered and trust their feet to lead them where they are meant to go.

In Staccato we physically practice the power of masculine energy. It is percussive and strong and promotes connection with the rest of the world. Staccato is the gateway to the heart. It shows us how to step out into the world connected to our feet and our feelings. This rhythm is the ruler of our linear world, the ruler of the warrior part of us, the part of us that shows up as truth and clarity. It is the part of us that stands up for what we care about, who we love, and what we love.

Staccato is the fierce teacher of boundaries. And it is the protector and ambassador of our fluid being. Visually, a man or woman fully embodied in the Rhythm of Staccato is defined, clear, connected and not fearful of the transparent expression of their heart. Whether dancing Staccato alone, in partnership, or in groups, it is always a powerful experience.

In Chaos we physically practice the art of fully releasing our bodies — we let go of the head, spine, hips and feet and move faster than we can think. Chaos breaks us free of our illusions and throws us headfirst into the beat. It takes us on the journey from 'I can't' to 'I will'. The simple practices of Chaos immediately bring us back to our bodies, to the moment. This rhythm liberates us from all ideas about who we are and gives us a real experience of being total, free, intuitive and creative.

Chaos is the gateway to the big mind. Dancing Chaos is the practice of going into the unknown, not fearing what's on the other side. Visually we look like a big, hot, giant, sweaty mess overflowing with cathartic energy. This is our big dance, our break out dance, our break through dance.

In Lyrical we practice the art of coming out of Chaos. It is the physical, energetic, emotional and spiritual dancing rebirth. The practice of Lyrical teaches us how to break out of destructive patterns and surrender into the depths of the fluid, creative repetitions of our soulful self, bubbling up from the deepest parts of ourselves, to the integrity and dignity that we often forget is within us.

Lyrical is expansive and connects us to our humanity, timeless rhythms, repetitions, patterns and cycles. Lyrical is more of a state of being than a rhythm, as it can be a crystal clear expression of any of the rhythms in their lightness. We become light in our feet, like birds flying in the air — but make no mistake, in Lyrical we are grounded and fully empowered.

Being Still and doing nothing are totally different. Stillness moves, both within and all around us. The dance is our vehicle, our destination is the Rhythm of Stillness; our challenge is to be a vessel that keeps moving and changing. Physically, in the dance of Stillness, we move in slow motion — like highly unpredictable meditative Tai Chi masters. Shapes from the past, the present and the future come through us — shapes of the Feminine and the Masculine and the magic dance they do together. Moving in Stillness and being still in motion fuses the accumulation of our bodies' life experiences into our true wisdom. Eventually we dissolve into sitting meditation, where all the other rhythms of our journey converge in the vital resonance of Stillness.

Each time we dance into Stillness, we practice the art of making humble and mindful endings interpreted by our higher connected self. This carries through to all of our endings in life — the end of this dance, this day, this relationship, or this life cycle. Good endings mean taking responsibility for the whole journey, distilling wisdom from our experience so that we may begin the next wave or cycle clean and not carrying the past with us.

Gabrielle summarises the Rhythm of Life as:

'Waves move in patterns.
Patterns move in rhythms.
A human being is just that
— energy, waves, patterns, rhythms.
Nothing more. Nothing less.
A dance.'

Deepak Chopra said:

> *'Our biological rhythms are the symphony of the cosmos,*
> *Music embedded deep within us to which we dance,*
> *Even when we can't name the tune.'*

Therefore, the Rhythm of Life is about…

- Music and motion creating emotion.
- Emotion is the power which attracts. For example, that which you fear strongly, you experience. So feel what you want to experience. I say, *'Put yourself in a constant state of bliss'.*
- Emotion is energy in motion, i.e. 'E-Motion'. When you move energy, you create effect. If you move enough energy, you create matter. If you focus your energy, you create your own effect. This is the alchemy of the universe, and secret to all life.
- 'E-motion' puts your thoughts into action. Every thought is pure energy, and each thought is pure creativity. The energy of your thought never dies; instead it emanates through the universe forever, manifesting your mind's creation through motion or action.
- Actions translate into experiences.
- Experiences create life.
- So orchestrate your experiences like a freestyle dance with a plan, and dance to your own rhythm and tune, and simply BEcome and LIVE THE LIFE YOU WANT,

Hence music can be used to understand combat, and combat to understand the rhythm of our life using motion, so we can transcend our understanding of rhythm (and broken rhythm) towards our end desires.

Rhythm of Life Drill

Using the mechanics of music (including rhythm and broken rhythm) and martial arts, think how you can apply these lessons to the Rhythm of Your Life, by filling out the right column of the table below.

Take sixty minutes to apply the mechanics of music and martial arts to understand the Rhythm of Your Life.

Music (Example)	Martial Motion	Life
Beat Strong Beat Weak Beat	- Single strike is 2 beats, extend (1-beat), retract & recover (1 beat) - Repetitive hard strikes - Repetitive weak strikes	
Bar	Succession of combinational strikes grouped together	
Time Signature (common time, cut-time, common 3/4 or 3/8 beats)	- Single speed strikes - Double speed of strikes - 1-2-3 strikes at single speed - 1-2-3 strikes at double speed	
Tempo (larghissimo or moderato)	Number of strikes per min	
Time Stretch (larghissimo to allegro)	Change speed of strikes 60-120-60 BPM	
Piacere	Broken rhythm at own discretion	
Styles (con dolcezza or con Fuqua)	Fight with softness fire or fluidity of motion	
Mood Tempo Markers (energico or vivaco)	Fight with low-energy to high-energy	
Tempo Change (accelerando or ritardando)	Speed up/slow down striking rate	
Notes & Rests (quarter-note & rest)	Vary length of timing of strikes and the time of rest between strikes	
Breaks (breath mark or caesura)	Take a breath &/or intermittent breaks between striking bouts	
Accidentals (flat or sharp)	Strike through target or snap strike	
Relationships (slur or phrase)	Simultaneous strikes or successive strikes played smoothly	
Dynamics (piano or forte)	Hit soft or hard	
Articulation (staccato or fermata)	Hit with a hop or pause on strikes	
Ornaments (trill or accianacatura)	Straight blast or a progressive indirect attack	

Music (Example)	Martial Motion	Life
Repetition & Codas (tremolo or repeats)	Repetitive alternating strikes	

Table 32: Rhythm of life mapping table.

The table below gives some examples of lessons transmutated from musical rhythm, to combative rhythm, to the rhythm of life:

Music (Example)	Martial Motion	Life
Beat	- Single strike is 2 beats, extend (1-beat), retract & recover (1 beat) - Repetitive hard strikes - Repetitive weak strikes	- An action - An action with intent - An action with little or no intent, which may be intentional or unintentional
Bar	Succession of combinational strikes grouped together	Series of actions leading to a well-formed outcome
Time Signature (common time, cut-time, common 3/4 or 3/8 beats)	- Single speed strikes - Double speed of strikes - 1-2-3 strikes at single speed - 1-2-3 strikes at double speed	- Natural rhythm, working pace, etc - Picking up your rhythm / pace - Rationally sequenced actions - Irrationally sequenced actions, which may be planned or unplanned
Tempo (larghissimo or moderato)	Number of strikes per min	Finding your natural rhythm, working pace, etc
Time Stretch (larghissimo to allegro)	Change speed of strikes 60-120-60 BPM	Adjusting to rate and pace of things happening, sometimes slow, sometimes fast
Piacere	Broken rhythm at own discretion	Be like water, and be flexible and adaptable to the outside
Styles (con dolcezza or con Fuqua)	Fight with softness, fire or fluidity of motion	Change your working style and pace towards your ends desires
Mood Tempo Markers (energico or vivaco)	Fight with low-energy to high-energy	Have passion for your major purpose in life
Tempo Change (accelerando or ritardando)	Speed up/slow down striking rate	Decelerate and stop things that distract you from your major purpose in life Accelerate towards your success goals

Music (Example)	Martial Motion	Life
Notes & Rests (quarter-note & rest)	Vary length of timing of strikes and the time of rest between strikes	Rest & recovery is as important as working towards your success goals, to ensure you are refreshed and reenergised
Breaks (breath mark or caesura)	Take a breath &/or intermittent breaks between striking bouts	Take a break to rest, recover and re-energise between tasks
Accidentals (flat or sharp)	Strike through target or snap strike	Find a way through or around obstacles
Relationships (slur or phrase)	Simultaneous strikes or successive strikes played smoothly	Develop relationships and share information and knowledge to connect your purpose
Dynamics (piano or forte)	Hit soft or hard	Work hard, then work a little more softly
Articulation (staccato or fermata)	Hit with a hop or pause on strikes	Attain small achievements which add up
Ornaments (trill or accianacatura)	Straight blast or a progressive indirect attack	Sometimes you need to take an indirect route to your goal, though it still get closer to it
Repetition & Codas (tremolo or repeats)	Repetitive alternating strikes	Keep persevering towards your end desires, having 'stickability'

Table 33: Rhythm of life sample map.

Dance to Your Own Rhythm

How Does Rhythm and Broken Rhythm Apply to Life?

One can think of 'rhythm' in your life being synonymous to 'being in your stride'. This is when you are in a resourceful state, and things are going your way, as you have established a certain pattern or routine which is serving you in some way, shape or form.

On the flip side, one can think of 'broken rhythm' being synonymous to some unexpected obstacle which 'throws you off your course', usually putting you in an unresourceful state.

Having a solid comprehension for rhythm in music and motion, you are probably already thinking about how you can apply your newfound knowledge to real life scenarios now.

Choose Your Song

In this section of 'Stay Ahead', you are going choose a song to dance to — or, to put it another way, you are going to take your Definite Chief Aim, as identified during the **'Power Side Forwards'** chapter or one of your preferred success goals, to help you **Orchestrate Your Success.** We are going to then use the idea of rhythm and broken rhythm to create tactics and strategies to help you Stay Ahead of your own success game, so you can dance to your own rhythm.

I say:

'There are those who dance to the rhythm that is played to them:
those who only dance to their own rhythm,
and those who don't dance at all.
Be a dancer, and dance to your own rhythm!'

If you would like more information on setting goals, then please refer to the 'Definite Chief Aim' and 'Goal Setting' sections in the **'Power Side Forwards'** chapter.

Taking your goal, we are now going to use a model called NLP PRESENT created by Tad James to help you, *'Be a dancer, so you can dance to your own rhythm!'*

Michael Jackson said:

'To live is to be musical, starting with the blood dancing in your veins.
Everything living has a rhythm.
Do you... ***feel your music****?'*

Firstly, I want you to find a partner to dance with. One person is going to act as the 'leader', and the other person will be the 'follower'. The leader is going to run the follower through the steps outlined below which they will follow, and you can swap over when you have completed the exercise one-way.

As they say:

'Life is a dance.
Sometimes we lead, sometimes we follow.
Don't worry about what we don't know,
What's important is we learn new steps as we go.'

The Leader is now going to take the Follower through the following sequence of steps of the dance to **discover your rhythm of life.** Here we go, let's dance.

Let's Dance

Stand in an open space where you can spread your arms out to your front and sides without bumping into anyone. Ensure you have ample space in front of you, so no one can walk across your field of view.

Close your eyes and ask yourself, *'If I were to point to my past, where would it be?'* Then ask yourself, *'If I were to point to my future, where would it be?'*

Point one arm towards your past, and one arm towards your future and ask yourself to just notice where your present is for you.

Now open your eyes and simply notice where your arms are pointing. This exercise identifies your timeline. There are two common types of timeline, which are:

- 'Through Time' — this is when people lay out their **past, present and future in front of them** usually from **left (past) to right (future)**, with the present right in front of them; or
- 'In Time' — this is when people have their **past behind them** and their **future in front of them**, with the present usually placed just behind their eyes.

If you have a **'Through Time'** timeline organisation (i.e. left-to-right), then I would like you to re-map it by turning it ninety degrees anticlockwise to **make it 'In time'**, so that:

- Your **past** is behind you.
- Your **future** is in front of you.
- You are standing in the **present.**

Standing in the present, visualise your goal in the future ahead of you. Can you see it? Wait for confirmation from the follower that they can see their goal.

Point to the goal in your future timeline. Leader — make a note of the location of your follower's goal in the future ahead of you, in relation to where you are now in the present. Ask them the questions listed in the table that follows.

	NLP Present	Ecology
P	Positive	• Is your goal positive? • How much do you want your goal out of 10 (1 being lowest, and 10 being highest)?
R	Responsible	• Are you responsible for your goal? • Do you own your goal?
E	Environment	• When and where do you want to be when you get your goal?
S	Senses	• What will you see, hear, feel, taste and smell to know you got your goal?
E	Ecology	• What will the impact be on you and others when you get your goal?

Table 34: NLP PRESENT and ecology model.

Ask the follower to act *'as if'* they have already achieved their goal. Then ask them to do the following:

	NLP Present	Ecology
N	Navigate	• Start to act 'as-if' you have already achieved your goal; • Find your rhythm and stride over to the point in your future where your goal is at a rate and pace that you are comfortable with; • When you reach your goal, start to see, hear, feel, taste and smell all the things you dreamt of before now; • You are now in the place where you always dreamt of being, now that you have achieved your goal
T	Talents	• Look back down your timeline towards the Past and ask your Follower these questions: - • What was the last thing you did to get this goal? • What did you see, hear, feel, taste and smell to know that you got your goal? • Give 3 things that surprised you about getting the goal? THESE ARE YOUR RHYTHM MARKERS • Was it worth it? • Give 3 obstacles that you overcame? THESE ARE THE POINTS WHERE YOUR RHYTHM IS BROKEN

Table 34: NLP PRESENT and ecology model.

Walk back to the present. Say to your follower, *'Ask yourself, now what are you going to do next now you've started the process?'*

Finally, ask them, *'How did you celebrate when you reached your goal?'*

Jack Kerouac, the Dharma Bums said:

> *'Jumping from boulder to boulder and never falling, with a heavy pack, is easier than it sounds; you just can't fall when you get into the rhythm of the dance.'*

A famous dancer, Isadora Duncan, quoted:

> *'Now I am going to reveal to you something which is very pure, a totally white thought. It is always in my heart; it blooms at each of my steps... The dance is love, it is only love, it alone, and that is enough... I, then, it is amorously that I dance: to poems, to music, but now I would like to no longer dance to anything but the rhythm of my soul.'*

Can you *feel it now?*

One Step Ahead

Some time later the daughter approached her father with reverence. *'Are you a magician?'* she inquired. *'Everything was just as you predicted. First he admired me, then he invited me out. Next the dear boy took me by his house, claiming he needed something from his bedside cupboard. Of course he invited me inside so I wouldn't have to wait outside alone, and once inside his apartment he offered me a drink, just as you had said. Then we listened to some soothing, relaxing music.*

But all this time I remembered your words, and I knew exactly what was about to happen. So, let me tell you how I am worthy to be your daughter. Just when I felt the right moment coming and he was about to make his move, I forced myself on top of him, and in this way violated him, shamed him and his family and ruined their reputation.'

Five Silver Stars

Five silver stars falling from the sky…

The first is for me for writing these stories down.

The second is for you for reading them.

The third is for all the storytellers from whom I learned these stories.

And the fourth is for all the storytellers who told my storytellers their stories, and ancestry stretching far back into the mists of time.

The fifth is for all of you who pass on, in your own way, these stories to someone else. When you pass on a story, giving it your stamp, you add to the sum knowledge in the world, and you confirm your own immortal creativity.

Conclusion

The mission of this **Stay Ahead** stage of your self-mastery journey was to:

Help you to **Understand Rhythm and Broken Rhythm, Understand the Rhythm of Life,** so you can **Orchestrate Your Success** and **Dance to Your Own Rhythm** towards achieving your own SUCCESS!

In this stage of your self-mastery journey we looked at:

1. Developing an understanding of rhythm.
2. Developing an understanding of broken rhythm.
3. Developing an understanding of the Rhythm of Life.
4. Orchestrating a plan for your success goal.
5. Dancing the dance to your own success by:
   - Identifying how to get into the rhythm of achieving your success goal by identify the three things that surprised you about achieving your goal.
   - Making your success plan bulletproof by creating tactics and strategies to stay ahead by identifying three major obstacles that you overcame to achieve your goal.

All so you can **Dance to Your Own Rhythm.**

And that brings us to the end of the **Stay Ahead** stage of your self-mastery journey. Before you embark on GETTING AHEAD and STAYING AHEAD, please answer the following:

Questions

1. Do you understand what **Rhythm** is? (Yes or No)
2. Do you understand what **Broken Rhythm** is? (Yes or No)
3. Do you understand what **The Rhythm of Life** is? (Yes or No)
4. Have successfully **Orchestrated Your Success** plan? (Yes or No)
5. Have you identified how to **Get Into the Rhythm** of achieving your success goal? (Yes or No)
6. Have you made your success plan bullet proof by creating tactics and strategies to **Stay Ahead**? (Yes or No)
7. Are you ready to **Dance to Your Own Rhythm** now? (Yes or No)
8. Are you **ready to stay ahead?** (Yes or No)

My friend, I would like to deeply thank you for giving me the chance to take you through this **Master Your Life journey**, and remember:

'ORCHESTRATE YOUR SUCCESS,

DANCE TO YOUR OWN RHYTHM, and

STAY AHEAD!'

'Self-conquest is the greatest of victories.
Mighty is he who conquers himself'

Bruce Lee

References

Introduction

- Artist of Life, Bruce Lee
- The Kung Fu Kitties: The Adventure Begins, Jeremy Roadruck
- The Magic of Metaphor, Nick Owen

Stillness

- The Busy Trap, Tim Kreider, http://opinionator.blogs.nytimes.com/2012/06/30/the-busy-trap/?_r=0
- Crime Index by Country 2014, http://www.numbeo.com/crime/rankings_by_country.jspentrepreneurship: A Working Definition, Thomas R. Eisenmann
- Welfare System in Denmark, http://medicolink.dk/welfare-system-in-denmark
- The Legatum Prosperity Index 2013, http://media.prosperity.com/2013/pdf/publications/pl2013brochure_web.pdf
- How Meditation Changes Your Brain, Dr Sarah McKay, http://higherperspective.com/2014/04/neuroscientist-explains-meditation-changes-brain.html?utm_source=hp
- The Magic of Metaphor, Nick Owen

Empty Your Teacup

- Think and Grow Rich, Dr Napoleon Hill, www.naphill.org
- Liberate Yourself, Chris Kent, www.personalliberation.com

Think and Become

- Interview with Anthony Robbins, Frank Kern and John Reese, https://www.youtube.com/watch?v=0lmluAvkUMo
- The Magic of Metaphor, Nick Owen

Waatah!

- Prochaska and DiClemente's Stages of Change Model
- Fear: The Friend of Exceptional People, Geoff Thompson, http://geoffthompson.com
- The Magic of Metaphor, Nick Owen

Possess an Eagle Eye

- OODA Loop, Wikipedia
- John Boyd, Wikipedia
- Human Eye, Wikipedia
- Visual Field, www.vision-and-eye-health.com
- Empty Field Myopia, Sky Brary http://www.skybrary.aero/index.php/empty_field_myopia
- Cyclopean Eye, Vision Plus Magazine
- The Magic of Metaphor, Nick Owen

Honestly Express Yourself

- Liberate Yourself, Chris Kent, www.personalliberation.com
- The Demartini Value Determination Process, Dr John Demartini, www.drdemartini.com

- The Magic of Influence, Jerry Clark, Club Rhino, www.clubrhino.com
- Albert Mahrabian, Human Communication Model
- The Science Behind Posture and How It Affects Your Brain, Bell Beth Cooper, LifeHacker, http://lifehacker.com/the-science-behind-posture-and-how-it-affects-your-brai-1463291618
- NLP and Hypnosis Practitioner Course Book, David Key, https://auspicium.co.uk/
- Guerrilla Marketing, J Conrad
- The Art of Selling Without Selling, Sukhi Wahiwala, www.sukhiwahiwala.com
- The Magic of Metaphor, Nick Owen

Be Like Water

- Liberate Yourself, Chris Kent, www.personalliberation.com
- The Hidden Messages in Water, Dr Masuro Emoto
- Vishen Lakhiani, www.mindvalley.com
- The Magic of Metaphor, Nick Owen

Power Side Forwards

- Paul J. Meyer, founder of Success Motivation® Institute, Inc.
- Three Feet from Gold, Sharon Lechter and Greg Reid with the Napoleon Hill Foundation
- www.mindtools.com
- The Magic of Metaphor, Nick Owen

Stay Ahead

- http://en.wikipedia.org/wiki/rhythm
- David Key, NLP practitioner Course Handbook, https://auspicium.co.uk
- Conversations with God, Volume One, Neal David Walsh
- Five Rhythms, Gabrielle Roth, http://www.5rhythms.com
- The Magic of Metaphor, Nick Owen

About the Author

Sifu Lak Loi is a true White Collar Warrior. He worked as a senior consultant both in the City of London and in Wall Street from 1997 before deciding to follow his own path to Self-Mastery.

Loi established the flagship Bruce Lee Jeet Kune Do ('The Way of the Intercepting Fist') martial arts school in the City of London, and has a direct lineage to Bruce Lee himself. Loi is a third generation instructor in Jeet Kune Do, certified by the famous Wednesday Night Group under the living legend, Sifu Tim Tackett, and his European director, Kwoklyn Wan.

Loi's purpose of his martial arts school is to:

> *'Preserve and promote Bruce Lee's martial art and philosophy of Jeet Kune Do, to help define and teach the core curriculum — not to confine us, but to liberate us — and to discover our personal expression of Bruce's martial art and philosophy.'*

His personal mission statement is:

> *'My chief definite purpose is to educate, inspire and empower people, so that they can live life to its truest potential... so they can align themselves towards their personal liberation, self-actualisation and achieve their personal success goals.'*

Loi uses Bruce Lee's teachings, fused with his personal development and elite fitness coaching credentials, as well as pioneering Dynamic Framing and Dynamic Anchoring mind-reprogramming technologies, to cultivate people's lives both mentally and physically through his process of Experientialism.

Loi calls it... Martial Mind Power.

Loi also holds a Bachelor of Science (Honours) degree in Computer Science/Software Engineering from the University of Birmingham, and is a fully qualified NLP practitioner and an instructor in hypnotherapy. He is also an associate of the Napoleon Hill Foundation (America's largest personal development organisation, founded by Dr Napoleon Hill, the bestselling author of *Think and Grow Rich*), having created their first ever iOS application called *Success Movie* (available on the App Store).

Check out www.MartialMindPower.com for more information.

Publisher Information

Rowanvale Books provides publishing services to independent authors, writers and poets all over the globe. We deliver a personal, honest and efficient service that allows authors to see their work published, while remaining in control of the process and retaining their creativity. By making publishing services available to authors in a cost-effective and ethical way, we at Rowanvale Books hope to ensure that the local, national and international community benefits from a steady stream of good quality literature.

For more information about us, our authors or our publications, please get in touch.

www.rowanvalebooks.com
info@rowanvalebooks.com

Lightning Source UK Ltd.
Milton Keynes UK
UKOW04f0257061016

284581UK00015B/507/P